Margaret ~
May your journey
be guided by the angels.
Joan Kilgen

KARMA AND YOUR SUN SIGN

Explore your karmic journey
through life

Joan Kilgen

Sunrise Press
Sayville, New York

Library of Congress Catalog Card Number: 95-68350

ISBN: 0-9645790-0-6

The author can be contacted through Sunrise Press, PO Box 271, Sayville, NY
11782.

Cover and illustrations by Laura "Lalla" Glasberg.

To Arlene who's being there has made all things happen.

TABLE OF CONTENTS

ACKNOWLEDGMENTS

Four years of preparation, writing and general obsession cannot happen without the loving cooperation of family and friends. First, I must give abundant credit to my mother, Gladys Rickmeyer, who spent endless hours reading, rereading, and editing this work. Her Leo pride in her work and steadfastness held her to her task with diligence and love. Our special thanks to Dr. Santiago Urmaza who's healing hands brought her from the darkness of glaucoma and cataracts to the miraculous ability to edit this manuscript. Her loving touch is upon this work. Other relations whose imprints are upon this work cannot be left unmentioned. My children and their loves, Susan the Gemini, Jenny and John the Leos, Georgette the Sagittarian, and Kevin the Virgo along with my grandchildren, Ashley the Capricorn, Gregg the Taurus, Karyn the Libra, Kevin, Jr. the Scorpio, and Timothy the Pisces, have all aided in the development of this work. They have often been my teachers.

Strangers became friends as they supported this endeavor. Linda Mittiga who tirelessly edited fresh copy and John Taylor whose writer's workshop spurred me on to completion. Both of these warm souls encouraged me strongly during the beginning when I might easily have fallen away from the challenge of such a work. And to Margarita Villoch who opened her beautiful home in Key West for me whenever I needed to escape the bustle of New York to retreat into the blissfulness of my soul's home. And Laura Glasberg whose creative energies adorn the cover. Laura's ability to reach inside my mind to create the caricatures for each sun sign is still a mystery to me. To Susan McIntosh of XRS, Torrance, California, who volunteered to scan all of Laura's line drawings as a birthday gift to me and Elaine Kirkland and Diane Darling for laser printer privileges. To my many clients, friends, and colleagues who never tired of asking me if the book was finished yet, supporting me along each step of the way.

And to Arlene Cramer, a special Pisces. No words can say enough. Her consistent encouragement can be felt on every page, along with her editorial eye and gentle advice.

No writer's work belongs to them alone. The angels have guided my walk down this path and I thank those known and unknown whose energy may be felt upon these pages.

FOREWORD

Many books have been written, and probably read by you, telling you the meaning and interpretations of the sun signs. They help us to understand our own personality characteristics and the behaviors of those around us as they walk us through the intricate realm of astrology. Karma and Your Sun Sign is designed to lead you down a different path by exploring the karmic journey of your soul. We each have our own unique path to follow which is carefully detailed within the complete interpretation of your chart. Yet we also have common destinations according to our sun signs and it is this route which is traveled in this book. Everyone born within a sign has similar lessons which they will experience with a multitude of diversity within cultures, lifestyles, aptitudes and interests. God has given us many tools through which to discover our soul's path, astrology being just one of them. Your chart is your treasure map, your sun sign being the beacon which helps to light your way. This book will help you to follow the markings of your map, illuminating the Xs that mark the spot, deciphering the hidden messages, counting off the paces in your march toward self-discovery.

You will not find the usual characteristic descriptions of other astrology books since not all of your sun sign's traits are directed toward your karmic fulfillment. This book concentrates exclusively on those karmic challenges which influence you as you evolve through your sun sign. You will discover why you are walking this planet right now and learn how to develop your soul's growth through a more complete understanding of your karmic needs. The language and terminology has been kept simple so that you may be able to interpret your sign without the need of an astrologer or any astrological training. There need be no mystery in reading your treasure map, since it is yours to read. For a more detailed reading of your chart, you will then need to consult with a professional astrologer. A word of caution, choose your astrologer carefully. Check his or her credibility. I suggest the recommendation of a friend or someone else who has had a positive experience with the astrologer as your best method of evaluation. The interpretation of your chart is important and needs to be handled with professionalism and skill.

In reading this book, you will notice that I make use of the pronoun, *he,* in some chapters and, *she,* in others. On the first page of each sun sign I make note of whether that sign is masculine or feminine in nature. When a sign is masculine, I use the pronoun, *he,* if feminine, I use *she.* I have chosen to do this for two reasons. By creating the continual tone through use of the appropriate pronoun, you are reminded of the energy through which your sign vibrates. This is especially important when discussing children since, for example, a girl born under a masculine sign experiences vast differences in society's expectations than a girl born under a feminine sign. A further reason for sharing the he/she pronoun equally within the book, is a tribute to the successful struggle of feminism to lift the generic male imprint from the printed word. This is my form of acknowledgment and thanks for the work of this movement.

Many years of work and study through the experience of counseling thousands of clients and teaching hundreds of students has helped me to gather all of this information together in the form of this book. The case studies and examples cited within these pages have been altered to protect the client's privacy; therefore any resemblance to a person or persons is purely coincidental. Clients files are totally confidential and that trust has not been violated. Only examples where celebrity names have been used are unaltered.

This book has called out to me for many years, demanding that the message of karma be written as it relates to astrology. I can only hope that I've done justice to this need. There are many truths for us in our world and multiple directions we may choose in our search for our soul's purpose. We must listen to our soul's whispers to understand and learn from one another.

HOW TO USE THIS BOOK

So many of us wonder why we are here; why we are alive right now, at this time and place. Why do we exist at all? We tend to ponder these thoughts when we are going through stressful or painful times and, it is during these times, that we are apt to consult authorities to get the answers which will help ease our pain. We span the journey through psychotherapy, clergy, support groups, physicians, and yes, sometimes psychics and astrologers in our search of the reasons behind our pain. Sometimes we seek out the answers to these questions in order to enhance our growth and understand our soul's purpose. We humans are a questioning bunch; our inquisitiveness and thirst for truth are remarkable.

This book deals with that search for answers through the use of astrology. Many of the answers to why we are here, karmically, are given to us through our astrological chart.

WHAT IS AN ASTROLOGICAL CHART?

An astrological chart is a picture of the sky, exactly as it looked, at the precise date, time, and place of your birth. Since we cannot take a photograph of the sky, we reconstruct all the planetary positions mathematically. This becomes our chart or map of life.

All the planets have their own unique characteristics depending on where they are positioned in the sky and within your chart. These characteristics or energies are analyzed by professional astrologers and can be used quite effectively to help you to understand yourself in greater depth. Many of us feel that our lives are all mapped out for us, that our destinies are written in the stars; that all the activities of our lives are preordained. It is important to understand that this is not true. We are all masters of our own lives and in control of our own karmic growth. It is essential that you assume this responsibility for yourself. Would you allow someone to completely take over your life for you? To make all your decisions for you? To take away all your choices? I do not think so. Then why would you think that you would let a planetary force have that same power? We humans are very complex and must take responsibility for ourselves and our actions.

An astrological chart is to be used as a tool to help you to understand yourself. You have choices and options throughout your life, and an astrological reading is designed to show you what *your* unique choices are in this lifetime.

There is a theory that your soul chose your current chart. Your soul chose this life with all its circumstances, strengths and weaknesses. We are all here on earth to learn. We are students within a gigantic school system, yet we each have our own individual programs of study. Your astrological chart shows you what your program of study is, the program of study that you chose for yourself during this lifetime.

Granted, there are times in all of our lives when we wonder why we are working on certain subjects. We are like the enthused freshman choosing his first semester of courses in college. We sign up with great confidence for those difficult courses of calculus, chemistry, world history, Russian I, advanced engineering. About midway through the semester we feel confused, overburdened, lost, afraid of failing, and looking to drop a course or two. That is how we can feel as we travel through life and live out the chart we have chosen. The reality is not always filled with as much confidence as the expectation. So, we exercise some of our options. We can look for escape (drugs, alcohol), we can drop out (suicide), we can blame our difficulties on inferior teachers (parents, spouses), or we can blame the administration (God). The list is endless.

However, to believe that you have chosen your own chart, that you have chosen your own course or direction in this life, brings the responsibility of your growth (success) directly back to yourself.

This book is designed to help you find those answers for yourself. It takes a reading of an entire chart to fully understand all your karmic reasons for being, but first you must understand one focal piece of yourself: your sun sign.

It is no accident that you were born under a particular sun sign. You chose this sign and the lessons that it will bring you. Each sun sign has its own characteristics and, most importantly, its own karmic life lessons. This book is designed to help you understand your own sun sign and, therefore, to help you understand another key to the puzzle of why you are here. Since each sun sign deals with its own karma, that same sun sign assures you of being exposed to particular situations to ensure your experiences in those areas. Taurus, for example, needs to have karmic experiences concerning money and material possessions. Therefore, a person born under the sun sign of Taurus will be naturally directed toward money and material issues in this lifetime. The Taurus person may have a tendency to spend a lot of money or squirrel away possessions or be geared toward materialism as a high priority. Eventually this obsession will lead toward a need for a life review and karmic growth will begin.

In reading this book, be sure to turn to the sun signs of those you love as well as those you have difficulty understanding. Everyone is involved in experiencing and growing through their own karma. Please allow astrology to help you understand the struggles of others as well as yourself.

SUN SIGN CATEGORIES

Each sun sign discussion is divided into five segments or categories: Primary, Evolved, Male, Female and Children.

PRIMARY

When we are new in a sun sign (those born in the beginning five days of the sign) we are like children on our karmic road. We may gravitate toward the more problematic tendencies of the sun sign until we get the hang of it. This is also true when we are actually children or young adults during this lifetime. The adage, *with age comes wisdom*, is true. We do learn from our mistakes, and we do grow toward the most divine and wholesome benefits of our sun sign as we develop and mature. This growth comes within each lifetime as we mature in years and it comes through each individual lifetime as we reincarnate over and over in each sign. The primary category discussion will show your tendencies when you are young of age and when you are fairly new within a sign. We all recognize parts of ourselves in these primary categories. These are often the tendencies that bring us in contact with the lessons we are here to learn. Our goal is to evolve beyond these tendencies to a more mature level. What a tremendous journey that will be for many of us.

EVOLVED

This category shows you what you are heading toward in this lifetime. It brings you to the higher consciousness of yourself, your highest potentials. It is here that you feel your most productive and where you can celebrate your greatest successes. You reach this level through years of living, trial and error, and through many lifetimes in a particular sun sign giving you countless opportunities for learning and growth. There is no set amount of lifetimes which you must live in each sun sign. In theory, you can learn the lessons all in one lifetime. In reality, you may tend to be a slower student than that and may journey through each sun sign at various paces.

MALE AND FEMALE

There are certain lessons to be experienced by all signs but sometimes a person's sex has an influence. These uniquenesses are discussed under these categories. We may be in an era when we are trying to remove sexual role-playing from our lives, but the different expectations of the sexes is still very much apparent in our astrology.

Each chapter will discuss what it is like to be male or female in each sun sign and will offer advice in handling the karmic lessons unique to each sex within the sign. Society's expectations of a female within a particular sun sign may be significantly different from what is expected of a male. These uniquenesses must be taken into consideration.

CHILDREN

On a personal level, I find this to be the most important category and I give it a great deal of attention. Perhaps one of the most beneficial uses of astrology is to help us understand, not only ourselves, but others around us. Who can be more important than our children? If, as an adult and parent, we can understand the needs and potentials of our children, then we are better equipped to help direct them toward their greatest potentials. Remember, we are only here to protect our children while they are young and to encourage them to follow their healthiest paths. We must learn to stand back as they grow older and let them live through the lessons they have chosen. Hopefully, by understanding and promoting their positive potentials during their youth, we will help them to equip themselves for their journey. However, the journey is still theirs and to protect them or save them from all pain into their adulthood would be robbing them of their karmic education. Enjoy this category; after all, we all want what is best for our children.

BELIEVE IN YOURSELF

In using this book, you must remember to always believe in the most positive parts of yourself. Life is not all serious karmic lessons and difficult courses of study. We also have some pleasant elective classes from which to chose. Along with calculus also comes theater arts. We all deserve recess and lunch break, so allow yourself to enjoy your walk through this lifetime. Life can be filled with some seriousness but it is always buffered with laughter and joy. Through your sun sign you can find your greatest avenues for happiness and karmic satisfaction.

KARMA

WHAT IS KARMA?

This is a question that could take volumes to explore, so let us look at an overview. A clear understanding of karma is important in order to gain the most benefit from this book.

Some say karma is a belief; others say it is a philosophy; still others see it as a religion. The answer is found in a piece of each of these thoughts. Do not look for rigid boundaries or simple truths in your quest for a definition of karma. Rather, leave your thoughts and instincts open for the truth that suits you best.

Karma is often compared to Newton's Third Law: for every action there is an equal and opposite reaction. This premise also plays a strong role in the concept of astrology itself. We all must deal with the oppositions and polarities in our charts. For example, Libra is opposite Aries; therefore, all Libras find a bit of Aries in their personalities, just as all Aries will experience their Libra tug. Many people have over-simplified this theory with regard to karma and automatically assume that they will experience a reaction equal to and opposite to an action they have performed. They also believe that this reaction will have a strong accent on punishment. For example, some believe that a person is born to this lifetime as an invalid because he has misused his physical strength in a past lifetime and is now being punished through the laws of karma. If we choose our own charts, then who is punishing us? Are we punishing ourselves out of guilt and remorse? This is a possible way of looking at karma and a popular attitude within Western cultures. The Eastern religion of Buddhism believes that karma brings with it several different levels of learning. Buddhists, like many of the Western cultures, feel that most souls are here on earth living out the reward-and-punishment principle. Do *good* and you will receive a life of blessings; do *bad* and you will pay the price in equal proportion. Buddhists also believe that there are a few select souls who have evolved to a higher level and are here to learn through life's self-chosen experiences. They also believe, as many religions do, that there are some souls who are here solely to help others, such as Buddha and Christ (a level which we are all capable of attaining through our lifetimes of spiritual growth).

Christianity and Judaism are deeply into the punishment/reward principle without even a mention of karma. Since most of us from these

Western cultures were raised on these religious principles, it is no wonder that we automatically assume that if our life is good, we are good, and if our life is troubled, we are bad.

Why not allow a different theory to mull around within your thoughts? Here you are, an energy, a soul, whose every intention is to evolve from student to teacher, *primary to evolved.* After the completion of each life, you review your experiences. If this time on earth is equated to schooling, you then evaluate your lessons learned, your course of study, but you do not grade yourself. This would put you back into the tendency to judge. Rather, you determine whether you have reached perfection in all these areas. If you deem that you have more to learn and wish to retake a class (experience) or two, you will choose your astrological chart accordingly and set up your next curriculum of study (life). If a soul comes back as an invalid it is because the soul has chosen to learn through the experience of this limitation, not because of a karmic punishment. The soul choses its next karmic step of growth consciously and with purposeful direction.

IS THERE CAUSE AND EFFECT IN KARMA?

Most assuredly, there is some degree of repercussion from past actions within our karma. We must be careful not to use the terms *punishment* and *guilt* while exploring *cause* and *effect*, for these kinds of thoughts take us away from the natural order of karmic events.

We have all heard of *instant karma.* How many times have you heard a mother say to her daughter, "I hope you have a kid just like yourself, then you'll understand what I'm going through with you"? Some years later we find that daughter pulling her hair out with her own child, just as Mom had wished on her. The daughter's soul had asked for a quick repercussion and learning experience similar to the experience she had given her mother. She was not being punished for her awful behavior as a child. She was willing to see both sides of the issue *instantly* or within the same lifetime. She could have chosen to come back in another lifetime to experience that lesson with her own child but she learns more through this instant karmic experience because she is able to relate one experience to another within a short framework of time. Many souls are now choosing to experience instant karma during current lifetimes simply because the evolution of earth and our souls seems to be speeding up. The world seems ablaze with karma but, then, it always has been.

We must realize that we study what we need to learn and we experience what we need in order to grow.

Be careful not to assume that a soul who is murdered is experiencing the cause and effect status of having been a murderer in a past life. We will all experience everything eventually. Let us continue using the analogy of murder as an example. We will all experience the pain of murder but our involvement may take various forms. For instance, we can be the victim, or the murderer, or someone who is associated emotionally with one or the other, such as a spouse, lover, or parent, or a juror in the trial of the murderer. We do not need to play each and every role to experience the lesson of one person taking another person's life. This teaches us many things: value of life, pain of loss, guilt, anger, and forgiveness. More often in the New Age we hear people say, "I forgive the murderer of my loved one". Remember how Pope John Paul II went to the prison and gave forgiveness to Mehmet Ali Agca, the man who had shot him in 1981? We must learn to go to the soul and to understand each involved party in order to learn the lesson of the experience. We are not here to judge others, or to have complete understanding of our difficult times. It takes great karmic evolvement to truly forgive our enemies and to realize that, in truth, we have no enemies. We need to be patient with ourselves in learning this lesson. We will all get there eventually.

THE STRENGTH OF THE SUFFERING

Many times we each have asked, *"What have I done to deserve this?"* *"Why is God punishing me?"* *"I must have done something really bad in a past lifetime to be suffering like this."* These thoughts of self-pity go back to our original leanings toward punishment and guilt. These questions do not need to exist in our understanding of karma.

I once did a reading for a lady who was in her mid-seventies. Her chart happened to be filled with difficult karmic lessons and she verified that she had had an extremely unhappy and difficult life. She felt this was because she was being punished by God for some wrong-doings in her past life. When I explained to her that her life was filled with difficult lessons because she was an evolved soul who had chosen these lessons herself, because she was up to that level of her soul's growth, she said she felt as though a heavy veil had been taken away from her. She was able to view her life's struggles with pride rather than cower under the guilt of punishment. We have kept in contact for many years and she continues to see light and love and hope in her life. The more we take responsibility for ourselves, the stronger we become.

MUST KARMA BE ALL PAIN?

When the average person is asked to define karma, they describe it as a punishment of past actions. In the sixties we had the phrase, *heavy karma, man*. However, karma is not always *heavy*. We see from the beginning of this chapter that karma is an equal and opposite reaction to an action. Therefore, karma will wear the cloak of all colors and hues.

It is true that some of our most important karmic learning experiences come from our more difficult challenges in life. It is also true that we tend to pay more attention to the struggles we are encountering than toward life's pleasures. This seems to be a part of our human temperament. No one keeps reminder messages around them, *take time to prick yourself with the thorns,* yet we do have to remind ourselves to *take time to smell the roses.*

When I am giving a reading to a client and I see planetary energy of opportunity coming up for them, I make a special attempt to stress this positive energy because it may otherwise go by unnoticed and, therefore, unused. Life is not all hard lessons and strife. It is equally filled with pleasure and joy. It is our *human nature* that we must struggle against, that *nature* that has us grumbling at the traffic on the way to work rather than noticing the beauty of nature that we are being forced to pass by more slowly.

To help us appreciate the positive karma around us, we must learn to still our whirling thoughts and tap into our spirituality and our creativity. Our sensitive natures are able to bring us not only pain but joy.

We human beings must believe that we deserve happiness, joy, beauty and comforts in our life or they will be lacking. How often have you heard yourself or someone else say, *"I'm afraid to even think about that wonderful thing happening to me; it may jinx it"* or, *"I never hope for the best, I expect the worse: then I will be prepared?"* How can we get what we ourselves do not believe we deserve? Karma, or life lessons, come in all shapes and forms from pain to pleasure. It is up to us to reach out for what we want.

WHAT IS REINCARNATION?

The philosophy of reincarnation is multidimensional and not totally agreed upon by those of different religious beliefs. There appears to be no definitive way of proving or disproving reincarnation and so it has been left up to the imagination of people from the beginning of mankind. The most widely acknowledged explanation of reincarnation is that a soul does not die when the body ceases to function, but goes on to a higher level where it remains until it re-enters into an earthly form and lives yet another lifetime on earth. This belief that life is perpetual is a vital aspect of the Eastern beliefs which state that a human soul can reincarnate into all various forms, even into the forms of animals. There are different "rules" concerning reincarnation in terms of the levels of evolution that the soul has attained. Some Christian doctrines oppose reincarnation, claiming that there is no credibility in this belief. Other Christians proclaim that Jesus himself talked about reincarnation and proved it himself in his resurrection from death. The Bible even refers to John the Baptist as a reincarnate of Elijah.

A common thread of unity runs among those who believe in the theory of reincarnation and see all life forms as an everlasting energy. Through the science of physics we know that energy cannot die. Everything on this earth is made up of living matter including trees, rocks and the chair upon which we sit. There is a belief that our energy force comes from a central energy power. I see it as a sparkler that a child plays with on the Fourth of July. The sparkler itself is the central source of the power and all the little sparks that come flying off that sparkler are live energy forces. On a sparkler, the little sparks appear to go out and disappear very quickly. Compare this to a human life. A human being lives its life and imprints upon itself certain lessons through its experiences in its life and then it dies. In the terms of reincarnation, it passes over. We all mourn the loss of that particular human being because that person played an important role in many other people's lives and we feel the loss of that person around us. However, its energy force, or its soul as it is called in many religious circles, does not die but continues on its journey by going to different levels of existence other than the earth. It is at these other stages of existence that the soul continues to learn and review its experiences and its process of evolution. It then chooses to come back to the earth in another form, perhaps another human form, in order to continue its quest for learning and growth.

The philosophy of karma is based on reincarnation, since karma is the actions and reactions that we encounter due to our experiences in each incarnation. For example, a man and a women decide, of their own free will, and of their own consciousness, to have a child and so the pregnancy develops. However, it is the free will of a particular soul that determines its need to reincarnate into that child's body. Life with those parents would bring to that soul certain experiences which it needs at this point in its evolution. When your teenagers look at you and say *"I didn't ask to be born,"* they really did! The parents decided to have a child; that was their decision. It was the soul's option to actually reincarnate into that child's bodily form. We could go into a philosophical debate over the point the soul enters the body and whether it is possible for us to reincarnate into the form of a rock or a cow or even whether the human soul is more *evolved* than animal souls. These sorts of questions are far too technical for the function of this particular book. The most important point to understand is that you are a living energy that has been around a long time and which will continue to be around an even longer time. In between your visits to this earth level you are meeting up with your source of power and other energy sources to strengthen you. It is like being part of a very tight-knit family and periodically going off to travel on your own. You always come back to that strong family bond. That is why you may feel a recognition of people when you encounter them on this earth level. These are souls that you know, that you are comfortable with, with which you have had other lifetime experiences and sometimes you may recognize them from that initial power source. It is my opinion that the term *soul-mate* is very much abused and misunderstood in the modern age. When we recognize someone and we feel particularly comfortable with them, that shows that there is a level of recognition. We remark how comfortable we feel with this person. This *soul-awareness* or recognition is quite common and need not be singled out as a relationship with a soul-mate or a once in a millennium experience. We will come into contact with many souls we have known before through our various travels in each lifetime. Sometimes they are the people we work with, our family members, our children, our spouses, even the person behind us at the grocery check-out counter. A soul awareness does not constitute the one and only love of our life.

The same is true with certain places where we choose to live in this world. You may travel to a foreign country and feel so comfortable there, so at home. Many people say that they feel they have gone back home when they travel to a particular place. That is because the soul has an awakening, an awareness of a past incarnation in this particular environment. Obviously, if we are happy there then it was a pleasant incarnation. Sometimes our souls jerk with rebellion when our bodies take them back to a place of unpleasant remembrances of past experiences. There are some places we go to or people we meet that we are very uncomfortable around and we do not know why. They certainly have not done anything or the area has not given us any negativities but we are not comfortable and that is an indication of an unpleasant experience in that area or with that person that we may not consciously remember but our soul is identifying the imprint of that past experience.

We would probably know much more about reincarnation, karma, our soul and ourselves, in general, if we allowed ourselves to listen to our inner beings. This is something we do not give ourselves time for in the twentieth century. Even when we are sitting alone we usually have a radio or TV on, or we are talking on the telephone or reading a book. We are very skilled at keeping our brains active yet it is only with inactivity, stillness and centering that we are able to go into ourselves and get many of the answers to the questions that this particular chapter in the book raises. Many people are actively seeking those answers. This book will hopefully help you to tune in to your karmic consciousness and help you to enjoy the discovery of your potentials based on your sun sign.

IS THERE A GOD?

There does not need to be any conflict between the philosophy of karma and your religious beliefs. Most modern religions touch upon karma in their doctrine, they simply call it something different. This is a subject that can fill bookshelves but let us just give it a simple answer here. In every aspect of life there is someone for us to answer to: a parent, a teacher, a boss. No matter what job we do, there is always some boss above us. Why should this not be true of the great cosmos? We tend to call this power God. We take responsibility for our own actions, we choose our next lessons, we review our own progress but that boss we call God is always with us.

The philosophy of karma can be easily assimilated into any traditional religious belief without conflict, even into a belief that there is no God. Remember, we are all here to find our own truth and we are all at different levels on that quest but the end of the path will be the same for us all: Nirvana. When we achieve this goal, we will have all the answers. Until then we can merely hypothesize and speculate and, most importantly, try our best.

SUN SIGNS AND KARMA

As stated in the Introduction, this book is designed to help you understand the karmic lessons coming to you through your sun sign. Characteristics of each sign are stressed because these special qualities help take you toward the directions your soul has chosen in this lifetime. Know yourself and know why you are here. Equip yourself with the right tools and always lean toward your strengths. You are on an adventure, but your adventure has a purpose. Your sun sign will help you to know that purpose.

ARIES

March 21 - April 19

Male Energy

KARMIC LESSONS

◆ Independence vs. I want it my way

◆ Dealing with leadership roles

◆ Diplomacy

◆ Sharing

◆ Dealing with aggressiveness

PRIMARY ARIES

You will be dealing with your primary energies when you are young, immature and first encountering your most important life lessons. You will find yourself acting and reacting on a primary level at different times of your life, long after you feel you should be more mature or above that basic part of yourself. Try not to be disappointed with yourself when your primary tendencies emerge. Look at this as a time in your life when you need to work a little harder. In fact, this may well indicate a significant learning experience on which your soul has quite purposely chosen to work. Knowing yourself through your astrology will help you to keep a finger on the pulse of your soul's needs.

In order to understand what your karmic goals are as an Aries, you need to get a clear understanding of what your primary inclinations will be. Rather than look at primary as a weakness, realize that some of the experiences which your primary tendencies will bring you toward will ultimately take you to your highest karmic lessons. As an Aries, you are working on understanding that this great strength and aggressiveness which you have naturally within you can sometimes be intimidating to other people. It is when you feel or sense that you are intimidating others that you should become aware that you are now working on your primary level.

As an Aries, you can sometimes say things in a way which can hurt other people's feelings even though this may not be your conscious intention. There is a primary Aries tendency at times for you to think of yourself first, to put yourself first; to use the words *I* and *me*, not only verbally but also within your thought processes. Another primary tendency is to be fiercely competitive. Now, it is an asset for you, as an Aries, to be competitive and to strive to be the best and the first. But, when you become competitive at the expense of other people around you, then you are working on your primary level. Also, this competitive, strong, aggressive part of your nature can sometimes get you physically hurt. When you are working on a project, full of enthusiasm, you may find you are hurting yourself. If you are cutting yourself, banging, bruising or physically doing harm to yourself, you are not paying attention to this primary Aries level which is working physically without giving mental or emotional thought to what you are doing.

You are working solely on the primary physical level of your Aries when you find yourself totally absorbed in a project or a goal, and unable or unwilling to think of the other people who are involved, which will be indicated by a lack of sharing or a lack of compromise on your part. You are being introduced to a karmic learning experience, again, through your primary level. When somebody is particularly strong and they have leadership ability, they tend to be somewhat *I* and *me* oriented. "*I'll take care of this*", "*leave it up to me*", "*I have confidence in myself to make that decision*", and that is an essential need of society that Aries will fulfill. But you are going toward your primary aspects of your Aries sign when you find that you are losing interest in other things and other people, and have become totally absorbed in your own self and your own endeavors. All fire signs need to learn about ego. All leaders need to learn about their egos. These primary tendencies you have just read about, will peek their little heads out at you throughout your life, and when they do, do not pull back and think that is a piece of yourself that should not be, a piece that you should avoid. Rather, think that this is a piece of yourself, your Aries, coming out in its fullest force, leading you toward a significant karmic learning experience. Be aware of yourself. The more aware you are of how often you say *I* or *me* in a conversation, the less likely you are to continue this pattern and the more likely you are to start consciously thinking in terms of *we*.

EVOLVED ARIES

You will be working with your evolved energies when you are older in years and after you have experienced several incarnations within your sun sign. (An experienced astrologer will be able to tell you where you are in your evolution.) We all learn from our early mistakes and experiences and this growth will show in the way we deal with our karmic life lessons. In an evolved state, you will lean toward your highest, most positive vibration. You will feel confident and proud of yourself and, certainly, self assured.

As an Aries, being in your most evolved state, people are going to be looking toward you as a leader, taking on leadership responsibilities. This can manifest itself on many different levels. For example, you could be a world leader, you could be a great general, you could be president of a country, or a dictator. You could be president of your local PTA, leader of a Girl Scout troop. You could be the one who organizes block parties in your community. Being a leader, as an Aries, will give you opportunities in many different areas of your life. It does not mean that you always need to be the leader, but don't be surprised if the people around look toward you when a leadership position needs to be filled. How you handle that position of authority is where your greatest abilities as an Aries will shine. First thing that an Aries needs to learn is how to delegate responsibility. That, in the evolved state, is how you will take away the *I* and the *me*. The primary aspect of you will say, "*I am the leader. I am the boss. Do it my way. Everybody, follow me. We're going up to the top of the hill.*" In your more evolved state as an Aries leader, you will take on the responsibility with the fullest confidence that you can handle it and then you will delegate responsibilities to other people while still remaining the focal point of leadership. You want to be able to take on a position of authority without being overly competitive in getting to that position nor overly ego-involved in maintaining that position. As an evolved Aries, your greatest asset will be to laugh at yourself and to own up to your mistakes. When you can do this you will know that you have accomplished and mastered a marvelous karmic lesson in your life. You will become quiet, you will become a listener and you will be surprised at how effective you will be as a leader when you become an interested listener.

Concerning your relationships, in your evolved state, you will be sharing and compromising with all the people with whom you share relationships. Not only will you be able to admit your mistakes as a great leader but you will also be able to admit your mistakes, frailties and fears within your closest relationships. Even here, you will be able to take more of a back seat when you are functioning through your evolved state as an Aries. That wonderful, fierce competitive nature that was coming out in your primary level is still there but now you are having fun with your competitiveness. You are enjoying your sports, your rise to the top, you are immersing yourself in the work of life without taking yourself too seriously. You see, as you take on additional responsibilities and challenge your world, you become more evolved and you begin to tone down your aggressiveness. You do not get less responsibility, in fact you get more, but you tone down the intensity behind that drive and you begin to relax. You become more comfortable with yourself. By the way, an evolved Aries will not be accident prone. You will become cautious and careful. Not to say, an evolved Aries will never have an accident, but that you will no longer have accidents because you are trying to do things too quickly. This aspect of yourself will dissipate and you will find much more fun coming into your life. An evolved Aries makes a wonderful partner, a magnificent leader.

REMEMBER, NO ONE IS TOTALLY PRIMARY OR TOTALLY EVOLVED. OUR KARMIC LESSONS ARE BEST LEARNED WHEN WE ARE DEALING WITH BOTH OF THESE ENERGIES.

INDEPENDENCE VS. I WANT IT MY WAY

As an Aries, you will be learning about yourself in relation to others. Our species stays within groups. We like to mate and form relationships within family and community units. You also are a part of this unity yet you like to go off on your own to fulfill your own needs. You enjoy adventure and excitement, competition and challenge. In the early evolution of man, you would have been the warrior, the great hunter. These settings can be lonely with no one to count on for advice except your own judgment. Therefore, the Aries in you brings with it an ability to make your own decisions that are very much based on your personal goals and ambitions. The rest of the group is left to huddle together and await your return from the great hunt or gallant battle. During these ancient times, the Aries male was honored for his bravery and was not expected to be a part of the group's unity. The Aries female was looked upon as a trouble maker who did not know her proper place within the group. She needed a strong man to keep her under control.

In our society today, we still need men and now women to leave the sanctuary of family and home in order to follow their independent goals. We still need our adventurers, explorers, hunters and warriors. But most of you are a part of the more everyday world of nine to five jobs, marriage commitments, children, and communities. Most of you must learn the lessons of coping with other people's wills around you. Aries can no longer simply leave the family with a grunt and spear without the need for explanation and compromise. The world of the Aries is different now and so are your karmic lessons.

If you are an Aries following your primary instincts, you will have difficulty establishing any relationships which lead to commitment. You will want things to go your way and will particularly want to be able to do the things you want to do without interference from others. This kind of primary behavior will set up situations which will force you to confront your role in relationships.

Here are some examples in case histories. See if you can find yourself or some Aries whom you know:

THE CHALLENGE OF COMMITMENT

Joe loved to live dangerously. He wanted everything to be fast and exciting or he wasn't interested in it. As a youngster he loved to speed downhill on his bike flinging his feet up in the air while the pedals spun wildly beneath him. He always left his friends behind as they coasted more slowly together as a group. As Joe entered early manhood, his love for adventure and independence led him toward driving fast cars, sexually conquering women, always living on the edge. Eventually, Joe fell in love with Ann, a woman who also loved fun things like waterskiing, parasailing and motorcycling. They married and had many years together enjoying these activities until Ann became pregnant and their first daughter was born. Ann could no longer "play" with Joe every weekend. They were no longer able to vacation as they used to, and Joe felt the difference. Ann was able to adjust to her new role because, even when she was a little girl, she would talk for hours on end with her girlfriends about growing up and being a mother. By now she had several friends who had already settled down themselves with families, and Ann was ready to sell the motorcycle and water skis and grow into her new role. Joe was not ready. He had never developed a close friendship with any of the other men his age who had decided to "settle down." He thought of them as boring. He had lots of so-called friends, but they were really just "guys" he would call upon for a game of racquet ball or a few drinks at the local hot spot.

Joe's primary need to run ahead of the pack had put him out front, in his eyes, but had also left him out of pace with his peers. He had become the lonely runner. Now his primary need for independence and doing things his way had set up a situation around him which would force him to

experience his karmic lesson of functioning responsibly within
a relationship. With moderation, Joe learned that he could
play racquet ball and parasail while still assuming his new
responsibilities as a father and giving husband. He eventually
became a part of a new circle of friends who also enjoyed
their independence and role as family-men.

Now we all know Joe could have gone another way
with his primary energy. He could have stayed out late night
after night. He could have been with many women to prove
to himself that he was still a free spirit. He could have
continued to drive fast, risking his life in spite of his loved
ones' needs for him to be alive. He could have always wanted
it to be his way.

When an Aries reacts this way, they are said to be fixated in their
primary stage. They will be exposed to karmic lessons dealing with
relationships over and over in order to give them the opportunity to learn
and grow. The Universe is so patient with us. The energies of the stars
never cease to extend themselves to us. And so, even if Joe were unable
to change his attitude immediately, the opportunity for learning would
always be made available to him as it is to all of us.

What if Joe should fail completely (although there is no concept of
total failure in the cosmos)? Then he would reincarnate and try again; the
answer lies in such a simple form. Through Joe's gradual acceptance of his
family responsibilities he, without conscious effort, brought his Aries soul
into an evolved stage of development.

THE LIBERATED WOMAN

Betty had many relationships in her life. They all ended by
Betty breaking them off - or so it always seemed. Her list of
ended relationships was quite extensive by the time she was
50 years old. She seemed to be repeating the same karmic
lessons each time. Finally, Betty turned to counseling in order
to gain some understanding of her problem. Luckily, her
counselor was a believer in the guidance of astrology in
therapy, and honed in on Betty's Aries life lessons.

Aries, like all Fire signs, is concerned with ego. She
had always been exceptionally independent with a highly
developed sense of self importance. It seemed she always
knew the right way of doing things. Her solutions were

always the correct ones. This attitude was causing a problem for Betty on all relationship levels including family and friendships. She felt it was her duty to take on a leadership role and lead everyone to the right path in life. She surrounded herself with people who were in need, people who were floundering. She had a sister with three children and no husband. Betty took this family under her wing with financial and emotional support. She maintained her independence by living apart from them but forced her ego upon them with her opinions. Betty, who had never had children of her own, became the expert on raising children and was quick to criticize her sister. Everything was to be done her way.

In her love relationships she also fought hard to maintain her independence and individuality, never allowing herself to fall comfortably into a total commitment. The men in her life were troubled or weak and Betty felt she had all the right answers for them. She talked fast. She moved fast. She became more and more critical of others. As her lovers matured and grew strong, Betty would end the relationship with great criticism of them and their weaknesses.

Betty was 50 years old and still fixated in her primary energy of Aries. It was right after this important birthday that she met her match. He also was an Aries and they fell into a fiery, passionate love affair. Now Betty had found, with the support of her therapist, her opportunity to face and learn compromise. She was able to give of herself in this relationship without fear of losing her independence. The fact that she was ready to exit her primary energy patterns was evident in her willingness to give of her love to a man who was strong and not needy of her. It also showed that she was becoming more comfortable with herself as she was able to love someone who was so much like herself. Her willingness to enter counseling was the first sign of her desire to change. This was a long learned lesson for Betty. She fought her growth for many years. Astrology and psychotherapy were both positive tools for her and she used them well.

A RELATIONSHIP WITH AN ARIES IS NOT FOR THE WEAK OF HEART!

As an Aries you have great strength, great courage. In an evolved state, you are able to direct those strengths toward the survival of a relationship rather than the destruction of it: the warrior who fights to protect his loved ones rather than seek the glory and adventure of battle; the hunter who enters the woods determined to make the swift kill and return with nourishment for his family rather than use the need of the hunt as his excuse to be away.

You are able to harness your energy and direct it toward a shared purpose, shared with any other relationship in your life. You are able to set up a relationship which allows you to maintain your individuality while you lovingly fulfill your share of the responsibilities. You have brought people into your environment who you respect and, therefore, will be open to their suggestions. You will not feel controlled or manipulated by these people because   you are the one who has chosen them. Most importantly, they will respect you and they will count on you. As an evolved Aries, you will be comfortable with this responsibility, you will not feel that your will has been broken. Aries is a powerful sign and you will find, with the support of a healthy relationship, you will able to conquer the world.

Even though it is important for you to maintain your independence, as an Aries, you still need to be loved. You need the warmth and security that a loving relationship can give you. As an evolved Aries, you recognize this need and will respond with great enthusiasm to a loved one. It is true that Aries energy can bring with it a wandering eye, a penchant for casual affairs which have no meaning to you. As an evolved Aries, you may face the challenge of such a temptation and you will bear the scars of any karmic consequences of your actions. Interestingly, astrology does not signify any judgements on your actions. These reactions will come from society and from within yourself. You will be learning the karmic lesson of putting other person's feelings ahead of your own immediate needs and whims. This can be an especially tough lesson because your ego will always be tempting you with it's need to be fed. You will establish healthier ways of supporting your ego without risking your significant relationships.

An evolved Aries will love hard and strong. Woe to any outside force which may try to hurt your loved ones.

THE LIONESS AND HER CUBS

Eileen's husband, Keith, was killed when his single engine aircraft crashed into a mountain top during heavy snows. Along with the tremendous loss of her husband's love, Eileen was now left with the sole responsibility of raising and supporting their five children ages seven through sixteen. She was always an active Aries, involved in the racquet ball league, tennis competitions and the high school PTA, but she had never developed a career. Her children were her career. Now, she was forced to find work, set up a new family routine and fend for herself and her children. Her Aries energy swung into gear.

Eileen was first confronted with the essentials of life...paying the mortgage, supplying the food, keeping the children's routines as normal as possible. Keith had left enough insurance to keep them afloat, but not for the long haul. Eileen saw this and, immediately, took charge of caring for her family. She drew from her basic, primary instincts which were to supply her family's needs. She worked long and hard hours in her new job in sales, advancing within the company, increasing her paychecks month after month. She set up an efficient system at home combining her efforts and those of her children to make sure home and hearth were running smoothly. The children had their chores, lists were posted all over the house with orders and rules; the older children took responsibility for the younger. Her children knew what their mother was doing for them and they loved her for the long hours she was working in order to keep up their standard of living. They each knew, in their hearts, that she was there for them. But, some of her children needed more than the maintenance of their large home. They needed more than the comfort of an older brother or sister when they skinned their knees or feared the monsters in the dark. They needed the warmth and love of their mother who was not there for them in that capacity. Eileen was now the warrior, the hunter, fending for her family.

Fortunately, Eileen's children knew that they could talk to her about their feelings and needs. They called a family conference. It was during that conversation that Eileen realized that she was struggling so hard to maintain a life style which was more important to *her* needs than those of her children. They made her aware that they needed her energy and force closer to them, in the home more than out. With the help of her older children, Eileen and her family moved from the beautiful, spacious house that Keith had been able to provide, to a smaller, comfortable home which they could more easily maintain. The reduced mortgage and fewer chores now took great pressures off the entire family.

Eileen had been working so hard, she had scarcely noticed how much she had missed the closeness of her family. She now realized that her children needed her to be around to help them with the challenges of growing up rather than keeping up their past standard of living. As an evolved Aries, Eileen was now able to put aside *her* need for status and *her* view of providing for her family. Her children had helped to show her exactly how they needed her strength and fighting spirit. They much preferred her rooting for them on the sidelines of their soccer matches or striding through the door with a glow of excitement as she initiated another issue on the PTA board. This time, children led an Aries to her evolved energy. They still looked to her for her leadership and strength only now it was in compromise to their needs and hers. She had accomplished her Karmic lesson of providing for her loved ones according to the needs of the entire unit. Most importantly, she had taught them, through her example, of the strength they all had within them. Eileen lovingly gave of her Aries strength to her children.

Each of the case examples shows how some Aries found themselves in a stressful relationship situation and how they chose to accept the karmic lessons these situations presented to them. These have been idealistic, success stories of Aries evolvement. Naturally, life's examples also are filled with stories of those who did not always make the right choices, those who experienced many struggles in order to grow.

For Aries, the lessons of relationships are more like riding a see-saw. There are many ways of playing on this ride. It's fun sitting on the ground holding your partner captive up in the air. It's also fun to be up high getting a good sight of the rest of the playground. But each of these are lonely positions with little give and take between you and your partner. When you see-saw back and forth with trust and confidence, neither one of you will be left high or low. You will find your eyes will always be on one another. You will both be experiencing the thrill of the ride and being relaxed together. This brings in the aspect of sharing which is also a karmic lesson for Aries and which involves their roles in relationships.

SHARING MAY NOT BE EASY FOR THE ARIES

As an Aries, you are born with a natural inclination to blaze new trails on your own. Your basic personality traits lead you to venture out on your own without the need for group support. In fact, you may find other people to be a burden, they may seem to hold you down. Your will is a strong will and learning to hear the ideas of others may take more time than you wish to extend. Sharing is not an easy karmic lesson for you, yet it is an important one if you are to learn how to work successfully within relationships.

For example, in the case of Joe, he may have gotten supportive advice from his friends in his struggle to settle down to being a husband and father. But Joe had not learned to share his time with friends when he was a child or an adult. Friends to Joe were people with whom he competed in sports and games and his attentions were always put on leaving them behind rather than walking with them. By deciding to share his life with Ann and their child, he found himself without experience or example in this behavior mode. Once he made the determination of his family commitment, he was soon able to extend this karmic lesson of sharing to his circle of buddies. Joe was then able to start making some long overdue friendships. Once an Aries learns to share within one relationship it becomes contagious and spreads throughout the rest of his or her life.

Please do not assume because you are sharing that you are automatically giving up your freedoms. Many Aries feel this way at first. Remember, Joe liked to ride his bike ahead of the rest of his friends. He liked speed, the adventure of the trip. His competitive nature pushed him to be the first one to get to the destination. Part of him could feel frustrated, held back, trapped by being enclosed in a group.

LEARNING TO SHARE DOES NOT MEAN GIVING UP YOUR INDEPENDENCE.

Learning to share means giving consideration to the feelings and needs of others. Sharing, to an Aries, can mean looking backward now and then to those you have left behind and checking that they are alright. By sharing, you will be giving   a part of yourself to someone else. Of equal importance, you will be allowing yourself to incorporate valuable lessons brought to you through other people's experiences. Sharing brings with it collective learning which will be invaluable to the evolved Aries.

DEALING WITH LEADERSHIP ROLES

Aries are born leaders. It is the first sign of the zodiac. It begins the Spring season, the initiation of life. We all expect the Aries individual to lead us and it is a mantle they willingly accept. It is the Aries karmic responsibility to deal with leadership. You must watch how you use this energy. It comes with a great deal of power.

THE CROWN OF LAUREL HID THORNS

Bucky was the star of the local high school football team; big jock on campus. Everybody looked up to him because he was a star in his sport and the game of football happened to be an important part of the community. Everyone admired him, parents, faculty, and his fellow students. So, at a very early age, sixteen years of age to be exact, he was commanding and holding the respect and admiration of many people. He was an Aries leader. Sometimes power comes to us too easily and this was the case with Bucky. When he walked into the local movie theater, all heads turned. Here was Bucky, the star of the football team. All the girls wanted to date him, so he thought. And he was able to ask out any girl he wanted and she would say yes, so he thought. And he really did not have to work hard at achieving good grades because the faculty needed him to be the star quarterback of the football team. All he need give to his studies was a mediocre piece of himself. The only place where he was expected to excel was on the football field which came naturally to him. It took no great effort for him to do this. He enjoyed being competitive. He relished plowing through other people on the football field because he was working on his primary level where he was fiercely competitive and often hurt. He also never had to learn how to share within his relationships. He felt that he was to be adored, after all, that is how every one was treating him. He never had to give in order to get. It all seemed right to him. The powerful force of his ego was always in control of his life. He thought that his team fully adored him since they always carried him on their shoulders after he brought his team to victory. Why, it was like a story book success for Bucky. In the fall of his senior year, during the Thanksgiving football game, two of the other major players who were a strong part of the team's defense system, were hurt while executing a routine play. They were playing a team they traditionally slaughtered with 20-30 point leads, so they were not feeling concerned about this game. But now they had two very valuable players knocked out of the game and, suddenly, things were not going well for Bucky. He was trying to drive some passes to his receiver and he was being ploughed back yard after yard, not being able to make any first downs. He was getting angry. The primary aspect of his Aries came raging through. Where was his defense system? How dare they get hurt! He was not looking good now. Within short order, the other team won, and Bucky's high school team left quite dejected from that Thanksgiving Day game. Bucky's image was not shining with great luster either. He was no longer the blazing hero because it became more and more evident to the fans in the stands that Buck wasn't alone in this team as the star. His dependency on the team's defense was powerfully evident that day. Bucky also had to start asking himself why he was a *star*, why he was a *leader* and how much he needed to share his success with other people. This karmic lesson was particularly strong because Bucky was forced to learn his lesson in public. He was forced to recognize that he was only *a part* of that football team. They were all sharing in the glory and, therefore, they all had to share in the loss. This happened to him in a friendly environment. The faculty and coach were sympathetic with the lesson he was learning. His friends remained his friends. He was particularly lucky that his ego had not gotten totally out of control before this crashing blow. Bucky learned at an early age that his success and leadership position came to him through a sharing of energies with the rest of his team. He brought this forward to other areas of his life which included his social and academic spheres. First, it came to him through the football game where he was given his opportunity to lead. Through his karmic experiences of leadership, he was taught the lesson of sharing. In this life, nothing happens to us without a purpose. The purpose for those two other players to have gone through the pain and agony of injury was, in the end, to enable Bucky to understand the responsibility he had with his leadership role. Also, he was lucky in that he had the support of his friends and community. It helped that he was quick witted enough to grasp the situation easily, that with leadership comes a responsibility to all the people around you. He learned that he was not the star without the rest of the team. With this realization came a growing appreciation of his fellow teammates. This karmic lesson enabled him to develop a sharing relationship with his teammates which led him to an even greater pleasure of the game of life.

THE TRUE PRIZE WAS SELF-UNDERSTANDING

At about the same point in time, there was a fellow student who had graduated high school and was now in her junior year of college. She was president of the top sorority on campus. Her name was June and she was going through some very similar karmic learning lessons as Bucky. Here was June, also a strong Aries, given this position of leadership and power by being elected president of her sorority. Her learning lesson came with swiftness to her. She was well liked by her friends and excelled in her studies and sports. June was given her Aries karmic test of her use of power through her role in her sorority.   Another girl, who June had known previously in high school and had not particularity liked, was seeking membership in the sorority. Her name was Sue. Not that Sue had ever done anything in particular to June. June just didn't think that Sue was sorority material. Of course we realize that sororities have bylaws and they do have certain criteria for picking their initiates but June's attitude toward Sue had nothing to do with these standards of the sorority. This had to do with June herself. And so, through her influence, June made sure that Sue did not become a member of the sorority. None of the other sisters questioned June's reasoning because she knew Sue from their past high school days where they had both played tennis together. The sorority sisters assumed that June knew something and was being lady enough not to slander Sue in any way choosing instead to quietly and swiftly eliminate her. They accepted her leadership judgement.

Time went by and June and Sue met each other on the tennis courts during a competition. They both played tennis superbly moving up in the standings until they were playing against each other for that top position, the tournament trophy. Both girls played their best games. It was during these matches that June recognized how much she respected Sue for her command of the tennis court: Her strong strokes, her steady game.

Sue lost that match and June once again held the trophy as the best tennis player in her region. Yet June earned more that day than merely being the recipient of another win. She learned something about herself. She became aware that she had ostracized Sue from her sorority because she saw her as a competitor. She saw her, on a subconscious level, as a strong woman, sensing Sue's equally strong Arian traits. She was afraid that Sue might take away her glory and, eventually, her leadership, just as she had now almost taken away that trophy. Once again, realization and the beauty of the karmic learning lesson came quickly to June just as it had come swiftly to Bucky. They were both given the ability to instantly remedy their past actions. June made sure that Sue became a member of her sorority. They were also able to develop a mutual friendship which they have continued to maintain to this day. Certainly both of these case studies show us that with leadership comes a strong responsibility to those who have given you the power.

It is important to note that not all Aries are aggressive, loud, overtly competitive individuals. The full extent of an Aries personality is based on the entire complexities of their astrological chart. Some Aries can be quite shy, withdrawn, choosing more of a back seat than you would normally anticipate from an Aries. But all Aries will be confronted with the issue of leadership at some point in their lives. Some may more aggressively confront that leadership power, others may do it in a much more subdued manner. Still others may have to be talked into it. Their karmic lesson of dealing with leadership will come upon them and they will have to deal with that lesson at some point in their lives. We can use the example of world leaders and how some people use and abuse their power. You can have dictators who only think of themselves and, therefore, show little or no concern for the people they govern. Their drive to be in power is simply to fulfil their own ego needs rather than to serve the people or to serve a cause.

Look at some of the leaders of the Third World nations, or at some of the resistance forces during our world wars. These leaders were made up of common everyday folk, who felt such a strong need to fight for their cause, to fight for their country or properties that they took the leadership call upon themselves joyfully, although they did not care whether their names were remembered, or whether they eventually sat on a throne of gold but they did care strongly for their beliefs.

Whatever the motivations behind the Aries drive for leadership and power, they still ultimately have to deal with their own truth of how they wield that power once it is given to them by others. We watch the aging process of our presidents in our country. Every president ages more than the four or eight years would have effected him if he were sitting in retirement or working in an easier job.

We know that leadership brings with it great burdens but an additional Aries karmic responsibility is to look at themselves and face these issues on the use and misuse of their leadership power; whether they are trying with all great intentions to be fair and just rulers or if they are "raping" the country of its financial resources, economic stability and morale. If an Aries is in power, that Aries is grappling with important karmic issues, beyond serving their cause.

There are Aries all over the world who are taking on leadership roles in much smaller fashion than our world leaders. These are the people I mentioned before who head committees, volunteer on the board of education, PTA, Girl Scouts, Little League, and company bowling teams. As an Aries, it is imperative that you, at some point in your life, assume leadership responsibility, whether it be in a miniscule or monumental capacity. Through this experience you will enable yourself to experience your karmic growth, the extent of which will depend upon your use or misuse of that power which you seek. The world needs you to be leaders. That is the role you fill to balance out our world. Because we need you to do what comes naturally to you we will call upon you to take responsibility. That is how karma comes to you. You have the natural inclination to be a leader. Other people around you will sense it and therefore they will point to you, *"Hey, you over there, Aries. Would you like to head this committee?"* It is up to you to choose what times you want to be a leader. You can not be a leader all the time. You would be exhausted if you tried. Once you do choose your time of leadership, the karmic lesson will come directly to you, how do you intend to deal with that power?

You are brave people you Aries. I know if I were a sergeant in the war and I needed someone to go up and take a strategic military position, I would turn around and find the closest Aries to me and command "*Go on up there and take that hill!*" I would know with the fullest confidence that Aries would perform to the best of his or her ability securing that hill. A competitive edge, the need to lead the group and fierce athletic and physical strength are given to you as an Aries. It is a wonderful combination which can bring you great success.

DIPLOMACY

All Aries need to learn the finesse and intricate style of diplomacy. As an Aries, you have a tendency to say things as you think them without sugar-coating or thinking it through very carefully. As fast as you are to physically rush into something, and take care of it, handle it and do it, you are just as quick to express yourself in words. And so, karmically, as an Aries, you must learn how to still your thoughts and think before you speak. There is a rash bluntness that can come across through your Aries nature. One thing is for sure, everyone around you will know what you are thinking. People will respect you for your honesty and truthfulness. But being blunt, and being diplomatic is not necessarily a contrast between honesty and dishonesty. You can be equally as honest being diplomatic as by being blunt. Usually it takes you some time to understand and recognize the fact that you are wounding peoples' feelings in the way you express yourself. Your Aries' tendency to walk over to someone at a party and say "*My God the color of your sweater looks awful on you*" can be devastating to that woman wearing the sweater but, as an Aries, you can continue walking by and never realize that you had said anything wrong. The Aries mind says "*I only said that to prevent her from embarrassing herself by wearing such an ugly sweater. I did her a favor*". That is the brashness of your Aries coming out, doing a "favor" for someone who did not really ask for your help.

I have been to many gatherings with Aries present and I have heard their mouths in action. If I were to go to an Aries and ask their opinion, I know I would get an honest response. I also know that I would have to prepare myself to hear that opinion in a form that may not be too easy for me to take.

As the Aries gets older, they realize that some people don't want to associate with them anymore. People back away from them. They may be afraid of hearing something offensive, or being told something in too blunt a fashion. The Aries, after a while, will start picking this up and maybe some people will have the courage to be honest with them. At this point, the Aries will begin to work on that issue of diplomacy.

In taking on a leadership role, you automatically find yourself needing to develop more diplomatic talents. Unless you choose to be that leader who is dictatorial in nature, you will be under advisement of different people and will want to maintain certain balances.

There are various levels of your own life when you will be working on diplomacy. As an Aries, it is important for you to understand that the opposite sign of Aries is Libra. Libra is the sign of diplomacy. In astrology we are always a part of our opposite, a part of our polarity. Therefore, you innately have a Libra sense within you, which will help you to develop this talent. Some Aries are born with it, they have already learned diplomacy through previous lifetime experiences. They seem to come into this world with a natural inclination toward diplomacy. And these Aries, when reading this part of this book, think to themselves, "*I can't identify with this. I'm not blunt like that.*" You will not, as an Aries, be able to identify with every primary quality that is being described here. These words are here for those of you who are able to identify with them. Your eyes will fall upon the words you need to read. Your minds will record the messages you need to hear.

ARIES MALE

If you are an Aries male you have chosen some specific learning lessons to work on in this lifetime. Our society not only allows, but also encourages, men to be aggressive. Aries is a masculine sign and therefore fits comfortably within the male form. If you are sitting in a restaurant with a group of people and the waiter refuses to serve you, some people at that table will look toward a man to speak out for them. Certainly, most people at that table will look toward an Aries man to take the initiative and handle the situation. Therefore, these Aries traits of leadership and aggressiveness can be used in a positive way by the Aries male. The key word in this sentence is "positive." Let us take the example of not being waited on in a restaurant. If you, as the Aries male, started yelling and screaming and pounding your fists on the table, you would be calling attention to the issue but in a negative way. You are expected karmically to use that energy to persuade the waiter to fulfill his responsibilities to your group by assuming a forceful, authoritative role as only an Aries can. In this way, you will be employing all the positive qualities of your firm, persuasive sign of Aries.

The Aries male who is the bully of the block is obviously using his aggressiveness in its most negative form. Sometimes that same man who was once the bully grows up to understand what it is like to use power in its positive sense. He could then, for example, become the policeman who helps the kids deal with the realities of the streets. There is a unique way in which an Aries man looks at an issue with resolute authority so that we may look up to him. Whether we respect him or fear him, he is intimidating. The Aries male is certainly being his most intimidating self when he is the bully or when he is choosing to frighten people with his fiery nature. After all, Aries can be filled with aggressive energy and combining that Aries force with the strength of a masculine body can be quite frightening to people. The Aries male is aware of this power. If he has any feeling of insecurity or need to intimidate other people, he has all the power he needs to act out in this manner.

This is obviously a karmic misuse of this energy. In a mature fashion, the Aries man is still strong physically but he holds himself with an air of authority. He is able to look someone right in the eye and say, *"I want it to be done correctly,"* or *"I want this done my way."* There is a sense of security derived from this kind of an Aries male. Instead of feeling intimidated by a misuse of power, this Aries can make people feel comfortable. He has the lead and they know he will take care of them.

The Aries man must also learn how to share his life, his time, and his money equally with his life partner and children. Remember, Aries has a basic nature to be self oriented; the tendency to be a loner. In our society and in our culture, we do not encourage men to show their emotions and to share their thoughts, time and feelings. After all, the man is supposed to be out there hunting, out there working, out there mowing the lawn. We do not think of him, especially an Aries man, as the one who is there to change the baby's diaper, to sit and read stories to his children. He is the warrior, he is the aggressive provider. He must learn to bring these gentler traits into his family life. Remember, karmically the Aries must also learn to share. When the Aries man is younger, he tends to be aggressive, out on his own, promoting his career, providing for his family being his full justification. But, as the Aries male gets older, he may feel something lacking in his life. He may feel the fear that his family has for him. Along with the respect he also feels the estrangement. As he becomes more aware of this loss, he will actively pursue a relationship of more depth with his wife and children. This level of relationship will come to him as he masters his ability to share.

The Aries male also has a wonderful gift to give to the people around him, that is to encourage them to seek their own independence. An Aries male may typically find himself in a situation where people are dependent on him. It is part of his own astrological makeup which encourages that kind of person to be near him. This is where you hear, *"My husband Joe died and I don't know what I'm going to do. I don't even know how to balance my check book. I have no idea how to turn off the water in the basement or where our insurance policies are."* The Aries man had taken care of all that and, in doing so, he had promoted a relationship of dependence upon himself by his wife. It was great in satisfying his need to be the leader, his need to be head of the household. It may also have been a product of his impatience; his inability to sit down with his wife and show her all these matters. Sometimes, it is easier for the Aries to handle everything himself. A mature Aries man understands that his life partner can truly love him without being totally dependent on him. He must learn the karmic lesson of earning the love and respect of those around him without encouraging them to be in a needy position.

An Aries male will also need to deal with his temper. Society allows a man to be angry. It is alright for a man to show his temper. After all, he is not allowed to cry, mope, or be depressed. But he is allowed to be angry. He is allowed to curse, scream and punch holes in walls. He is allowed to drive fast when he is angry. He is encouraged, to hit that racquet ball with all his might if he is angry at his boss. Since society is encouraging the temper within the Aries, which really does not need much encouragement, it may take a while for a mature Aries man to enter into the realization that his temper may become an obstacle to him. He will, therefore, learn to control his temper as he works on fine-tuning his other karmic lessons of diplomacy, sharing, and patience as well as dealing with his own aggressiveness.

ARIES FEMALE

Aries is a masculine sign which is not always comfortable in the female form. Society, in many respects, still expects a woman to take a more passive role. But society is changing as a result of our economics and our social structures, certainly in western cultures. Women are now, not only expected, but needed to go out and work. They are needed to take a much more aggressive role within our society and within our culture. Years ago, Aries women had a much more difficult time of it. It is so unnatural for an Aries woman to take a passive role. She is woman who is filled with independence and leadership ability, aggressiveness and competitiveness. These are not traits of passivity. The karmic lessons for an Aries woman can be especially difficult. She must learn how to live with strong masculine energy while, at the same time, maintaining her femininity. Very often, Aries women are tomboys when they are young. They enjoy playing out in the playground climbing trees, and playing stick ball in the street. They like being around their brothers and their fathers tinkering with the car, mowing the lawn, sweating and getting dirty. A wonderful outlet for the female Aries is athletics. She should allow herself to develop her aptitude for athletics and work out her healthy energy through sports. She needs to realize, whether her immediate environment accepts it or not, that it is alright to be aggressive, strong, and physical. If she likes things which society usually categorizes as male, such as football or fishing, she should pursue them. Karmically, she must be true to her Aries self. She would be doing herself a disservice if she pretended that all these strengths did not exist and tried to play a prissy role by wearing flowery dresses and sitting primly on the veranda. An example of an Aries type woman was Scarlet O'Hara in *Gone With The Wind.* She knew what she wanted and she aggressively pursued it. Another example is the pioneer women in America who were not afraid to get out in those fields and work shoulder to shoulder with their men. Many of our female leaders in history were tapping into their Aries strengths and potentials.

An Aries woman will be following her karmic direction by entering into masculine careers as lawyers, doctors, firefighters, and police officers. They also enjoy climbing the corporate ladder, usually very successfully. Take note, the most difficult karmic lesson for the Aries woman is that she is a threat to other men. Men who feel this threat may try to keep her in her place. They may tend to fear her potential to excel. The key for the Aries woman is to be so totally confident of her own femininity that she is able to allow these more masculine Aries traits to develop to their fullest potential without being a threat.

The Aries woman must also learn to deal with her temper. She can use this energy in a positive way by asserting herself and not allowing other people to take advantage of her. Once again, society does not allow a woman to show temper tantrums. Remember, the Aries man is allowed to punch holes in the wall, the woman is not. She is supposed to sit in a corner, crumble, and cry. Ah, but not our Aries woman! She finds it impossible to play such an impassive role. Therefore, the Aries woman has the karmic lesson of proudly brandishing her Aries strength within the limitations put on her by society. She must learn to moderate her anger and her aggressiveness. And the Aries woman, like all Aries, must learn how to share. She must adapt to sharing her space, power and positions of authority.

If you are an Aries woman, you have a wonderful capacity to help other woman take a more active role in today's modern world. You are able to join men in their own competitions and hold your own. You are an inspiration and a role model to many others and, most importantly, you will enjoy your leadership role.

ARIES CHILDREN

If you are the parent of an Aries child there are many ways in which you may help your child to best develop his strong Aries traits. It is important to recognize that an Aries child has a temper. Karmically he is here to learn how to deal with that anger. You offer the first guidelines which he will be experiencing to show him his limits. Therefore, it is important for you not to give in to the temper tantrums of your Aries child. You must accept the fact that he has a temper and that you cannot deny its existence, nor can you eradicate it from your child's personality through your own sheer will. You are not here to change your child's personality according to what you want him to be but to help your child by encouraging him to use his assets and modify his weaknesses. You are able to show your child how he is able to take that same energy force and use it in a worthwhile way. You can help him by showing him immediately that he will not gain approval or attention through negative outbursts of energy. Every child throws a temper tantrum at some point in his life. All children test their parents to see how far they can go. The Aries infant, for example, may cry furiously for his bottle. You will not be teaching the Aries infant any positive lesson by attempting to teach him how to learn patience by holding back that bottle from him. But you can help him by being soothing to him rather than reacting with great stress and anxiety while that bottle is being warmed up. If you sing to your Aries baby, and you coo to that child while the bottle is being warmed up, you are giving him a far healthier message then by reacting to his angry screams with your own anxiety...."*alright, alright, I'm coming!*" The Aries infant will sense your discomfort and anxiety and incorporate that message of stress within his own consciousness. Your response of anxiety will show him, at an early age, that he can use anger as a tool to make people uncomfortable and to make them give into his demands. This is a pretty powerful tool to give your child. It is also setting up an unhealthy personality pattern for that Aries child to deal with as an adult. So, when he cries, you do not want to run quickly for the bottle, rather, at a steady pace, warm the bottle and calmly help him to learn how to wait. This will be the beginning of a wonderful lesson of patience.

It is also important for you to realize that it is hard for the Aries child to share his toys. This is an *I* and *me* sign, not a sign of easy sharing. Karmically, your Aries child is here to learn the lesson of sharing. If the child has difficulty with this lesson, it means that he needs to possess certain things around him. As a parent, for you to deny that your child has this need, would be an unrealistic view. You would not be helping your child by making him share all his toys with his friends or siblings. He needs to own and possess certain toys which are all his in combination with encouragement to also share other toys which are not of such importance to him. You are unable to change the specific personality and karmic traits of your children. That is not your job as a parent. Rather, you are here to help and encourage him to best deal with the karmic lessons of his sun sign.

It is important to get an Aries child involved in sports or some kind of physical activity at an early age. Please do not differentiate as to whether you have an Aries girl or boy. All Aries children are best served if they are involved in a physical activity. This means playing with your child when he is an infant; playing ball, taking him outdoors frequently. Aries children need fresh air and the freedom of the outdoors. Get him involved in dance lessons, acrobatics, Little League baseball, football, soccer. Whatever direction he seems to be taking, encourage him. If you like fishing, take your Aries child out fishing with you. Remember, do not categorize whether this is a "male or female" activity. One way to help your child to deal with the aggressiveness, anger or temper which is in him, is to lead him to the healthy outlet of physical activity.

As the parent of an Aries child, it is best for you to encourage this child to assume responsibility and independence at an early age. Not only responsibility such as making his bed, and doing the dishes, but also responsibility for other people. You can help your Aries child in several ways. If you say, *"I want you to teach your little brother how to hit a ball,"* you are taking his natural talents for physical activity and sports and combining it with his karmic need to fulfill his responsibility toward others. In terms of household chores, it is important that the Aries child be given his own responsibility within the family unit so that he learns how to share in the communal living that a family unit provides. It would be unhealthy to say, *"Well, my Aries child doesn't have to wash the dishes because he's the star of the football team and he really needs to practice everyday after dinner."* That is excluding him because of his successful leading position on the football team from participating in his sharing responsibilities in a family unit. He must have both.

An Aries child will desire independence at an early age and sometimes that can be frightening to a parent. An Aries child can often be quite wiry. You leave the door unlocked one minute and that two year old is tottering down the block exploring the railroad tracks. So, there is a tendency to try to keep them fenced in for their own protection. You will find out early that it is almost impossible to confine an Aries child. They learn how to climb that fence right away. It is important to teach your child independence by giving him your trust to explore but this must be inter-woven with guidelines. These guidelines must not be limiting to his karmic needs. Keep in mind that society will also give him limits. You will be helping him to deal with this karmic lesson of independence versus restriction by acclimating him to guidelines in his youth.

Be aware that Aries children tend to be accident prone. Therefore keep them away from knives, guns, poisons...anything which may harm them. If you give birth to an Aries child, immediately "child-proof" your home. Try to remove all potential dangers. Keep sand under your swing set in your backyard, not cement. Realize that your Aries child is athletic, adventurous and a bit of a dare-devil and, therefore, may get hurt. You may not be able to always protect this child from injury. You certainly do not want to stifle him with a lot of no's and limitations for fear that he will hurt himself. There may be more damage to him psychologically and karmically by not allowing him to climb a tree than there would have been to him physically by falling out of the tree. This is not an easy awareness for you as a parent.

It is important that you do not teach fear to an Aries child. At the same time you must teach him a respect for danger. If your child is interested in boating, prepare him by teaching him the rules of this sport. Insist that he wear a life jacket. The Aries child is the typical child who says, " *I don't want to wear that life jacket...it's sissyish, it's too hot, it's too confining.* " You, as a parent, must show that these are the guidelines for safe boating and must insist that the Aries child wear his life jacket. Even if he goes out on the boat alone you need to give him the message that you will trust him to wear his life jacket even if you are not there to make him wear it. If you feel that you are not authoritative enough to do this then take him to boating classes, coast guard meetings, and give him books on safe boating. Use whatever means you can to show him the importance of respecting the danger of water along with the fun and adventure it can bring, without initiating any fears. All this guidance will help the Aries child to move more quickly toward his positive karmic lessons.

If you are lucky enough to be the parent of an Aries child, hold onto your seat. Your child is strong of body and mind and will love to test your parental authority. You may be raising a future leader of society or a star athlete. You are certainly the parent of a child with great potential. Enjoy his adventurous nature. You have paid the ticket for the ride, now hold on.

TAURUS

April 20 - May 20

Female Energy

KARMIC LESSONS

◆ Dependability in relationships

◆ Learning to adapt to change

◆ Stubbornness vs. determination

◆ Laziness vs. motivation for ambition

◆ Dealing with money and possessions

PRIMARY TAURUS

You will be dealing with your primary energies when you are young, when you are immature and when you are first encountering your most important karmic life lessons. You will find yourself acting and reacting on a primary level at different times of your life, even after you feel you should be more mature or above that basic part of yourself. Try not to be disappointed with yourself when your primary tendencies emerge. Rather, look at this as a time in your life when you should work a little harder. In fact, this time will be an indication of a significant learning experience on which your soul has quite purposely chosen to work. Knowing yourself through your astrology will help you to keep a finger on the pulse of your soul's needs.

In order for you to consciously work on your karmic Taurus lessons, it is important for you to get a clear perspective of what your primary inclinations may be. Every soul existing on this earth plane is dealing with the realm of materialism. Granted, we will all experience different levels of comfort, or discomfort, in our materialistic experiences depending upon our social standing, country of origin, family wealth and group karmic directions. Each one of us, regardless of astrological sun sign, must bear the responsibilities of our material environments. We must all pay our way in life. Most of us need to earn our keep through daily toil and weekly wages. Whether we are earning currency or decorating beads or digging clam shells, we all must learn the lessons of accumulating our form of earning and using that cultural form as payment for our needs. In this way, we all have karmic lessons similar to those of the Taurus. And, as much as our integrity in the material arena is important to us, it is ever more important to a Taurus.

When you chose to enter this world level as a Taurus, you opted to face some heavy testing of your materialistic values. The segment of this chapter on materialism will display all the various forms this can take in your life. To think that life's test for you in materialistic awareness ensures a life of poverty is a misconception. It is most often through wealth and materialistic success that your hardest lessons will emerge. You cannot avoid your responsibilities by living the life of a hermit, devoid of monetary transactions either. Your tests will then come to you through the animal world. For, if a Taurus slays a deer for food and clothing but hoards the meat beyond his capacity to eat, he is denying nourishment to the rest of the animal kingdom. By taking only what he needs and leaving the rest for the buzzards, rats and ants, he has fulfilled his karma. As a Taurus, you must understand your need to maintain enough accumulation of the material to sustain your emotional need of security and physical need for survival. This you cannot deny yourself. It is extremism in either direction which may injure your karmic growth.

Taurus is a fixed sign, which means that you do not feel comfortable with change. Hence, you will be challenged by change at various times in your life. You chose the lesson of experiencing change in your life with a natural reluctance to accept change. You are functioning in your primary stage when you flatly refuse to accept or flow with change to the point of your own unhappiness. Planetary transits will periodically set change in motion in your life as a test of the development of your flexibility. There are ways to help yourself adjust to these uncomfortable times. One way is to try to keep yourself in control of the changes. This can be done by initiating the changes yourself. It is when you dig your heels in and refuse to adjust to change that the changes themselves can be most hurtful to you. It may help you to recognize this inflexibility as fear of the unknown, which it really is, and to acknowledge that your reaction of stubbornness is your primary tendency emerging. Acknowledge your fear and then face it by initiating a change of your own initiative rather than exhausting all of your energy trying to maintain the status quo. What a difficult lesson this can be for you. Yet, the rewards of change are greater for you than for anyone else for it means you have overcome a powerful primary fear. You need not try to turn yourself into a nomad or whirling dervish of inconsistency. Your karmic lesson is to overcome your *fear* of change.

Which brings our awareness to your basic nature of stubbornness. Yes, you. Simply put, you are working on your primary level when you are displaying your characteristically stubborn nature. You are functioning on your evolved level when that stubbornness transforms itself into a spirit of determination. There is no stopping a Taurus who has his mind set in a certain direction.

Taurus is ruled by the planet Venus, the planet of peace, love and harmony. Venus brings a loving warmth to Taurus which can be manifested in all relationships. You are working on your primary level when you hold onto relationships, regardless of their merit, simply because they are now a pattern in your life. You are used to them. You fear the change that a breakup in a relationship would bring into your life. Always remember, that Venus is available to bring you great love and contentment through your relationships. Do not settle for less because of your fear of change.

EVOLVED TAURUS

Your life lessons will always center around money and materialism whether you choose to vibrate on your primary or evolved energy. The evolved Taurus may still be surrounded by materialistic issues but has chosen to face them rather than be overcome by them. As an evolved Taurus, you will be involved with financial dealings either through your work, family, or personal life. You have developed an excellent judgment in these dealings and will be respected and relied on for your financial talents. At work, you may be involved in bookkeeping, accounting, real estate, banking or some other form of employment which demands good business judgment. At home, you have successfully balanced your need to save and your penchant to spend. You are always aware of where your money is and how much your possessions are worth without being consumed by the materialism around you. Yours is no longer a home of clutter created by accumulation of unnecessary objects. You are, by nature, a generous soul who has learned to share your material world graciously and lovingly with others. You are able to throw things out or give them away. As an evolved Taurus, you are able to deal effectively with financial transactions both in your personal and business worlds. Few people can be trusted more than an Evolved Taurus when it comes to materialism. Many people will discover this integrity within you and entrust you with many of their financial matters.

In your evolved state, you have also developed your ability to adapt to change. Sometimes you have had to hold your breath and simply hold on during times of crisis and upheaval, but you have learned that you are able to survive and once again create balance and stability in your life. You have become wiser due to the unexpected occurrences of life and are no longer fearful of the state of change.

You have learned to use the strength of your willfulness to establish the personality trait of sheer determination instead of allowing yourself to be paralyzed by the immobility caused by your stubbornness. People around you know that if you have set your mind on a goal or course of action, there will be no stopping you. And, as an evolved Taurus, they have full trust and confidence in the credibility and constructiveness of your goals. You are a loving sign who easily brings the strength of your love and the dependability of your devotion to those closest to you. It is easy to trust an evolved Taurus with both your heart and your wallet.

REMEMBER, NO ONE IS TOTALLY PRIMARY OR TOTALLY EVOLVED. OUR KARMIC LESSONS ARE BEST LEARNED WHEN WE ARE DEALING WITH BOTH OF THESE ENERGIES.

DEALING WITH MATERIALISM: MONEY, CAREER, POSSESSIONS

As a Taurus, you will be dealing with the material aspect of life on this earth. Your everyday issues will not be much different from those of everyone else around you. It is because of these over-all similarities that you may lose sight of the importance which materialism plays in your soul's evolution. After all, most of us need to work Monday through Friday to pay the same bills of rent, food, electric, telephone, etc. So, let us ask the typical questions that would come to your Taurus mind: Why should it be so important an issue for you as a Taurus? Isn't it hard enough as it is to make ends meet? Why is the great cosmos singling out you poor Taurian working-stiff, for a harder challenge?

Actually, you are not being singled out for any above average difficulties in your finances simply because you are a Taurus. Some Taurians are a part of the struggling working class, and others are powerful millionaires. The issue is not how much or how little money you have. It is your attitude toward money and materialism. Keep in mind that possessions may represent a feeling of emotional stability to you. You may panic if you have too little. You may become a hoarder to stave off the possible starvation which poverty brings. And your definition of poverty may be quite different from someone else's. After all, their emotional well-being may not be as involved with materialism as yours.

Each Taurus is unique in his placement on the evolutionary scale of materialism. But, there are two common categories to which many of you belong. Perhaps you will see yourself or a loved one here.

ECONOMIC DEPRESSION/WAR SURVIVORS

There have been eras of hardship in our modern times, namely World Wars I and II and the Great Depression of the early 1930s. Taurians who lived through these eras experienced significant difficulty. Their natural need for economic security was unmet and their fear of material deprivation remained with them long after prosperity returned to society. A typical example was Leah, a Taurus, whose life of poverty began in Europe in the late 1800s.

LEAH'S FINANCIAL TREK THROUGH LIFE

Leah was born in Germany long before the time of modern technology and financial wizardry. Her mother had died when she was a child, and her father had left her with her grandmother in a small German village on the Alsace-Lorraine border while he journeyed to America to find the better life. Leah was a Taurus whose natural need for material security was left wanting as she lived with her desperately poor Grandmother. But Taurians are also earth people. They are comfortable with the laws of nature so Leah adjusted easily to living off the land and the nearby woods. She used to tell stories of how she and her grandmother lived on frogs legs, out of necessity, in their hungry years, and she would laugh to see frog's legs years later on the menu of expensive French restaurants.

When Leah was 16 years old, her father sent for her to join him in America. This would be her opportunity for financial security. But even this venture in her life was not an easy one. She was placed into servitude and worked in people's homes for several years. She was used to hard work, so that did not bother her. And she did have a room of her own and good food always available. She never had to forage in the woods again for her evening meal. Still, a

Taurus needs her own financial independence and the comfort of her own material security. As a servant, she was totally dependent on her employers for everything.

Soon she met a young man, Eric, who had also escaped from the poverty of his European birthplace and was now gainfully employed by a steady, reputable firm in New York City. They wed and parented a large family, quite common for those times. Not only did Eric move up successfully within the company, he also invested his savings in real estate, and soon, owned a substantial number of apartment buildings throughout the city. Life was just grand for this Taurus named Leah. She was able to relax now and not worry about her financial security. She had certainly come a long way from that little town in Germany.

Leah's karmic testings came with World War I and then the stock market crash of 1929. As the country had needed to pull in its belt and adjust to doing with less during the World War, Leah again slipped easily back to the Taurian resourcefulness she had learned from her grandmother. Yet her hardest test was the Great Depression, for it was during this financial crisis that she and Eric lost all of their investments including every one of their real estate holdings. Thankfully, he still had his job, and there was some degree of financial security, but not nearly to what she had become accustomed during her recent years.

Leah always saved for a rainy day. She never stopped clipping coupons and searching for bargains. She saved everything from pennies to string. Nothing was ever thrown out or wasted during any period of her life. Leah had passed through the karmic testing of material security via many stages of her life. She knew what it was like to have nothing and what it meant to have a lot. She saw that life was like riding a wave and she always prepared herself for the trip down.

Taurians who lived through these eras are instinctively of a saving nature. They naturally abhor the waste which is now so accepted in American society. These Taurians may react to such an extreme that they cannot let go of anything material. They become hoarders, scavengers. They cannot throw that lone shoe away; after all, one day they just may find its' mate. They keep their basements, attics and closets filled with their lifetime accumulations because they are afraid of one day being without. They are afraid of one day needing something that they once had but had haphazardly discarded.

A Taurian need not be of this "older" generation to be a compulsive saver. Any Taurian who has suffered loss of material security in his life is likely to react in this manner.

The karmic lesson for you, as a Taurus, is to learn to let go of unnecessary accumulations. Holding on to too many "things" is akin to *materialistic constipation*. They will bind you, hold you down, limit your spiritual growth. If you have the storage areas of your home stuffed with accumulations, give them away. That's right. Give them away to someone who can use them. If some of your possessions are of too much monetary value to just give away, then sell them. But, it is your motivation behind the transaction that is important. If you are selling in order to buy more, you are then encapsulating yourself in a never ending circle of material constipation. Be generous. Give to others in need. Taurians are loving, giving people by nature. It is only fear of being without that can block that generous spirit. Herein lies your karmic lesson.

Many times, a Taurus who has been deprived of emotional love and support can substitute materialism and possessions for this emptiness. Be aware of this possible connection.

This bring us to the second kind of Taurus. This person needs to buy anything and everything they see in order to fill their lives with the comfort of possessions.

THE TAURIAN GADGET LOVER

Sue is a Taurus of the modern age. She has lived all her life with necessary comforts and financial security. Her mother died when Sue was three years old and she was raised by her father and older brother. They always provided her with a comfortable, middle class home, beautiful clothes, plenty of food. Sue was not brought up lacking any of the practical, Taurian material needs. What she was lacking was a mother to nurture her childlike needs. As an adult, Sue often responded as a child to life. Her Taurian instincts of materialism led her to buy everything she wanted, when she wanted it. She filled her home with toys that her father had not even thought to buy her. Her bedroom had a large bubblegum machine in one corner, always stocked with fresh gumballs. Her living room had toy dogs that barked, wind-up ducks that waddled along the coffee table, and a pinball machine against the far wall. Her mania to buy did not stop with toys. Sue always had to be the first to own anything new that came on the market.

She had one of the first microwave ovens, VCR's, camcorders, and a mammoth screen TV. One would think that a record had to have been set by how many gadgets had been purchased on Sue's charge cards. Naturally, Sue's karmic Taurus lesson was coming to her through her overspending. She was suffering the lesson of debt in the age of easy buying.

Notice that the end result is not much different for Sue then it was for Leah. Both Taurians eventually accumulated a great amount of possessions. Each was partly motivated by an emotional need and sought a materialistic solution to that need. Each woman suffered from *materialistic constipation*. Sue was eventually in such debt that even her closest friends got tired of hearing her woes as she continued her spending frenzy. Sue, like Leah, had difficulty parting with her possessions which she, like a child, tired of quite easily.

Unlike Leah, Sue did not store her accumulations in a basement or attic. She had them displayed, collecting dust, throughout her house. Sue's possessions were being used as a substitute for a feeling of comfort, the comfort of the mother's love she lacked in her childhood. Sue's karmic lesson was to identify the role materialism played in her life. This is not always an easy lesson for the Taurus.

Money and possessions play an important role in the life of the Taurus. It is important for you to identify the role it plays in your life. Be patient, this may take time and some assistance from a relative, friend or therapist.

Hopefully, from these examples, you are now becoming aware of the subtle role materialism plays in the life of the Taurus. It is most important to understand that your karmic lesson, as a Taurus, has absolutely nothing to do with wealth vs. poverty, much vs. less. Your karmic lessons have to do with your *attitudes* toward materialism. Your value system. Your ability or lack of ability to let go of unnecessary monetary ties.

You must acknowledge that you need some financial security in your life in order to feel safe. Some people find this by saving newspapers, or string, others find it through large savings accounts and CD's, others through the amassing of many possessions. There are countless number of ways in which a Taurus can work through their karmic, materialistic lessons.

The important questions Taurians need to always ask themselves is how their materialistic lessons are manifesting themselves in their lives and most importantly, why! Your answers to these questions will be different from those of another Taurus but the importance of the answers will always be equal.

INTEGRITY

The integrity of a Taurus is paramount in their quest for karmic evolution. We all have a responsibility to pay our own way in this life on earth, or, at least to cover our trail. As a Taurus, you have an additional overseer - karma. A karma, I must add, that you chose. Taurians have a responsibility to use sound judgment in their monetary dealings. You are to learn the value of work and the responsibility of money and possessions. A Taurus should always attempt to pay their bills on time, not overextend themselves financially; to take proper care of their possessions and to rid themselves of what they no longer need or what may be better used by someone else. There is an interesting metaphysical theory that the more you rid yourself of clutter in your life, the more security of materialism will come your way. Think about this. If you were about to go clothes shopping but your closets were already full, where would you put your new clothes? If you had nowhere to put them you would not be able to bring them home.

As a Taurus, you should clean out your home. Rid yourself of unnecessary clutter so that you can create room for the new to come into your life. Every kitchen has a junk drawer. Clean out your "junk drawer" today. You will be surprised at what will now enter into your life; it could be a check in the mail or a new love relationship. Do not barricade yourself behind the walls of materialism. You karmic lessons will always find you.

Taurus, you also have a responsibility to not only pay your bills while you are alive but to also leave a clean slate when you pass over. I always recommend that Taurians leave the means to cover the expenses of their deaths. Life insurance policies are one source of meeting this need. This does not mean that a Taurus has failed his karmic lesson if he leaves this life with debts. We, as onlookers, have no idea of the accomplishments of any soul during their sojourn here on earth. We only have the responsibility of working on our own karmic lessons rather than judging others.

As a Taurus, you may also need to deal with other people's money. You may be responsible for writing out the bills in your household, or settling estates, or keeping the books for your company or investing other people's money in the stock market. Your integrity with money can, and will, take many forms.

VALUES

You will be dealing with the karmic challenge of determining your own individual values. Obviously, values will include your attitudes toward money and possessions, and these areas of your life will be highlighted. But, you will also need to confront your values on many other issues such as relationships, work, and spirituality. You are working on your primary level when you refuse to move beyond material values thereby neglecting these other aspects of your consciousness.

What is success? What does success mean to you? These are questions the evolved Taurus is always asking himself. Your natural inclination will be to list income, job title, and financial accumulation as tokens of your success. As you evolve and grow, these material standards will diminish. You will amaze yourself as you watch your new list of successes grow as the material need lessens.

WORK

Taurians are, usually, hard workers. Yes, you can be lazy, if you are too embedded in your primary level. But, usually, your drive for accumulating material security pushes you toward the stronger work ethic. Karmically, you need to "sing for your supper." It is important for you to earn your money through gainful employment.

Taurians have a magnificent ability to bear with jobs which require repetition. You are able to work a slow, steady pace following projects through to completion by plugging along. Many an Aries and Gemini can learn a karmic lesson or two by following your example. *(See chapters 3 & 5)*.

You are the sustainers of our world. You are able to take a project and guide it slowly, and masterfully to its completion. You are like the turtle who finishes the race by continually plodding along. You are like the beaver who takes on the masterful job of building a dam through hard work and perseverance. You deal well with routine and repetition. Be aware that you also need job security and a job that pays well. Do not feel that you are betraying your spiritual side of self because of your needs for job security. Also keep in mind that your karmic role is to deal with materialism. This is a vital part of your life. You must work within the framework of materialism, not avoid it.

On a primary level, you may have difficulty adjusting to changes on a job. A change of any extreme may throw you off, from changing the position of your desk, to changing jobs completely. You are also dealing with the karmic lesson of adjusting to change and these challenges may appear to you within your work world. Be flexible. Too much struggle and control to keep things as they always were can be hazardous to your karmic self and so exhausting.

Do not think that you are stunting your karmic growth if you are a sustainer of home and hearth instead of out there in the workforce. This is also important to any Taurus who is unable, for any reason other than laziness, to hold an outside job. As long as you are on this earth you will be confronted with the karmic lessons of materialism. This will not pass you by. No soul would be here on earth without the opportunity to confront his karmic growth lessons. This is the natural law.

ADAPTING TO CHANGE

Taurus is a fixed sign. You have a natural inclination to want things to stay the same. Karmically, you have chosen to have instances in your life when you will have to bend with change while you will naturally feel fearful or threatened by that change. You can count on the fact that major change will come into your life. You must learn to allow change and, also, initiate change yourself. It's like going swimming on that first summer day. The water is very cold. You can either walk in slowly until you are finally all the way in, or, you can jump in quickly and get the shock over with fast. In this analogy it is significant to understand that, if you do not go into the water on your own, there is somebody waiting on shore who will surely throw you in. Guaranteed, you will get wet. It is always easier to control the action yourself and you can control the types and circumstances of the changes in your life most of the time. In fact, the more you initiate change, the easier it will be for you to adjust to those times when change comes into your life outside of your control.

BREAKING UP IS HARD TO DO

Jill was totally resigned to her life as an unhappy and unfulfilled wife. She and Sam had long ago given up on even the social facade of their marriage being a satisfying one. Jill's friends had stopped trying to give her moral support to leave Sam and start a new life without him. Truth was, they were tired of hearing her complain without making any motions to better her situation.

Jill was a Taurus who feared the unknown that change brings with it more than she hated her life with Sam. She had seven children, a high school education and no job experience. What could she do? Sam had been her high school sweetheart. She even lacked dating skills and here she was 38 year old, trapped. Granted, this would be a frightening situation for anyone but, to add to it, Jill was a fixed Taurus. Her fear of change and her need for financial security kept her where she was...year after year. She knew she should initiate a divorce, but couldn't bring herself to do it. In the Spring of 1984, Sam brought the jolt to her. He had found someone else. Within a short three months, Jill was on her own to care for herself and her children. Sam's support payments were not nearly enough to carry all her expenses now, but somewhere, with the moral support of her friends and family, Jill began to adapt to the change. She entered a Junior College and studied business administration. She entered the workforce in a low level position, but soon was able to branch out on her own. She opened a florist shop which, very quickly, flourished economically. The change was forced on Jill. She tapped into her Taurian resources to obtain financial security and persevere. Within five years, Jill appeared to be a totally different woman. These were difficult years but they brought her to a level she may never have obtained had she remained fixed in her unhappy marriage. Initially, the change in her life put her into a tail spin. The end result was a new woman filled with self-confidence and pride.

Change may be especially difficult for a Taurus. You must have confidence that the liberation of change allows you to face your karmic challenges and brings you the impetus for growth. People who are fearful of change to the point that they avoid it at all costs, usually are prone to phobias and neurotic disorders. An example would be a recluse who refuses to face the challenges of the outside world by confining herself to her own home. What a loss for such a loving creature as a Taurus.

STUBBORNNESS VS. DETERMINATION

We do not say, stubborn as a bull, for no reason. As a Taurus, you can certainly be stubborn. You do not need anyone to tell you that. Some of that stubbornness comes as a result of your fear of change. Karmically, you are here to turn that tendency toward stubbornness into the stronger trait of determination. Interestingly, this development seems to manifest itself as the Taurus gets older. At whatever age it happens, it is a time when you will feel masterfully strong and in charge of your life. You will feel the power of control working more strongly as you cease to be stubborn. This is an interesting twist as you may feel that your stubbornness is an aid to you in controlling your life but, instead, it becomes a deterrent. There's the example of 16 year old Dawn.

GETTING OFF THAT STUBBORN WEIGHT

Dawn had been heavy most of her childhood but the pounds really came on when she hit puberty. During her sophomore year of high school she was tipping the scales at 200 pounds. Everyone tried to help her with suggestions and different diet plans, but Dawn refused to even acknowledge that her weight bothered her. Her stubbornness and control over her family and friends gave out a clear picture to all...do not talk to Dawn about her weight!

There came a point, and no one knows why, when Dawn decided she wanted to diet. She joined a diet center and, with total determination, stuck faithfully to their diet plan. The pounds disappeared month after month until Dawn had the shape she had always wanted.

Stubbornness held Dawn back from acknowledging her weight problem to those who loved her. Her angry responses to anyone who did try to mention it to her were her form of control. Yet, determination became the positive force of her stubbornness and proved to be a stronger control, in the form of self-control, which enabled her to stick with her diet. As you can see, sometimes there's a fine line between stubbornness and control. This is a subtle karmic lesson for the Taurus. When you are being honest with yourself, you are totally aware of when you are being stubborn and when you are being determined.

LAZINESS VS. MOTIVATION FOR AMBITION

When the Taurus is young in years or a soul which is newly entered into the sign (an experienced astrologer would be able to give you this information), he is likely to be lacking in ambition. The fixed quality of the sign can subdue the person's vitality. The Taurus's karmic responsibility is to establish his own individual motivation for ambition. Materialism is often the catalyst which starts the Taurus going. Let us not overlook some other equally important motivations for you Taurians. Relationships are also extremely significant in your life. Taurians will work hard with their love of family as a powerful motivation.

Many Taurians have a special love for nature, including animals and these forces may prove to be strong motivation for taking action.

It is important to identify your motivation, also acknowledging that the motivations may vary depending on your stage in life. Once you have set your goals, it is important that you take a slow, steady course of action. Moderation, steadfastness, and sure-footing are all positive methods for you to rely on in your pursuit of your ambitions. Your laziness will be overlooked when you are a child, but can be your downfall as you grow older. This is a karmic lesson which will come to you with maturity.

DEPENDABILITY IN RELATIONSHIPS

Relationships are important to a Taurus. You are a fixed sign which does not tolerate change. Therefore, you desire a permanent relationship with as few changes and surprises as possible. Your ruling planet is Venus, the planet of love, and you have the potential of a kind, lovable nature. The people around you will almost always be able to second guess you. You do not like surprises, so you do not give surprises in your relationships. The Taurus is a steady, nurturing force which can bring great love and stability to all relationships. What a beautiful gift this is for you to give to the world. We need stability in this time of transition which is all around us. The Taurus is the one we will go to when we need a safe haven and steady embrace.

If someone is looking for an exciting, adventurous relationship they need not align themselves with a Taurus. To this kind of person, the Taurus will seem boring and dull. With the Taurus comes predictability rather than excitement.

As a Taurus, you have a special strength to bring to all your loved ones and a stability to bring to the world, and that is your steady dependability. We all need someone to come home to, someone to keep a steady hand on the till of our ship. Taurus offers the world that stable comfort.

Taurians usually make wonderful parents. You offer your children a consistency which may be lacking in their outside world. The children of a Taurus may often complain, "Oh, I know exactly what Mom will say about that and there's no changing her mind." What is more important behind those words of seeming complaint, is the comfort of the predictability of that mother's nature.

The Taurians' loved ones will always know that they are there for them. The ability to love can pour out of every fiber of the Taurus. Naturally, not all Taurians display such a fine, loving nature. One's physiological background and life's experiences can alter the potential of a Taurians' loving nature. It is the Taurians' karmic goal to develop this steady, constant energy to the best of their ability. One way is to surround yourself with people who will appreciate these qualities within you. Be around other people who also value family and home and who admire your fixed, steady nature rather than feel that you are a hindrance to the fast pace they choose to maintain. To generalize, an Aries may find a Taurus too slow, whereas a Cancer may fall comfortably into the same values of family comforts.

FROM HAWAII TO HOOTERVILLE, USA

Mary, a Taurus, was first married to Jim, a U.S. Navy Pilot. She saw him to be a fun-loving young man who loved her with as great a passion as his love of the great jet planes he flew. Here, thought Mary, would be a great opportunity for a happy marriage. They had love and the stability of a respected career in the Navy. The first year they were stationed in Norfolk, Virginia and it took Mary almost that whole year to adjust to being away from her family and friends. It was also hard to adjust to making new friends who were constantly leaving for different ports, and to her loneliness when Jim was gone, as he was for weeks at a time. It wasn't the aloneness that was so difficult to tolerate, it was the constant adjusting this life made necessary. Within five years they had lived in Virginia, Florida, California and, finally, Hawaii. The financial security that Jim's career brought them did not outweigh the emotional insecurity she suffered from all these moves. Their marriage deteriorated to divorce and Mary went back to her small town of Hooterville, U.S.A. She basked in the comfort of her family's warmth and stability. Nothing ever changed in Hooterville, only the trees grew bigger.

She started dating Roy, who owned and operated the local car repair shop. At first she missed the excitement of her first days when she was dating Jim, seeming like a lifetime ago now. Soon, the dependability of Roy and Hooterville relaxed Mary and she was able to find another, wonderful passion with Roy. Their love for each other grew with the sureness of the roots of the Elm trees that engulfed the town. As the whole town expected, they were married in the spring. Here Mary found another kind of security, the loving security of routine and familiar surroundings.

Eventually, Mary and Roy built a cafe alongside the auto repair shop and Mary ran the restaurant. They parented four children who always knew where they would be living tomorrow and always knew where to find their parents today. It was here that Taurus Mary learned to appreciate the dependable aspects of her life. She gave freely and plentifully of her love to her family and to her small town.

This does not mean that Taurians are totally unable to tolerate change in their environments. Many of you are able to create a homelike stability wherever you go, and this is a wonderful gift you bring to your family. But, Taurians are certainly creatures of habit. It is important for you to acknowledge this need for pattern and routine and not try to deny who you are. The world needs the stability you offer.

You also have choices in the relationships you choose. It is important for you to be aware of the karmic reasons why each type of person may be in your life. For example, a Taurus may find himself with a fiery person whose purpose is to fire the Taurian's ambitions, taking them from laziness or stubbornness to a point of action. Even after the Taurus has become "activated" though, he will then try to level off to a stable position as soon as possible. This will then help show that fiery person how to maintain their strength without burning themselves out.

Taurians are able to offer a marvelous gift of security and stability to their children. The child of an emotionally healthy Taurian will be comforted through the parent's dependability.

Through these examples you can see that, as a Taurus, you have an important karmic lesson of learning how to deal with routine and stability (emotional and financial) in your personal life along with the task of bringing these traits out to help fortify the rest of the world. Where would we be without the stable nurturing offered by you Taurians?

TAURUS MALE

Taurus is a feminine sign and therefore, allows the men born under this sign to tap into the feminine, more passive sides of their nature. Do not be misguided into thinking that this creates a weak, easy pushover of a man. Some of your most aggressive men in the field of finance are Taurians. Here, we must call attention to the motivation behind the ambition. Men who are uncomfortable allowing the expression of that feminine part of themselves, will lean more toward the materialistic aspects of Taurus. After all, isn't that what society encourages them to do? Karmically, it is important for the Taurus male to express both sides of himself. There are many ways for him to do this. He can combine his material and feminine self through his choice of careers. He could build empires in service kinds of careers - working with hospital care, nursing homes, beauty saloons, flower shops, nurseries, restaurants. Taurian males make wonderful lawyers who cater to family needs and real estate, for example.

If the Taurus male does not find his blending of both selves within his career he is able to find it at home. Here is a man who can work feverishly at the office in order to provide his family with all the "things" in life he thinks they need. (By the way, sometimes the family doesn't need all those "things" as much as *his* ego needs to provide them.) Then, after his day of work, he can come home to a steady routine with his family. He may enjoy gardening, maintaining the upkeep of his home, playing ball with his children, camping, baking, nestling on the floor with his dogs. One trait a Taurus male must beware of is becoming a couchpotato. Activity is important to keep his body in shape. Activity with his family and pets is especially healthy for him.

If the Taurus male's company tells him they're relocating to a different state, this can truly put him into a tizzy. The company needs to give him ample time to adjust to the change and promise to relocate him to an area where he can set up as comfortable a home situation for his family as the one they will be leaving. To remove the familiarity of work and home for a Taurus all at once can be very hard on him.

A great amount of his feeling of self-worth is wrapped up in his job title, income and possessions. Many a Taurian male will be forced to confront this issue in order to help him focus on his karmic responsibilities in these areas. He has a karmic need to fulfill his material obligations to himself and to his family without becoming a slave to materialism; a hard lesson when society is continuously stressing materialism to him while minimizing his need to nurture his feminine, passive side.

TAURUS FEMALE

The Taurus female is very often the drive behind a successful husband. Her need for financial security will enable her to marry with her head, not only her heart. She is certainly not a cold, calculating money hunter. She simply has the ability to choose her mate cautiously to be sure he is able to provide properly for their family. If a Taurus female does not choose a man who is ambitious, she will go out and work herself. She will not do without or have her family do without. Again, like her male Taurus counterpart, she must be cautious not to give materialism too high a priority in her life. Her karma is to learn the balance of materialism and emotions.

A woman is obviously comfortable with the feminine energy of Taurus. She is a natural born nurturer. Karmically, she has much to learn and to teach to others about the importance of a stable home. In a stereotypical sense she may choose to be the mother who has fresh baked cookies ready for her children when they come home from school, and greet her husband with a settled homefront when he comes in from a hard days' work. A regular *June Cleaver*. We all recognize that life is not this simple. The Taurian female will have many challenges thrown her way to help her face her karmic lesson of materialism vs. emotions. Still, her ability to be loving and nurturing is a gift she has to share and, as with all gift-giving, her rewards will be great.

In this economy, most women are out there working either to support themselves or to help support their families. Many Taurian females are single parents. They are strong women. Even if their stature may be short, they are long on stamina particularly if they are providing for children. In their evolved state, they are hard, dependable workers who are not afraid to get right in there and tackle a necessary job. If a Taurian woman is lazy, she has great karmic need to face this challenge. She is too strong to allow herself to deteriorate through laziness.

Remember, karmically, Taurians must learn how to handle their finances. The Taurian female must either earn her own money or have full knowledge of her financial circumstances. She must not leave this all up to her mate. Nor should she simply go on daily shopping sprees with a charge card and have all bills paid by her mate or an accountant. It is important, karmically, for her to be attuned to the financial aspect of her life. If someone else takes full care of her financially, even if this is done with the most loving intent, she is still being robbed of her responsibility to learn about herself through the material world. No one can shelter, nor should they try to shelter, a Taurus from these opportunities of learning.

Change is a karmic challenge for a Taurian female no matter what the origin of that change may be. She needs to be able to ask for help in adjusting to any change around her. If that change affects her whole family, they may be apt to lean on her since she is the steady rock of the family. It is important for her to acknowledge any fear of change she may be experiencing and seek the help of others. The experience of change is there to teach her about the necessity of adapting to transition. It is not here to make her life miserable. She needs to spend time examining her reactions to change and the benefits change can bring into her life. This is not an easy karmic lesson for the Taurian female.

TAURUS CHILDREN

Taurian children have the ability to give and receive great amounts of love. The proper nurturing of a Taurian child is particularly important to her being able to develop to her greatest potential. Even if your Taurus child sleeps a lot and is not demanding of your attention, it is important that you hold her and give her an abundance of your love. This is a child who is ruled by Venus, the planet of love. Her first example of a loving experience will come to her through her parents, siblings and extended family. I call Taurian children the rocking-chair children. They loved to be held and rocked to sleep. It is even important to stroke and hold them after they're asleep. They are aware of this love on a subconscious level. In fact, it would be great if you talked to your Taurus baby even before she was born. She needs the tone of a soothing, steady voice...sugar sweet. This Taurus has the wonderful potential of being a loving adult and she will begin learning of her potential through you.

One of her karmic lessons is to learn how to deal with change. Do not feel that you can start teaching her this lesson early in life by creating constant change in her environment. Quite the opposite. She needs the comfort of routine and steadiness around her. If, for example, there is arguing going on around her and she does not appear to react, do not think that she is oblivious to the dissension. She is very aware and can be incorporating this disharmony even as she sleeps. Give your Taurus baby a healthy routine with great amounts of love tossed in. And, keep in mind, that if there is any change going on in the life around her, she is well aware of it even as an infant. An older Taurian child is more likely to voice her discontent. But, even if she does not, you, as a parent, need to be ever mindful that your Taurus child is threatened by change. She is feeling frightened and insecure and needs your comfort.

If there is a divorce or separation between parents, do not be too quick to say, *"she's too young to understand."* She is not too young to feel. That child needs extra attention given to her routine and strong comforting arms around her to assure her that she will not be abandoned.

If your Taurian child is older and the family is planning to move to another town, keep in mind that this move is hard on her whether she voices it or not. Reassure her that many of the family routines will continue even in your new location. Help her by taking her to visit her new school and never, never throw out her old toys rather than pack them up. Take everything familiar with her. Do not feel that you are overprotecting her from the realities of change. She **is** experiencing change. She is confronting a karmic lesson no matter what her age. You will be showing her loving care, which is in itself, a wonderful lesson for her.

Food is important to the Taurian child. She can easily equate food with love. All food should be lovingly prepared for her but not used as a substitute for love. She needs to be taught healthy eating habits and, very important, minimize her intake of sweets. One of her karmic challenges will be dealing with inertia and excess weight can be a burden in learning this lesson.

Your Taurian child will probably love nature and animals. Let her feel the grass under her bare feet. Teach her the wonders of nature. She will love pets, particularly dogs. With a pet, she will begin her development of learning the lessons of giving love and nourishment to others.

The lesson of dealing with materialism is significant to your Taurus child. Allow her to deal with materialism at an early age. Open a bank account for her and put in all the money she may receive as gifts. Show her how the banking system works. But also allow her to experience the handling of money. One natural tendency is to tell her what to do to protect her from losing or wasting money. Your job is to instruct, teach and then let her try on her own. She will learn easily if the lessons are peppered with great amounts of love and encouragement. She can learn the value of money through chores, jobs, such as paper routes, at an early age. Encourage this type of experience. It is important to show her how to give of her time and money to others. You can do this through your own example.

Remember, it is important for Taurus to learn how to let go of possessions but you will not be helping her to learn this lesson by forcing her to give away toys and possessions which bring security to her or have sentimental value to her. Her possessions should be disposed of with her permission...granted this will take some prodding from you!

If you have a male Taurus child, encourage his feminine side. Introduce him to the beauty of the fine arts, music, and literature. All Taurian children, male and female, will benefit from these experiences. They are children of beauty and love but they are not fragile. Their way of protecting themselves is to dig in and to stay with the known entity of their lives. Their karmic lessons are focused clearly on materialism and inflexibility and their greatest tools for survival are those of love and beauty.

Your main role as a parent of a Taurian child is to love her unconditionally and to help guide her through her times of transition with a gentle, loving hand.

GEMINI

May 21 - June 20

Male Energy

KARMIC LESSON

♦ To educate yourself through schooling and life itself

♦ To communicate with integrity

♦ To find your own identity

♦ To develop socializing skills

♦ To complete goals

♦ To get in touch with your feelings

PRIMARY GEMINI

Gemini is an air sign which means that it is primarily concerned with all forms of communication. We human beings have a marvelous capacity for letting our thoughts be known and we call this communication. We are all here on earth with a special capacity for communication. This is, supposedly, one of the factors which puts us "above" the rest of the animal kingdom (definitely an example of *human conceit*). People of all sun signs have a responsibility to develop their minds and communicative powers throughout their lifetime. But Gemini has an even stronger obligation toward this development of self. As a Gemini, you will periodically experience your primary tendencies which will become an indication of where you must grow and mature.

Gemini, working through its primary level, can bring out communication of a rather immature flavor....talk, talk, talk, talk, talk....mostly about self-oriented issues. All Geminis enjoy working with their minds on some level. The primary Gemini is often found busy talking about themselves and gossiping about others. This can run the line from harmless chatter to hurtful mudslinging.

There is a childlike quality within the Gemini which can follow a self-oriented direction. After all, a child sees only his own little world as it revolves around him. A Gemini, on a primary level, can also be consumed with this self-concern.

Schooling is ever so important to the Gemini. When a classroom bound Gemini is vibrating on his primary level, he will do much more talking in the class rather than absorbing information. He will be flitting from one thought to the next, unable to settle down to the teacher's lesson for the day. This can certainly create a behavior problem in the classroom. We may picture a Gemini child in this stage, but I can usually pick out a Gemini student in my adult classes when they too are functioning on their primary level of talkamania. They are fun to be around, yet so hard on a serious-minded class of adults trying to learn.

Geminis, like all air signs, have a special need to be liked by others. This gives you a need to develop social skills at an early age. You can be found flitting around from person to person, group to group, socializing, entertaining, and hopefully, absorbing information through other people. On a primary level, you seem to have no set personality of your own. Like a chameleon, you change the hues of your personality to blend comfortably with the people you are with at the moment. This can lead to bewilderment for everyone including yourself.

All of this activity and chatter without a strong sense of self-identity can lead to a shallow personality. As a Gemini you must develop the skill of communication and thought processes in order to mature and develop the full depth of your personality.

IS THE GEMINI TRULY SCHIZOPHRENIC?

Gemini is probably one of the most misunderstood signs of the zodiac. The Gemini has the same statistical chance of being schizophrenic as any other sign may have. This preoccupation with your sanity can rob you of your potential karmic growth. Think of yourself as that beautiful monarch butterfly dancing from one flower of interest to another. That is what you are here to do. Your karmic direction is to experience and taste many different flavors of life without necessarily settling down to one particular nectar.

If a subject interests you, as a Gemini, you will find yourself drawn to learn about and experience that subject - for the moment. Hence the social stigma, *Jack of all trades, master of none*. As an inquisitive Gemini, your karmic road will lead you toward many avenues of interest. You justifiably earn the title, Jack of all trades. It is society that demands you to settle down to one interest and specialize in that one direction. How many butterflies have you seen settling on one flower and resting there peacefully without moving? Ah, but society demands of you to make a choice and settle down, to choose one area of interest and make it all yours, to wear the shackle of a label. If you do not, society says you are split in too many directions, unable to decide what you want to specialize in for this lifetime. Your mind is unable to concentrate; it is split in too many different directions. You have a split mind!

You Geminis also blend in comfortably with many different kinds of people, a gift enjoyed by so few other people. When you are with your bowling team friends, you wear casual clothes, relax with a glass of beer perhaps, chew gum, and let correct diction escape your grasp. Your conversations will center around work, property taxes, football stats. The next day you are with your socialite friends taking in a night at the opera. Now you are wearing formal attire, sipping champagne from crystal, sitting straight in your chair and discussing arias, national politics, and the stock market decline. Who are you, Gemini? Are you the jock relaxed at the bowling alley or are you the intellectual with season tickets to the Met? Society wants to know. Society, in its own limitations, needs to put labels on everyone. Each person needs to fit neatly into a category. That is the order of things they say. Why Gemini, your personality seems to change according to the person you are with at the time. If you refuse to choose who you are, then society must then find some kind of label for you. Here's one - Schizophrenic. That will do.

No, Gemini, you are not schizophrenic. And, if you ever feel that you are, it may be because you also feel you must compromise your flight of interests and choose a label for yourself.

Karmically, you are here to spread the pollen of social interaction from one group to another. You are here to help the world to understand the versatility of mankind and help erase the barriers of group lines.

EVOLVED GEMINI

As an evolved Gemini, you will be well-educated either through formal schooling, lectures, seminars, books, TV, radio, tapes, or through experiencing life with other people. It is important for you to experience as much as you can of life in any and all areas which interest you. This does not mean intellectual snobbery. Quite the opposite. An evolved Gemini learns simply for the fun of learning, never to lord their accumulation of knowledge over others. You will be an interesting and kind conversationalist. A rapt listener. An inspired teacher. All of that information which you amass throughout your life will be joyfully and excitedly shared with others as a gift. The intellect of the evolved Gemini is never used as a weapon. This kind of enthusiasm soon becomes contagious and your love of learning will be spread to other people of all sun signs.

An evolved Gemini still has the intellectual wanderlust of the butterfly enabling you to handle more than one project at a time, but you will also have developed the skill of follow-through in enough areas to give yourself a feeling of accomplishment.

Karmically, you are here to develop yourself to your highest intellectual capacity. Your karmic role on earth is to share these accomplishments with others. There is a wonderful childlike quality in the evolved Gemini which can enrich our world through literature, dance, music and a general fun-loving spirit.

REMEMBER, NO ONE IS TOTALLY PRIMARY OR TOTALLY EVOLVED, OUR KARMIC LESSONS ARE BEST LEARNED WHEN WE ARE DEALING WITH BOTH OF THESE ENERGIES.

STIMULATING THAT WONDERFUL MUSCLE - THE BRAIN.

In this lifetime, your primary karmic lesson is to learn as much as possible through your schooling and/or life itself. Many times, Geminis are of above average intelligence but this can not always be assumed. You are here to learn how to work with what you have. That includes basic IQ levels and educational advantages. A Gemini of the 1930's who was forced to quit school at the third grade in order to help support his family during the depression, has karmic opportunities equal to that of a Harvard graduate in his quest for mental development. Only humankind has put labels of success on classroom achievement. Karmic lessons of communication go way beyond mankind's restrictive barriers.

A young Gemini likes a lot of stimulation - noise, activity. As a child, you enjoyed music around you, lights, colors, people's voices. These kinds of stimulations wake up the Gemini's mind and start it into gear. As you mature, you need to learn how to respond to a quieter stimulation - reading, meditation, imagination.

WHY ARE SENIOR CITIZENS SO DAMN QUIET?

Mickey's mornings, before catching the bus to his high school, began with a blast from the local radio station. His head bobbed to a resounding base beat of acid rock while he showered, brushed, ate and dashed off with his boom-box to another day of school. His nervous system never quieted as he donned his earphones from class to class, his pulse never missing a beat of the vibrant rock and roll. His Gemini mind amazingly still maintained a C+ average which got him into a fairly decent college in a metropolitan city.

Here, Mickey found rock 'n roll frowned on by his peers. After all, this college was in the midst of a sophisticated city. Mickey soon had his ears tuned to jazz as it wafted out of his friends' dorm room. He also found himself frequenting jazz bars and fancied himself quite an expert on sweet jazz by the time he graduated college.

Mickey entered the adult world of work all day, car radio on the way home and TV at night until he slept in preparation for another day. He had learned well in school. He was advancing in his career. He was married, had children. Wasn't he like everyone else? He had plenty of intellectual stimulation necessary for a Gemini.

Then Mickey discovered quiet. He found he appreciated the times when his wife was out with the kids and the TV was off, the phone wasn't ringing. He even refused to turn on the radio during those precious moments. It was then that Mickey learned how to think. He then discovered the most relaxing yet most exercising times for his mind. He learned to feel his thoughts; to be alone with himself and the person he had created through years of constant audio and visual stimulation. Mickey was now able to experience his greatest karmic lesson. He was able to communicate with himself.

Why are older people able to enjoy quiet? Because they are brave enough to let their thoughts become their conscious reality. When a Gemini keeps himself constantly stimulated by music, talking, noise, TV and more, he is not only ingesting positive information, he is also avoiding the fine tuning, polishing treatment his mind truly needs. Too much stimulation around the Gemini is an escape; an escape from his own thoughts and his own truths, his own realities. If you wish to truly cross over that bridge to your highest karmic, intellectual lessons, learn to sit quietly with only yourself for stimulation...no books, newspapers. No music, TV or conversations. Be still. Be meditative. Your karmic lessons come from that wonderful muscle, your brain. Be alone with it. Be in tune with it. Now you have opened your mind to your karmic truths.

GEMINI IS LIVELY

You Geminis are the communicators of the zodiac. Your need, at times, to be quiet does not mean that you are to be hermits. You are a wonderful part of this social system that we have here. And you have a valuable part to play with your ability to communicate.

Knowledge comes in all forms and all sizes. As a Gemini, you should be open to various mediums of brain stimulation. When we think of communicating, we automatically think in terms of talking. And talking is a comfortable mode of communication for you Geminis. Be open also to your wonderful gifts of writing, music, poetry, sign language, dance and all forms of gesturing. Each and every one of these symbols are important to you.

An evolved Gemini will do a great deal of writing and reading. As little as thirty years ago, everyone read, talked and wrote. We talked during dinner, we read after dinner, we wrote to our family and friends far away. Now, with the marvelous inventions of radio, TV and telephone (Gemini inventions by the way) we have lost many of our old-fashioned communicative skills. This has created a difficult time for Geminis. You will need to discipline yourself in order to develop the skills of writing, reading and conversation. You, Gemini, are like Hermes, the winged messenger. Your job on this earth is to keep communication aglow. This is done quickly and accurately with the Gemini inventions of the wireless, telephone, TV and radio. Not to forget the VCR, computer and Fax machine. It is your karmic role to also nurture the beauty of the written word; the rules of spelling, grammar and pronunciation. Some of our greatest writers and public speakers were Geminis. Therefore, you have a need to read and write whether it be published writing or letter writing, national speeches or notes on greeting cards. The safety and security of the skill of communication lies in your hands. We are all depending on you.

This may not be easy for you in this time of communication shortcuts. It is far easier in this fast paced world to read the abbreviated cliff notes rather than the whole novel. And it is even simpler to watch the movie than read the notes. You can not really read a book while commuting bumper to bumper on a major highway to work and back every day, but you can listen to a talking book. These are all legitimate forms of communication comfortable to you, the Gemini. They should not be ignored. They are a part of our modern age. They are simpler and they are legitimate ways of communicating. Karmically, you may also find yourself forced to practice the old, slower ways for these are also the ways of your soul. The fact that you are reading this book shows that you have not succumbed to the phobia of words on a page. Reading a book, magazine or newspaper takes time, patience and the discipline of sitting down and slowing your pace. You have many senses to use in your quest for learning. Your karmic drive requires you to use them all.

COMMUNICATING WITH INTEGRITY

As you have seen, there are many different forms of communication, each of which can be comfortable for the Gemini. You will find your own most compatible mode of communicating and will even experience changes in your techniques and interests as you evolve. But one factor must remain evident in any and every stage and that is your penchant for integrity.

If you are coffee klatching with your neighbors when the children are off to school, be aware of the direction of your conversations. The Gemini in you must talk, but what do you choose to talk about? Beware of malicious gossip and mudslinging. This is a Gemini tendency, especially when bored. If you find yourself drifting off in this direction, remember you are now experiencing a karmic test.

Most Geminis are knowledgeable in many different areas. For example, if you once had an interest in sailing, you would have taken a course in boating, read a few books and associated with some people who were able to teach you something about sailing. Perhaps you have abandoned that interest by now, but the information is still stored in your cranial muscle. Now, you see your next door neighbor pulling a new sailboat into his backyard. Your natural instinct is to go over to him and share everything you have learned about sailing. You are a natural born teacher! Jack of all trades, remember? The karmic, integrity issue is raised when your neighbor asks you something you are not sure about. You may be tempted to bluff your way through it rather than admit you do not know the answer. It is to the credit of your karmic advancement to be able to use the phrases, "*I don't know*" or "*I can look it up for you*". Beware of intellectual   conceit.   An   honest,   forthright   approach   in   your communications along with a thoughtfulness of other people's feelings would be a safe route for you to take.

Geminis make powerful writers and public speakers. Some of our greatest orators and authors have charts flavored with creative Gemini energy. Of course not every Gemini decides to use their communication skills in these areas but, if you do, please be aware of the powerful tool you place in your hand when you wield the mighty pen. You are able to bring information and pleasure to your fellow citizen with your talent. Obviously your karmic attunement to integrity will be strong if you choose this direction.

FINDING YOUR OWN IDENTITY

You have a remarkable gift for being able to blend into many different environments. There is a mimicking, aping characteristic which allows you to be comfortable with many different kinds of people in various situations. This marvelous adaptability enables you to enjoy various experiences throughout your life. This trait is childlike in nature and can be quite unnerving to other, stuffier people. Remember, society wants so desperately to categorize you but you may want to refuse to conform to their need, just as a child refuses to color within the lines until they are forced to "follow the rules".

People will be jealous of that Gemini nature and reprimand you for being immature and flighty. You have two karmic tests going on here. First, is to be able to establish your own unique individuality without allowing yourself to be forced into a role. Secondly, to be able to nurture and enjoy the childlike part of your nature without succumbing to the Peter Pan syndrome.

WILL THE REAL ANNIE PLEASE STEP FORWARD

Annie was a Gemini who always loved people. She was a popular honors student through high school and went on to receive her college degree in Communication. She was versatile and adaptable and thrived on having her days brim over with activity. It seemed natural for her to become a traveling, independent reporter for a local cable news station. Annie's days were filled with running, cameraman in tow, from story to story. At first she was primarily absorbed in her technique, and style. She needed to learn her craft and she learned it quickly. Later, as she became more comfortable with her job, she was able to relax and enjoy all the people she was meeting on her daily travels. She ran to report on a fire in a nursing home and got to know the local volunteer firemen. She covered a mugging in the downtown district and got to meet the cops on the beat. Once she covered a major sports event when the sportscaster was down with the flu. She did a particularly impressive interview with the manager of the home team that day. As she moved up the ladder of success she was given her own human interest stories, made permanent staff reporter, and was well on her way.

Annie was a Gemini who was establishing her identity in her career of communication. She was also meeting different kinds of people and found herself establishing many positive relationships along the way. She got along well with everyone she met. Annie had breakfast with the firemen at their fundraisers. She had tea with the socialites as they planned the latest fashion show. She had become fast friends with the wife of one of the younger cops on the beat and the two of them loved to see the latest movies with a large, buttery popcorn for two. Annie was unaware of the fact that each of her new friends brought out a different aspect of her personality. She only knew that she felt comfortable and relaxed with each of them.

Annie's rude awakening came when she decided to have an open house to celebrate her move into her beautiful new apartment. She invited all of her new friends that night, excited to share her good fortune with them. But, instead of the party being a circle of warm friends, she found herself feeling more and more strained as the evening wore on. She realized she had to entertain every one. No one was mixing. By the end of the evening, Annie was fully aware that she was the only factor any of these people had in common. They were painfully uncomfortable grouped together in her new apartment, which was feeling smaller and smaller by the hour. What Annie was now learning was the Gemini flexibility which enabled her to have many varied friends also forced her to examine her own sense of self-identity. Who was she? She noticed her behavior shift as she moved from group to group, yet it was still her. Did she have to choose which group of friends she preferred? Did she need to adapt one mode of behavior above the others? It was these questions which exhausted her the most. It seemed everyone was looking at her demanding her to choose.

Annie's eventual choice was interesting. She chose to maintain all of her friendships and, most significantly, she decided never again to try to blend all of her relationships together in one room. Annie refused to be categorized. She refused to choose one aspect of herself above another. And, most importantly, she refused to question her own self-identity.

IS THE CHILD WITHIN YOU ALIVE AND WELL?

Modern psychiatry tells us we are made up of three parts, the parent, the adult, and the child. The Gemini also has these three aspects of self but it is karmically important for the Gemini to keep the child within alive and well. This must be done against the forces of society which is always telling you to "grow up".

It is your responsibility to mature, to become goal oriented and take on responsibilities just like every other adult around you. But it is your karmic duty to continue to maintain the wonderment of a child. There is no need to become stuffy and overly serious minded. Most of life's joys are seen and experienced with the eyes of a child.

Once again, society demands you to conform, to leave that wonderment of childhood behind you and enter into the serious world of adulthood. Be categorized! Conform! Choose one above the other! Do as we do!

You are here to keep the child alive in all of us by exposing us to the merriment of your nature. You are here to laugh, to dance, to sing. You are here to bring the bubbles of your voice into the all too serious concerns of our lives. You are the child of the world. This does not mean immaturity or responsibility-resisting. You are the magical quality of life that is available to everyone and you, the childlike Gemini, are here karmically to lead others to the magic of fun and merriment.

If you are expecting people to encourage you in this course, forget it. They will be demanding that you conform, act your age, and fit into their neat categories. But the child shall lead them. Karmically, you are here to see and enjoy this world through the eyes of a child and to show others how to do the same. You are to bring laughter and frivolity into your life and the lives of all around you.

Music will play an important role for you, especially expressing yourself through dancing. These are valuable forms of communication for the Gemini. At times you will be the life of the party dancing and singing for the world around you. Other times, the world of music will be a private special place for your soul alone. But it will always be nurturing to your karmic growth.

SOCIALIZING WITH SKILL

As you have seen, Gemini is quite a socializing energy. People are important to you. After all, why would there be a need to communicate if there were no other people here but you?

The child within Gemini can be immature at times and you must learn how to use that gift in a way that does not put off other people. The child loves to use the words "I" and "me". We accept that from a child. But, as you age into maturity, it is karmically important for you to widen your scope of interest to include others around you. Your conversations need to focus on issues which involve people other than yourself. A valuable karmic test of your evolvement would be to keep a tally on how many times in a day you think and say those words, "I" and "me".

Becoming a good listener is also a karmic lesson for Gemini. Many times when we first think of communication we think in terms of talking, at which you are wonderfully talented. Be cautious though, an excess of talking can lead you toward that "I" and "me" syndrome. Therefore, you need to concentrate your communicating skills by listening. Geminis are here to learn and you can incorporate much learning through simply listening. This skill also enhances your socializing energies and fine tunes your relationships.

Gemini is a mutable energy which means you are able to flit from one subject to the next. It also means you are able to flit from one relationship to the next. Thus is created the social butterfly, an apt description of a socializing Gemini. Keep in mind that moving easily from one relationship to another also brings with it a degree of detachment, a trait which is commonly found in the Gemini. Sometimes, this behavior trait will save you from unnecessary hurts, other times it robs you of the quality of a deep and meaningful relationship. You are here karmically to learn about feelings and depths of relationships. You will still have your ability to jump from one person to another just as your mind can jump from one thought to the next. But you will also have your greatest learning and self-awareness through your ability to settle down and gamble your emotions on one relationship. This will mean concentrating on sharing, compromising, and giving...mature Gemini traits.

You can see that you are here to keep the childlike wonderment in our universe but you are also expected to accept the responsibilities that come with maturity.

COMPLETING GOALS

You, like everyone else, need to have the feeling of satisfaction that comes with accomplishment. Therefore, it is important for you to follow through on some of your goals so that you may experience an end result. The trick for you is to be able to move from one interest to another without always seeing each goal through to fruition yet, to have enough accomplishments around you so that you can feel good about yourself. You, the butterfly, are supposed to experience a variety of interests. The butterfly enjoys flying from flower to flower as its whims may take it. If you watch a butterfly with scrutiny though, you will see that it always seems to go back to one favorite flower in particular. There is also a pattern the butterfly is following. There is definitely order to its seemingly erratic behavior. It is not quite as fickle and noncommittal as it may appear.

This is also true of the Gemini. Your interests will be varied (Jack of all trades). You will also experience the accomplishments of certain goals which are of significant importance to you. Your completion of these goals will become possible because they will peak your intellectual interest. You will want to learn as much as you can in the areas that interest you the most. You will want to go a step or two beyond a mere interest or casual attitude. Certain goals will grab your interest and lead you through your karmic path of goal completion.

Wherever there is an area in which you must experience your karmic lessons, there is also a tendency to experience difficulty in that same area. Keeping this in mind, it is important that you allow yourself to enjoy the many varied interests that captivate your mind throughout your life and not feel that you must follow each and every one of these areas to full completion. Trust your instincts to let you know when one goal of your life becomes of karmic significance. You will feel a need to pursue this goal with a stoic fortitude which will surprise you. Your Gemini resourcefulness, intelligence and creativity will come bounding to your aid, and although accomplishment may not be easy, it will certainly be rewarding.

FROM DIAPERS TO Ph.D.

Pamela had always had an active life. In high school she maintained an A average, belonged to a multitude of clubs, ran for the office of class president in her senior year and worked part-time at the local fast-food shack. She was never strained by all of this activity. She thrived on it. Right after high school she married, and within twelve years, she had become mother to six children. Hers was not a fairy tale marriage. Pamela found herself abused physically and emotionally. She felt trapped with the responsibility of her children's welfare. All that exuberance of her childhood was ebbing away. She was losing her enthusiasm and her confidence in herself.

Pamela's best friend, Jane, suggested she take a college course to get herself out and stimulate her mind again. Slowly and steadily, Pamela added courses to her transcript until she had completed her BA in English Literature. The college experience brought this Gemini to life again and she decided to go for an even higher goal, almost bigger than life goal. She decided to go on for her Ph.D. and become a college professor herself. But Pamela had never really been goal-oriented before this. She always did whatever she wanted to do at the time. This was the first time she had to plan out her life and some of the obstacles were seemingly insurmountable. How could she continue her education to such a level with an oppressive husband, the demands of six children, and the financial burden? How would she find the time and the energy? Her karmic need to complete this goal pushed her forward. It was an unseen energy that worked as a gentle friend constantly filling her with the warmth of confidence.

Pamela was lucky in terms of her marriage. Her husband's boss at work took him aside and strongly suggested he enter an alcoholic rehab center which would be paid for by the company. Knowing that he had no choice, he signed himself in and was finally able to find peace within himself upon coming to terms with his problem with alcohol. This peace became incorporated into their marriage and he became supportive rather than abusive to Pamela. The road was long but worth while.

With this renewed support, Pamela was able to fulfill her goal. She graduated with her Ph.D. the same day her youngest child graduated from high school. Now that took perseverance for a Gemini!

Geminis are certainly able to complete the goals of their choices. The easiest will be the goals which are Gemini in nature: education, writing, music, communication. The trick is to keep your spirit young, confidence high, and patience in tow.

MALE GEMINI

Gemini is a masculine sign and fits comfortably with the male spirit. It also has a strong creative slant which allows the Gemini male to bring out the feminine, passive side of his nature. This combination strengthens his ability to reason with full compatibility of right and left brain thinking. He is able to direct his attentions to several areas at once which is a wonderful asset to him at work. He needs a job which has great variety and leaves him with space, freedom, and versatility within his work day.

Male Gemini energy creates the natural salesman. A man with a natural sales pitch. Obviously this talent can be used at work. Think of the traveling salesman. That is Gemini. He's on the road, using his wits, meeting many kinds of people and situations. A job made for Gemini, particularly men (although not exclusively). Even in a more restricted area of work, such as corporate work, the Gemini nature will emerge. He needs freedom and respect from his superiors. He certainly needs great variety in his work. A boss need not be afraid to confuse the Gemini with too many responsibilities. He not only can handle them, he will relish them. Diversity is the name of the game for him. Give him a project that needs some problem solving, an object that needs some tinkering. A Gemini man can be an asset to any business or line of work. He simply needs to be left alone with as few rules as possible.

His mind is the key to his success. At an early age, the Gemini male needs to be encouraged to get the most out of educational advantages. He is learning everywhere, not only in the classroom. The depth of his mind can be bottomless. Once settled into a career, he should learn as much as possible about his field. He needs to keep up with any new information as years go by. He may even become the teacher or writer who instructs others.

Communication is important to him. He will be talkative around his friends and family and will constantly be ingesting information from them. Sometimes the Gemini male has trouble with his communication or his learning process. If this is the case, this is a definite karmic experience to focus his attention on his mind and the quality of his communication. For example, a Gemini man could have a stuttering, stammering, or hesitation pattern in his speech. This could become a device to slow down his thoughts and certainly to slow down his words. This calls attention to his communications, and eventually, gives him an opportunity to better develop his thoughts. This can also happen to Gemini women, but for some reason, is more common with men. All Geminis can succumb to foot in mouth disease and need to slow themselves down in some way or another.

The companionship of other people is significantly important to the Gemini Male. He needs the stimulation of other people around him. He has a karmic responsibility to choose his friends wisely and to be discriminate in his conversations with them. He must be cautious of the "ole washwoman" syndrome. Gemini men can be quite the gossips!

A key to success for the Gemini men is to keep active on a physical and mental level. Their karmic lessons come to them through their minds but they must keep its' housing, the body, in good shape. Physical activity is another healthy outlet for their abundance of energy. The sedentary duties of reading and studying need to be blended with the physical activities of sports, dancing, walking and daily exercise.

GEMINI FEMALE

Even though Gemini is a masculine energy, it sits comfortably within a female spirit. A Gemini female can easily focus her Gemini talents into areas which are sociably accepted as "female".

Music is a powerful force for all Geminis. Society feels it is natural to send a little girl to dance classes and piano lessons. Little girls are encouraged to sing. Because of this sociological structure, Gemini females most often direct their communication skills first toward the medium of music. This is certainly an effective way for her to communicate her feelings and begin to exercise her intellectual muscle, the brain. Unfortunately, in some areas of society, the Gemini female is discouraged from other forms of communication.

She is expected to be bright in school but her opinions and thoughts are not always respected in "important" areas of politics, business, finance, etc. This double standard can be particularly frustrating to the Gemini female. Her karmic objectives are unique. She needs to learn how to express herself within the guidelines of society's structures, while also breaking through some of those barriers without losing her status of femininity. The Women's Movement of the western cultures has been a blessing to Gemini Females, but there is still a long way to go in all areas of the world. We may very well see Gemini females as forerunners in these kinds of movements.

Father is significantly important to the Gemini female. She identifies strongly with him and needs to develop an understanding of the role he plays in her life. An ideal situation would be a loving daddy's little girl relationship but this is not always the good fortune of the Gemini female. As she matures, men will play an important part in her adulthood. She may still be seeking the daddy she never had. She certainly has a need for the respect and admiration of the men around her either in personal or business relationships.

The Gemini female may also gravitate toward masculine careers or areas of interest. She may desire to be a lawyer, doctor, musician, mathematician. Society says it's alright for her to go to school and get a job. In the past, Gemini females flooded the field of teaching, a socially acceptable position for a nice Gemini girl. Now they are opening the doors to explore possibilities in areas previously denied to them. They dare to aspire to more exciting and lucrative careers once tightly closed to them. They are competitive with the best because of their learning abilities and they feel comfortable in the male world.

Socializing is so important to the Gemini female. She must have many friends around her when she is younger and many men attracted to her as she grows older. She is truly the butterfly who enjoys socializing, dancing, and dating. She also has the ability to detach herself emotionally from an unsuccessful relationship. She has a karmic responsibility to become more in touch with her feelings and the feelings of others and will be exposed to situations which ask her to display her loyalty to one person. This very often comes about through her children, although the Gemini female can also detach herself from them if she feels her emotions are threatened. She was, or wanted to be, daddy's little girl, yet it is her sons who are likely to win over her heart. Many of her karmic lessons will be coming to her through these close relationships.

GEMINI CHILDREN

Sing to your Gemini child! He loves music. Crooned and sing to him. Toys with music boxes, chimes, radios or teddy bears with tape cassettes in their bellies are gifts that the Gemini child will love. As he gets older, be prepared to pay for music and dance classes, and please do not differentiate between girl or boy stereotypes. Let them choose the instrument or style of dance they want to learn. Music is soothing to their soul and stimulating to the communication center of their brain. These children are here to learn about communication and this lesson may start with their introduction to music.

As an infant, it is beneficial to prop him up in front of the TV, even if you do not think that TV plays a positive influence on children. The stimulation of TV and radio is wonderful for your Gemini child. He loves to be in the center of noise and activity.

As he grows older, adult stimulation is important to him. A family setting where everyone sits around the dining room table together for meals is healthy for him since he thrives on the stimulation of conversation. He will want to hear your views on all sorts of matters and will want to be able to express his. Be prepared for a verbal, vocal child. Most importantly, do not stifle his curiosity. Discipline will be a must since he can be most active in his vocal physical manner. The trick for you is to discipline his unruliness without quelling his inquisitiveness. There is a childlike quality to him which can be frustrating as he grows up but this same characteristic will be his greatest asset if he learns to handle it properly. It can be difficult, as a parent, not to restrict him too much while not spoiling him through too much freedom.

Education will be important to your Gemini child. Start immediately to set up an education fund for his future. We all know we should read to our children, and it is especially important to the Gemini child. It is good for him to see you reading too. Have subscriptions to book clubs, magazines, newspapers around the house. Encourage him to do well in school. Be supportive as a parent by attending open school functions perhaps even becoming active in the PTA. Include him in conversations, stimulate his mind. Then let go. Your Gemini child may decide to go on to Harvard or he may decide to quit high school at 16 years of age. Of course, higher education is ideal for him but this realization may come to him later, or he may decide to get his education through on-the-job training or through the classroom of life. Your role is to always encourage him to learn in any way possible. Put the tools of education in front of him, show him how to use them by instruction and by your example and then walk away. The Gemini child has a free spirited mind which may take a direction totally unthought of by you.

Father plays a significantly important role to the Gemini child, particularly to the female Gemini. His thoughts, attitudes, and opinions will help mold the mind of his child. A female Gemini wants to be daddy's little girl. She needs a great deal of his time and attention, and most importantly, his love. Her relationship with her father will have a powerful effect on all her future relationships with men. If, as a mother, you are not satisfied with the father-daughter relationship your Gemini girl is experiencing, it will be necessary for you to step back and recognize that this is a karmic relationship over which you have very little control. It is the mother's duty to protect her children from any possible hurt, as much as possible, but you will not be able to substitute for any loss of love and affection between them. Certainly, try not to be jealous if you see the budding love between the two of them. This would be an ideal relationship for her.

Friends are important to your Gemini child. They are constantly learning through all kinds of mental stimulation, and the conversations and relationships with friends will advance the necessary skill of socializing. Most Gemini children love birthday parties with all of their friends. They love the stimulation of a clown or magician, lots of colorful balloons and plenty of musical games. As your Gemini child gets older, you may find yourself worried and concerned with the kinds of friends he chooses. This can be a realistic concern because Geminis are easily influenced by their friends. There is a childlike, immature quality in Geminis that makes their parents always want to protect them...to think of them as children. The more respect you give them, the more adult they will respond in their behavior. Ideally, this maturity will show itself in his choice of friends. Again, some of the people around him will be of karmic significance to his development of communication. You may not always be aware of the reasons why someone is in your child's life at any particular time.

By the way, I usually recommend putting a lock on the phone within hands-reach of a Gemini teenager. Have you ever seen phone bills the size of mortgage payments? Visit a Gemini's home!

Follow-through is another karmic lesson for your Gemini child to learn, since he has the temperament of the butterfly, flitting from one interest to the next. As a parent, you certainly do not want to destroy his wonderful, inquisitive mind, yet you also need to teach him how to follow-through on goals. For example, your Gemini child will most probably want to take music lessons. He will come home from school with a trumpet under his arm all excited about starting his lessons. You will be handed a bill to pay for the trumpet. His practicing may begin with enthusiasm and dwindle to total quiet. Then he will come home with a flute under his arm, another burst of enthusiasm, and of course, a bill for you. Here begins your dilemma. He may need to experience many instruments until he finds what he likes. Or he may only need to learn a little of many instruments without ever becoming accomplished on any one. Meanwhile the bills are piling up for you. The trick to parenting a Gemini child is to encourage his curiosity and need to touch on many aspects of learning (Jack of all trades) and also to know when to draw the line and force him to develop one interest above another (master of one). He needs to have both aspects of his personality nurtured. As he gets older, he will have more difficult karmic testing in the areas of completion and obtaining his goals. The examples you set for him as a child will serve him throughout his life.

Your Gemini child is exciting, vibrant, fun-loving, sociable and intelligent. He may not always fit into the norms or categories that society wants for him and that may be his greatest attribute. Help him to develop his own uniqueness and support him to follow his own destiny. He is a beautiful butterfly who needs to be free and frolic in the winds of life. Do not try to categorize him or encase him in a display box. Your Gemini child can be a breath of fresh air rushing into your family. Enjoy him.

CANCER

June 21 - July 22

Female Energy

KARMIC LESSONS

♦ Dealing with emotions and mood swings

♦ Insecurity vs. self-confidence

♦ Family issues as a child and as an adult

♦ Children

♦ Eating habits

PRIMARY CANCER

Everyone on earth is dealing with their emotions and their relationships with others. We are a species that enjoys living together in groups and family units and it is within these relationships that we develop emotionally. Cancer is a water sign, which means that all of you who are born under this sign are governed strongly by your emotions. The reactions you receive at an early age by those around you teaches you how to govern and control your emotional state. If, as a baby, you get your bottle faster when you throw an emotional tantrum, you will continue throwing tantrums even into adulthood in order to get what you want. If, as a child, you get people's attention when you cry, you will continue to cry as an adult in order to control people around you. Obviously, these emotional patterns become more sophisticated with age. Their root beginnings and primary reasons for development also become further and further removed from your consciousness and complex, emotional patterns develop which may eventually require psychoanalysis or great introspection to uncover. It is because of this complexity which accompanies your emotional self, that it may take painful, honest scrutiny on your part, along with a good dose of courage, in order to truly face your primary Cancerean tendencies.

You are emotionally vulnerable as a Cancer whether you are vibrating on your primary or evolved levels. This is a part of yourself which you must acknowledge. Be kind to yourself. Even when you find yourself behaving in an emotionally immature manner (which you will from time to time), it will help you to realize that this is the child part of yourself which is in need of recognition and attention. It is when you deny this insecure, frightened part of yourself that you enable an emotional cover-up which may take years of hard work to undo.

Patterns: You will learn most about yourself by observing your patterns in relationships. On a primary level, you will find yourself repeating many negative, self-destructive patterns with various people. You will suffer emotional hurts and have a tendency to blame others for your hurts, while recognition of your patterns will bring you back to your childhood relationships where they originated. It is through understanding of your past that you can adjust to your present.

Karma plays a powerful role for the Cancerean person. You have chosen a life of significant, karmic relationships along with a tendency to be quite vulnerable within these relationships. It is important for you to realize that most of your karmic lessons come to you through your emotional patterns more than the actual people connected with them. For example, if you tend to date or marry alcoholics, it is not the alcoholics themselves who carry the karmic connection for you. It is your pattern of attraction to addiction, lack of self-worth and issues of deprivation which are your karmic issues.

When you are behaving like or feeling like a child, you are then tuned into your primary level. Interestingly, it is by touching on this primary part of your sign that you will be able to hone into and experience growth through your karmic lessons. This is a complex sign, so let us take it step by step...one karmic lesson at a time.

As a Cancerean, you are acting on a primary level when you are allowing your moods to erupt completely uncontrolled, acting exactly as you please without regard for other people. It is on this level that you can be sullen and moody, consumed solely with your own feelings and needs. This kind of behavior can be quite unnerving to those around you. You yourself can feel as though you are on an emotional roller coaster experiencing rapid ups and downs within short time periods. This kind of behavior can lead you to a life of great loneliness and isolation. If you got away with this emotional power play as a child, you may try to continue it in your adult relationships. It can become a habit. You must keep in mind that habits can be broken, even emotional habits.

You have the ability to be crystal clear in your emotions. The emotional confusion you may feel from time to time is an indication that you are protecting yourself from a painful realization. A little of this protection is all right, too much is a fearful avoidance of your karmic lessons. This is where the zodiac symbol of the crab fits you well. Picture the crab in the bottom of the sea. Along comes an intruder moving in its direction. The crab instinctively puts its claws up in a menacing fashion, pinching at its potential enemy. It then side steps away, never taking its eyes off the intruder, finding it's nearest hiding place. Cancereans can do this also. You can be so afraid of being hurt, that you can assume that anyone who tries to come close to you emotionally is a potential enemy. You can keep that hard shell on your back and menace people with your moods, never allowing them to come close enough to hurt you - or to love you. Remember, even the crab has to shed its hard shell in order to mate. You are fixed in your primary stage when you allow your moods and fears to keep you from experiencing relationships with others. Your karmic growth comes to you through identifying and correcting your patterns in relationships. This is hard to do alone. You may want to share this quest of self-inspection with a trusted loved one or trained counselor. You must trust, whomever you choose as your confidant, enough to remove your shell of protection.

When you find yourself identifying harmful, disruptive patterns within your relationships and emotional swings, you are then recognizing, not only your karmic lessons but also your primary tendencies. If you continue to remain immersed in these depths of destruction, you can be assured that you have failed to rise to your evolved potential.

EVOLVED CANCER

Your Cancerean energy, in its evolved state, gives you the ability to bestow unconditional love to those around you. You have the loving and nurturing power of a mother for her young and this love can be your focal characteristic when you are vibrating to your evolved state of Cancer. You are capable of the highest form of unconditional love without being overly protective, smothering or succumbing to the martyr syndrome. You will keep a comfortable home for yourself and your loved ones, a place of sanctuary and warmth.

As an evolved Cancer you will gain a keen understanding of yourself as you exist in relation to others. In this way, your emotional energy will be directed in a loving, giving manner to all those around you.

You will learn your karmic lessons through understanding the emotional pain of your past and will then be able to convert these lessons into positive, constructive emotional patterns. The trick to obtaining this knowledge, is your ability to assimilate the truths in your experiences with your ability to let go of the unnecessary hurts and angers of your past. This ability to discriminate positive from negative emotions will be your signal that you have progressed through your most difficult karmic experiences.

REMEMBER, NO ONE IS TOTALLY PRIMARY OR EVOLVED. OUR
KARMIC LESSONS ARE BEST LEARNED WHEN WE ARE
DEALING WITH BOTH OF THESE ENERGIES.

DEALING WITH EMOTIONS AND MOOD SWINGS

The heavenly ruler of Cancer is the moon which we associate with our
emotions. Even the shepherds thousands of years ago noticed that their
sheep behaved differently during the various phases of the moon. Women
also seemed to be particularly affected by the moon both with their
emotions and their monthly cycles. The moon's pull creates the tides of the
oceans, the ebb and fall of the seas. Since our bodies are made up of 90%
water, the moon also affects us and this effect is manifested most
noticeably in our emotional state. No wonder, as a Cancerean, you are so
concerned with your emotions.

As a child, you will be prone to emotional swings, from high to
low, with a great swing toward the low. People near you may have
difficulty with these fluctuations. As you go out and make friends, they
teach you just how far you can go with your mood swings. After all, who
wants to play with someone who is always moody or crying? People begin
to condition you early in your life. The choice becomes yours immediately
whether to come to terms with your emotional state or to hide your
emotions behind a protective shell. As a Cancerean, you probably did a
little of both. The difficulty comes as you place layer upon layer of
unresolved emotions without identifying your feelings. These layers then
manifest themselves into fears, phobias, and neurosis which become
increasingly more difficult to identify as the years progress.

There is a keen sensitivity which comes naturally to you. If your
emotional state becomes too complex, you will find yourself totally
involved with yourself, self-absorbed rather than extending this sensitivity
outward to help others. The way a Cancerean is treated as a child, along
with emotional complexities of that early childhood family unit, greatly
affects the emotional outcome of the Cancerean's temperament. We can
say this is true of all signs, but the Cancer is particularly vulnerable to
childhood and family dynamics.

ANGER + ISOLATION = DIVORCE

Nancy was an only child caught in the web of her parents' selfish relationship. Her mother and father were as mismatched as two people could be. He was of Italian descent, from the northern industrial city of Chicago and she was a Baptist country girl from a small town in Georgia. No one ever figured out what brought these two unlikely souls together in marriage. But, here they were, trying to maintain a marriage as each year together reminded them of how little they had in common. When Nancy was a child, they lived in the heart of Chicago. It was in this thriving, populated city that Nancy learned to cope with isolation. Her mother, always the country girl, was frightened by this hustling bustling crime-infested city. She would never venture out of their apartment, not even to stroll Nancy through the beautiful park which was directly across the street. Nancy spent most of her preschool days staring out the window watching other children play and listening to their laughter. Her evenings were spent primarily in her room as it was the custom, in her father's belief, that children should be kept quiet when the man was home from a hard day at work. Truthfully, Nancy preferred the sanctuary of her own room to being in the living room with her parents who fought every night, neither one willing or able to change their customs or their needs. Nancy was indeed a lonely child.

She also was an angry child. She had developed her father's temper and was easily prone to attacks of violence and destruction. This was not considered a favorable trait for a little girl by either of her parent's standards and further increased her stays in her room, which by now had become both her haven and her prison.

Obviously, Nancy's school years were difficult for her. She had never developed social skills with other children. As a Cancer, she had tremendous mood swings which fluctuated from tears to anger, with many levels in between. Her parents had taught her to stifle these emotions. Her fellow classmates also had little tolerance for her lack of social skills. Nancy became shy, quiet. She was the good little girl. Not very friendly. Not a joiner. But, she made no trouble, so she was considered a good little girl. With this kind of labeling, Nancy was being encouraged by the system to contain her emotions, stay isolated and deny her anger.

Nancy dated very little through high school and married the first man who showed any serious interest in her. In a sense, this was her chance to escape her prison but it also put her into a world of relationships which were alien to her. She had no healthy examples of marriage in her childhood, she had no idea what her place was within this new relationship. Before long, her ability to contain her frustration, anger, and insecurity disintegrated into fits of temper and violence. Her husband was shocked to see so much anger within his shy, withdrawn wife. She was particularly quiet when in groups or any kind of socializing environment yet he actually felt his life threatened when she hurled her years of accumulated anger at him in the privacy of their home. Her tremendous frustration in finding a suitable outlet for her suppressed emotions became a focal point in their relationship.

In one important sense, Nancy was lucky. Even without a favorable role model from her childhood, Nancy had found love in her marriage. This was one emotion which had survived her early life unscathed and was to become a source of strength in her uphill battle to face her buried emotions. Her anger was not inherited from her father, as was assumed by her mother. It was a product of her years of suppressed feelings, her forced isolation which left her unprepared for functioning in the world outside her room. The ultimate goal for Nancy and her husband was for her to be able to recognize this anger and its source. It was important for her to learn about her feelings and emotions as a child regardless of her age now. She had to learn to express, feel and assimilate all of her Cancerean emotions - past and present - in order to function as an emotionally healthy adult. This was to be a long, challenging project for both of them.

Nancy's karmic lessons were particularly difficult because they were so efficiently hidden behind years of defenses and layers of denial. Her violent outbursts after marriage were, although frightening, a healthy sign of her refusal and inability to hide any longer. She was at last ready to come out of her room and take her place in society.

In the Cancer's normal progression in dealing with emotions, you begin by interacting emotionally with your parents, grandparents, siblings, aunts, uncles, cousins, and then you add to these skills through your relationships with friends, teachers, and classmates. Further development then evolves through dating, employment, marriage and with your own children. Very often there is a snag in one or more of these stages of development which can be especially difficult for you Cancereans. It is through both the ease and difficulty of these experiences that you learn your karmic lessons of emotions.

INSECURITY

All Cancereans are emotionally vulnerable. You each have your own methods of covering up or protecting yourself but the sensitivity is still there. Here is where the example of the "crab's shell" used early in the chapter best applies. I know when I am teaching astrology and there is a Cancer in my class, I must be careful in my use of sarcasm. I also know not to call unpleasant attention to that student or to ask them to reveal anything about themselves which they do not offer voluntarily. This is a sensitive sign. It is because of this sensitivity and insecurity that you, as a Cancer, learn at an early age, how to protect yourself. Remember, too much protection can rob you of the opportunity of happiness as well as hide you from emotional hurt. Your karmic lessons will come to you through both of these avenues. Hiding from the possibility of hurt will not protect you from your karmic reasons for being here as a Cancer. It is important for you to acknowledge your insecurities and vulnerabilities and then strive to rise above them rather than hide from them. This, admittedly is much easier to say than it is to do. Yet, this is the karmic challenge you have opted for in this lifetime.

Many times, the people around us seem to smell out our fears and insecurities. Other times, we expose them freely, of our own accord, to our trusted loved ones. This leaves us vulnerable, yet is an essential ingredient in establishing a fulfilling relationship. Your greatest fear, as a Cancer, is to have this knowledge of your insecurity used against you in a power struggle or love argument. It is because of this reluctance to expose yourself easily, that you need to take your time in relationships, to choose wisely and with great discretion. Trust must be developed and nurtured for love to blossom. You are a loving soul, by nature, and you function best when you are amongst loved ones; therefore, you will instinctively learn to deal with your insecurities if they are holding you back from fulfilling relationships.

Your insecurities can also hold you back from fulfilling your goals in life. It is your fears which stop you from going on to college, going on that job interview, asking the boss for that much deserved raise, volunteering for that committee or playing the lead role in the class play. Your insecurities keep you behind the scenes in most of your work and play roles.

I was active in the local Little League Baseball organization when my son was young. I will never forget one meeting of a room filled with women when the chairperson asked for volunteers to work in a role which would reap little or no recognition but would best serve our children. 80% of the women who volunteered to help were Cancereans. The other 20% were Pisces. (*Chapter 14*). The gentle, loving nature of the Cancereans, along with their aversion to the limelight, made them perfect for the job.

DOS AND DON'TS FOR THE INSECURE CANCER

DON'T:
• make a Cancer sit in the front of the class
• ask a Cancer to talk about their most embarrassing moment
• make a Cancer play the piano at a party if they do not want to
• discuss a Cancerean's family secrets with others
• throw a Cancerean's insecurities up at them in an argument
• call attention to a Cancerean's weight problem

DO:
• show a Cancer that they can trust you with their emotions
• encourage them toward their goals with your love
• be gentle with a Cancer's feelings
• give your Cancer plenty of hugs
• be kind to a Cancer's family
• keep the potato chip bowl on the other side of the room

Your insecurities are stronger when you are a child and early adult. As you grow and get further involved in relationships with other people, you will have to face your deepest fears. Obviously, the more you are willing to confront these insecurities, the faster they will disappear from your life. Be patient with yourself. You Cancereans are a strong bunch...particularly when you are reaching out to help or protect others. It is through your involvement in loving others that you will develop your greatest strengths and overcome your deepest insecurities.

FAMILY ISSUES AS A CHILD AND AN ADULT

As story-book-like as it may seem, all you want as a Cancerean child is to have a happy family around you with Mom baking cookies for you when you come home from school, Daddy scooping you up by the front white picket fence when he comes home from work, you and your brothers and sisters laughing around the dinner table and singing songs around the piano in the living room in the evening. As an adult, you crave a loving marriage, children, a house in the country and a cat and dog in the yard. Ah, you say, doesn't everyone want exactly this kind of life? The answer is twofold. One, No, not everyone wants this for their life. Many think it would be boring. Two, although other people want this kind of life, they do not crave it emotionally as you do; therein lies the difference.

The little Cancerean child has a strong emotional need for stability and security in the home and family structure. The karmic lessons come early to this child when this sanctuary of family and home is shattered in any way. This disruption comes in various forms, divorce, death, poverty, alcohol abuse, personality conflicts, physical, sexual or emotional abuses. Here we have a Cancerean soul who craves stability in the home and very often has the karmic lesson of coping with stress and disappointment in this area. Any difficulties experienced by a Cancerean through family and love relationships are karmic lessons designed to bring strength and independence to the soul.

Even if happiness is not a part of your childhood, you can still strive to obtain this peace and stability in your adult life by creating a warm, comfortable home for yourself. One of the characteristics of your Cancer energy is to hold on to past hurts, allowing them to fester within your subconscious, thereby creating patterns which become repeated in your adult relationships. Your childhood and your understanding of your family dynamics, play an important role in the degree of healthy patterns you will establish as an adult. To truly understand yourself as an adult, you must allow yourself to acknowledge your hurts and disappointments from your childhood and, most importantly, you must give yourself the right to assimilate what is necessary and let the rest go! Your karmic lesson is to feel your pain, learn from your past and then move on to your future unbridled by the past. This is not easy. It is easy for you to withdraw from the possibility of future happiness because of any painful experiences in your childhood, early dating or even an unhappy marriage. Once again, you can hide beneath that thick shell of the crab and sidestep yourself away from any possible happiness. With the story of Nancy in the beginning of this chapter we saw how childhood experiences affected her future relationships. Another example is Celeste, a client of mine for many years.

FROM BOARDING SCHOOL TO BORING LOVE

Celeste was raised in a middle class, suburban neighborhood. Her parents struggled hard to maintain their home and social position in the community. Celeste was their only child but she was not their primary interest. They were rather selfish people who enjoyed socializing with their peers, traveling and being by themselves. When Celeste was eight years old, they sent her off to boarding school where she was to remain throughout the remainder of her educational years. Now, Celeste was a Cancer who craved the warmth of Mommy's arms and the security of Daddy's lap. She cried and pleaded to be able to stay home with them, but they insisted this was for her benefit. They assured her that the quality of her education meant everything to them. She saw how they struggled to pay her tuition, which they made known to her, so she tried to believe them. Still, the feeling, intuitive Cancerean energy within her told her all the facts did not fit. They did not seem to miss her. They were not faithful in their writing or visiting her. They traveled, they socialized. They became inseparable as a couple, but Celeste did not feel she was a part of their "family". As she grew up, she felt even more unloved. She felt unworthy. She felt ugly. She was a Cancer who was not a part of her family. They wanted to live their lives without her.

Upon graduation from college, she married a man much older than herself. Here was a stable, mature man who would provide that home she had always craved, and he did. Soon she had a beautiful house, far prettier than her parent's home. Her home was surrounded by a white picket fence, she quickly added a dog and two cats, and soon her perfect dream came true. She gave birth to a beautiful baby girl. Everything seemed perfect for her Cancerean happiness. But, had she truly studied the lessons of her childhood? Had she gone within herself to confront the emotional pain of her childhood? Had she let go of her hurts?

It became obvious she had not as her marriage began mirroring images of her relationships with her parents. Her husband, it turns out, was cold. He was focused on his career and his main concerns were with himself and his own needs. Slowly, he pulled away from Celeste; first isolating himself emotionally, then maintaining a stubborn, inflexible attitude toward her pleas for love, until soon he was living his life as he wanted, giving her no explanation of his whereabouts. Once again, Celeste was in a relationship which left her unloved, isolated and abandoned. Karmically, this repetition of relationship patterns gave Celeste an opportunity to strengthen herself and take control of her life but she was not ready yet.

Celeste choose to immerse herself totally in her daughter, Kim. She was going to make sure that Kim knew that she was loved by her mother. She kept a warm home, baked cookies, cooked healthy foods, helped Kim with her homework, showed interest in Kim's activities in school. She seemed the perfect mother. But was she? As the years went on, Celeste made Kim a substitute for her missing parents and husband. Kim now had the responsibility of playing many roles for her mother and this is a lot to ask of a little girl.

Celeste was coming in for annual astrological readings through all these years and the psychology of her relationships were becoming more and more pronounced. It became evident that no one in that household was happy. Each was a product of their own emotional confusion and this was becoming an increasingly complex family unit. Celeste was angry at her parents, hurt by her husband, and worried about her daughter. It was finally her love for Kim which gave Celeste the courage to face her emotional past. She entered an intense therapy program, and much to her credit, stuck with it, first for her daughter and finally for herself. It was at this point that she began to find some self-worth. She was able, after a considerable amount of time, to see her parents for their weaknesses and frailties and to confront the pain she had hidden away for so many years. This was not easy for Celeste; she was unaware of the extent of her anger. She chose to let go of any semblance of a relationship she had maintained with her parents. She also divorced her husband. Celeste now maintains a healthy relationship with her daughter and is ready to bring some new relationships into her life which she hopes will be much more satisfying to her Cancerean needs.

It is through the recognition and then the breaking of old relationship patterns that new, healthier relationships can come into the Cancerean's life. This karmic road can be a long hard one yet it is one which must be traveled if you are unhappy with your past and present.

CHILDREN IN THE CANCER'S LIFE

Cancer is a maternal sign which brings with it many complex issues concerning children. Children will play a significant karmic role in the lives of all Cancereans, male or female. Children are the continuation of family and family roots are the basis of the Cancerean's karmic concentration. Naturally, not all Cancers have children of their own. In fact, procreation itself is not a requirement for the Cancerean to fulfill karmic involvement with children. As a Cancer, you are required to experience an involvement with children, be they yours or someone else's. You will have contact with the minds and emotions of some children in your life which will teach you something about yourself. Children will be a mirror to your soul and your soul's needs.

In the Cancer's desire for family and roots, many decide to have large families. Others seek the love they felt deprived of by their own parents through the love of a child. Children are used to bring love into an otherwise emotionally starved Cancerean's life. Therefore, you must be cautious not to use your children as a substitute for, or an escape from, your adult relationships.

Many Cancereans become overly protective of their children. They suffered so much loss of love in their lives that they become desperately afraid of losing their relationships with their children. They foster dependence. They behave like mother or father hens, not allowing their children to wander too far, thereby robbing their children of the adventure of life's experiences.

Children can come into the Cancerean's life through various relationships such as nieces, nephews, stepchildren, or students. Cancers make excellent teachers. Do not feel that the children who bring you to your karmic lessons have to be your own. Your karmic growth comes through your loving, nurturing and sharing with a child. You are able to achieve the wisdom of unconditional love through the children in your life. Wise spiritual leaders have said the relationship closest to attaining unconditional love is a mother's love toward her child. This state of love is the karmic objective of any Cancerean - male or female, fertile or barren. It is a condition of the soul not the body.

CULTURAL BACKGROUND AS AN ASSET

I had watched Bobby grow from child to manhood. His parents had asked me to do an astrological reading on him when he was a schoolboy and here he is now, a grown man with children of his own. (Oh, how time rushes forward). Bob and Sarah, Bobby's parents, raised their four children in a small town on eastern Long Island, New York. Bobby was the second oldest and the first son. The ancestry of this family was mixed with much European and a large dose of Southwest Native American Zuni. Although they were far from their tribe in location, they held the values of their Zuni heritage deep within their hearts.

Bob and Sarah were parents who deeply loved their children and they wove this love and sense of family spirit tightly within their lives. Children are revered traditionally by the Zuni Indians. It is not unmanly for a Zuni father to spend his leisure time feeding, holding, and playing with his children. Bob showed this love openly to his children. Theirs was a home of much love and laughter.

When Bobby married and had children of his own, society of middle class Long Island expected him to provide for his family, mow the lawn on Saturdays and bowl with the company team on Tuesday nights. Bobby, a Cancer by birth and a Zuni by heart, felt more comfortable in what was considered to be a motherly role. He entered a socially accepted profession as a New York City firefighter, thereby satisfying all male standards necessary for respect by his friends. But, in his spare time, he preferred to spend his time with his children. He enjoyed feeding, bathing, dressing and playing with them. Unlike many fathers, Bobby was not uncomfortable with his children as newborns or infants. As his children grew, Bobby's interests with them changed. He was involved with his son's drum and bugle corps and was equally comfortable playing bingo with his daughter in her Brownie troop fundraiser.

Bobby had the example of his parent's family-oriented home environment, the ancestral influence of his Zuni Indian culture, and his own Cancerean inclinations to draw him comfortably toward his karmic responsibilities toward children. His were experiences of joy and great satisfaction because he was comfortable within himself. His whole life had always been geared toward his Cancerean directions. He was a fortunate man.

As a Cancer, it is important for you to be conscious of the role children play in your life, and equally important, of the responsibility you have toward the children around you. Your karmic lesson may involve learning about yourself through your involvement with children. Their needs may be symbols of your own childlike needs that have never been met. You are the adult, you are the teacher, but do not be surprised at the wisdom and lessons which will come to you through the youngsters. They have much to teach you.

EATING HABITS

As a Cancer, you need a great deal of loving and nurturing, particularly as a child. In order to survive infancy, we all must have the security of a mother's protective arms and the nourishment of her milk. Our cries are silenced by food and love. Cancers are particularly affected by the abundance or scarcity of loving nourishment.

If, as a Cancer, you did not feel satisfied with the amount of love and security you received as a child, you may find yourself craving food, as an adult, in order to nourish the unloved child within you. You are prone to substituting food for love.

If you were abused physically, emotionally or sexually as a child, you will tend to use food as a source of security. If you were not satisfied with the amount of "mother's milk" you received when young, you will crave large amounts of food as an adult in an attempt to give yourself the love you lacked. Excess food also puts on extra pounds. Obesity can become your security blanket protecting you from any other relationships coming into your life which may also bring you pain or disappointment. After all, who will want to date someone who is fat? Who would want to sexually abuse someone who is obese?

It is your karmic responsibility to look at your eating habits as an indication of your emotional state of mind. In order to shed unwanted pounds, you may have to be willing to also rid yourself of buried hurts and emotional denials. This is not easy in our American culture where there's a food commercial every ten minutes on TV, where there's a fast food restaurant on almost every corner, where meritorious behavior and special occasions are always celebrated with a meal. Do you remember when you were a child in your school's spring concert? Everyone went out for an ice cream sundae after the performance to celebrate.

Your society is working against you in this one, but the lesson is still there. Many of you become health food addicts, strict vegetarians, vitamin poppers. Others of you become enmeshed in eating disorders. Moderation is a key to your success in this area. You must be aware of your eating tendencies and painfully honest with yourself concerning the connection between your emotions and these patterns. Your karmic lessons may appear to you through the kitchen but they may have originated in the family den or the bedroom. Do not be afraid to ask for help with this karmic route. Your answers may lie within deep-seated, psychological sources. It may not be as simple as a temporary diet.

CANCER MALE

Cancer is a feminine sign in nature. It involves emotion, maternal instincts, vulnerability, fears, insecurities, and intuition. Our society does not encourage these traits in our boys and men. They are considered sissy or girl-like. Therefore, a man born of this sign could have a harder time with his karmic lessons than a woman would, or so it will appear to the man. He must learn to feel secure enough in his own masculinity that he is able to enjoy the feminine side of himself without fear or shame. He is learning through this sign to encourage the maternal, nurturing side of his nature. Men who have succeeded with this struggle have no difficulty taking on responsibilities of babies, cooking, cleaning, and other household tasks. They can also lean toward careers in fields such as pediatrics, home improvement contractors, and chefs.

A Cancer male needs to closely examine his family relationships, especially with his mother, grandmothers and any sisters. His attitudes toward these women in his early life greatly influence his adult relationships with women. It is his father, though, who can have the greatest affect on the Cancer male's acceptance of his intense emotions. He ideally needs a father who is affectionate and nurturing and who is unashamed of his own emotions. The Cancer male needs a father who is not afraid to hug and kiss him, a father who is not afraid to shed tears both of sorrow and joy. If he has a father who shuns him because of his feelings, who makes him feel "unmanly" because of his emotions, he will need to concentrate on the karmic ramifications of this relationship. He may tend to close down emotionally until he identifies his relationship with his father as the source.

A Cancer male is learning how to be honest and open with his feelings in spite of the many obstacles which may come his way. He may be quiet, moody, unable to express his emotions in a healthy manner. He may lack the motivation to delve into his psyche until he experiences several unhappy relationships, each one with similarities to the other. He will eventually need to look at these patterns in order to experience happiness and inner contentment.

Because of a possible succession of relationships, the Cancer male may be separated from his children by divorce. He still has a karmic responsibility toward his children. It is important for him to continue emotional, physical, and financial support and to play an active role as their father. He may want to pull away from them because to stay a part of their lives would open him to possible hurts. He may fear abandonment of them more than they would fear it from him. If he sees another man entering their lives he may first feel a possessiveness toward his children and then he may abandon them before they emotionally abandon him.

Cancer men are masters of passive-aggressive behavior. They have not been encouraged by society to express their feelings freely, so they learn at an early age to get their way or their revenge through passive behavior. This emotional response can be found in any of their relationships, even with their children.

A Cancer male must also exercise integrity concerning all aspects of materialism. Money and possessions can become substitutes for unfulfilled relationships. Materialism can fill the emotional void, for a while. They can be especially successful in the business world since this is where society allows them to express themselves. Therefore, the Cancer male has a karmic responsibility to understand himself in relation to his needs for materialism. He must show honesty and integrity in this area of his life.

He also has a need to acknowledge and trust his marvelous intuitive nature. He need not wear a turban and promote himself as a wizard, but his intuition is keen and enables him to easily size up people and situations. This unique ability will be an asset to him in his personal and professional life.

Generally, women love Cancer men. They are able to understand women. They think in similar fashions. Women love the sensitive and nourishing traits of the Cancer male. He can feel comfortable with most women who desire marriage, family and a stable home.

CANCER FEMALE

The Cancer female has a great deal of loving energy to give in a relationship. She has a need to nurture, protect and serve those she loves. Although this is a basic part of the Cancerean female's make-up, she may have withdrawn from these characteristics if she has been denied love or abused as a child. The need to love and be loved is still there, it is the layers of protection she has put around herself that she must karmically work through in order to find her happiness. Traditionally, the woman has been the lesser sex, abused and ignored, undervalued. The Cancerean female may have experienced deprivation or abuse which will force her to close down emotionally. If she closes down to her past, she may also shut herself off from her future. Sometimes this karmic lesson can feel like a "*Catch-22*". If a Cancer female experiences emotional hurt in her past she tends to hold onto that pain in order to protect herself from ever being vulnerable to that pain again. Yet, by holding on too strongly to the pains of the past, she robs herself of any opportunity for happiness in her future. And so the patterns of self-destruction can continue. The goal of the Cancer female is to break through her defense mechanisms which she has built in response to past hurts, to feel the pain upon examination of any past relationships, and then to let go of these painful remembrances so that she can move forward to a new and healthier life. She needs to penetrate her complex system of denial in order to free herself from the past. Forgiving and forgetting can be difficult karmic experiences for the Cancer female. It is not uncommon for a Cancer female to judge future men in her life by the painful experiences she had from men in her past. That can lead her toward feeling that all men are like her father or ex-husband, or no men are any good. With this belief, how can she lower her defenses enough to trust any man or let any happiness into her life. There can be such a rewarding relief for her as she learns to let go.

Of course, not all Cancer females have unhappy childhoods or unfulfilling relationships. Many women are fortunate to have experienced a strong, loving bond with their childhood relationships and these women are eager to pass this positive energy on to their children.

Children are particularly significant to Cancer females whether they be their own or someone else's children. There is a nurturing, protective quality inherent in this sign that breathes life into the souls of our children. They are able to put great parts of themselves into the caring of our young. It is because of this magnificent intensity of emotion that they are able to bring a vulnerable baby from its infancy through to its adulthood into its own future. Sometimes this intensity of emotion can get stuck along the way. The Cancerean mother sees her child as a substitute for her loveless childhood or empty marriage. She can then become overly protective, and fearful of losing the one love of her life, failing to let her child grow to a point of independence. Many cartoons and jokes have been made of the overly protective mother who then becomes the notorious mother-in- law. Once again, this bring her to the karmic lesson of letting go.

The ultimate goal of the Cancer female is to gain self-confidence. She needs to love herself enough so that she is able to give of herself unconditionally, not only to others but toward her own best interests as well. This is a loving woman who must first learn to love herself regardless of messages she got from her past. She is the mother of our race.

CANCER CHILDREN

Cancerean infants need an abundance of physical loving and emotional security. They love to be held, stroked, bathed, powdered, kissed and schmoozed. They feel wonderful with their blanket tucked tightly around them. They feel best when they are in your arms or sleeping against your body. Take your time feeding and tending to your Cancerean infant. She soaks in all your love and savors the touch and smells of you. You will feel her need for you and dependency on you immediately. This is a child who may feel very nervous if thrown up in the air or left with a baby-sitter, too much time out of Mommy's arms.

Feeding is an important time for the Cancer infant and child. She loves the time spent in Mommy or Daddy's arms as they feed her. She also enjoys food. This combination can lead to extended nighttime feedings, a hard time giving up the bottle, and a battle of the bulge. Remember, she needs those feedings for more reasons than simply the intake of food. You must be attuned to her need for nourishment on many levels. This is a child who needs your emotional energy. But, do not worry, she has an unlimited amount of love to give back to her family. She is not simply a taker. You will be able to read the love in her eyes and her smile.

Family is the most important part of the Cancer child's life. She is not selfish. In fact, she enjoys being a part of a large family - brothers, sisters, grandparents, aunts, uncles. The more love the better. But, do not be surprised if she is quiet and withdrawn sometimes in large groups even if they are family. There is a shy, introverted part of the Cancer child that enjoys watching the interaction of others without being the focal point herself. Of course, there are many outgoing Cancers, but be aware of the times when your child needs to pull back from the crowd. This is a sensitive child, remember, who may be ingesting some emotional input and needs the alone-time to assimilate her feelings. Respect of her privacy and need for quiet time is important to her well-being. When alone-time seems to be too frequent, it is important to gently open the lines of communication with her. Let her know that she is able to discuss anything with you. Ask her how she feels about situations in her life. She works on a feeling level and must be at ease with this part of herself.

This is where the men in a Cancerean boy's life play a pertinent role. The Cancer boy needs a male role model who is not shy about expressing his feelings, particularly his fears and sadness. He is sensitive and easily hurt. His society, friends, peers, will give him guidelines at an early age as to how much emotion he can comfortably show in public. But what is he to do with all these feelings and emotions if he is unable to express them freely at school or at home? He will begin, at an early age, to bury his feelings, to deny them, and this is where the Cancer child's problems can begin.

The perfect environment is a family unit where feelings, good and bad, happy and sad, up and down, are shown openly; where there is trust and confidence of acceptance. With this kind of a solid base, the Cancer child, male and female, will be well-equipped to handle their sensitivity in the other areas of their life. This sensitive and emotional nature will become the asset it is meant to be rather than the source of discomfort it can be.

You see how important family is to this child. Be aware then, that any disruption to that family unit can be very upsetting to her. If the family has to move, if she has to make new friends, if there is a divorce or death of a family member, any of these changes will be especially difficult for the Cancer child to handle. As a parent, it is important that you be kind, loving, gentle, and reassuring to her during these periods of emotional stress. It is fine to admit that you too are frightened or sad or angry. She needs to hear that other people are feeling something too. She also needs to feel confident that she is still loved and will continue to be protected.

Do not be overly protective. Because a Cancer child is a family oriented person, they may tend to stick close to home and other family members. They need to enjoy the adventure of life and develop their independence. If you refuse to allow her to cross the street when her other friends are, she will take this as a message from you that she is not capable, that you do not have confidence in her. You see, they really are emotionally complex people. My rule of thumb is when in doubt, ask! If you think your Cancer child is upset or perhaps misreading a meaning behind your actions...ask her what she is feeling. This kind of openness will be one of the greatest gifts you can give her.

Cancer children are also highly intuitive, creative and inspirational. Nurture these qualities and listen to what your child has to say. She may know more than you realize. If she says a leaf should be purple do not force her to see it as green. You may find that purple leaf on one of her paintings hanging in an art gallery several years later. If she tells you that she does not feel that the family should get in the car that day and drive to Grandma's, maybe you should put off the outing for one more day. She may know something on an intuitive level that you do not. Trust her to know her feelings.

If you see your child gaining too much weight, becoming physically ill frequently, (especially with nervous stomachs) or becoming excessively reclusive, question her. Find out what is bothering her. There is most probably something going on or something that has happened to her that she is holding in, afraid to tell. Once again, open communication is the key to the Cancer child's emotional well-being.

Most importantly, enjoy this loving child. She will be as close to you as you allow and her love can be with you throughout your life. All that nourishing you gave when she was a child will be saved to give back to you in your twilight years. She is your offspring who will investigate the family tree, sustain the family traditions, and gather the family together. Your role with her is so very important. The happiness or misfortune in her early life will manifest their results in her adult life. Love is the key to this child's success.

LEO

July 23 - August 22

Male Energy

KARMIC LESSONS

- ◆ Dealing with ego

- ◆ Wielding power and authority

- ◆ Learning to be flexible

- ◆ Developing creative potential

- ◆ Succumbing to life's pleasures

PRIMARY LEO

Everyone on earth is born with an ego and must learn to deal with this self-oriented part of themselves. There are times, for our individual self-preservation, that we must rely on this ego in order to maintain our unique identities and, perhaps, our self-survival. It is also evident that our egos, at times, can be the cause of our own destruction - the source of our greatest grief - our enemy within us. Each of us will find the power of our ego tested through various degrees of challenges throughout our life. This is the nature of mankind as it progresses through its karmic schooling on this plane we call earth.

Yet, as much as this expression called ego is common to all of us, it brings particular, pertinent learning lessons to Leos. Leos are here with a strong, karmic responsibility to learn and grow through their understanding and control of their ego force, and what a difficult lesson this can be. If you are a Leo, I suggest you try this little experiment. Try to go through a twenty-four hour time period without saying or thinking the words "I" or "me". You will realize, as all sun signs would, that this challenge is difficult if not impossible. Therefore, rather than teach you not to think egotistically, this exercise will help you to become aware of how often your thoughts and motivations do turn toward your own best interests and concerns. It is through this awareness that you will be able to focus your attention toward your karmic lesson of ego.

Leos are, by nature, loving, giving people and you enjoy sharing benevolent relationships with those around you. It is because of the caring glow of this sign that you will attract many friends and loved ones to your life. It may help you to think about this sign through the symbols which have always surrounded it.

Leo and the Sun. The astrological sign Leo is ruled by the sun, the most powerful body in the heavens. Since the beginning of time mankind has worshipped the sun as its source of power, its source of being...a god. My, what an ego reflection that brings to you. By nature, you are used to being worshipped and respected. You have the power in you to be a ruthless or benevolent ruler, depending on your whim. The immature, primary part of you can feel justified to sit upon your throne of ease and luxury, and expect all those around you to do your bidding and cater to your comforts. From this attitude comes the philosophy that the world owes you a living. You expect much to come to you with little or no effort on your part. This is the fundamental concept of ego on the primary level.

When the Leo "king" or "queen" bestows a kindness he or she may follow the good deed with an echoing pounding of the chest, demanding recognition..."*look what I did for you.*" This shallow stage of ego can wield great power and destruction through the thunder of pompous authority. It can be a mighty power to reckon with particularly if it is left unrestricted.

Leo the Lion: We also think of Leo as the lion, the king of the jungle. Other animals fear the lion, therefore, it has captured the title of ultimate ruler. We do not see the lion having great ambition or an industrious nature. It is a creature of great physical power, usually pictured lying down or sleeping, certainly moving slowly through the jungle. Its reputation is established, therefore it does not have to spend too much of its time proving power or establishing respect. This, too, is the innate attitude of the primary Leo. There is that tendency to begin life expecting care, comfort, and luxury. The ego seems to incarnate with full potential for inflation. Thus, the karmic challenge begins at once.

Leos need a great deal of attention. This is an astrological given. As a Leo, you need attention. This is a simple fact which must be totally accepted by you and all those who are a part of your life. Your karmic testing is activated by the means in which you demand that attention. On a primary level, you will captivate people's attention by creating scenes, crying, yelling, showing-off, tripping, falling, whistling, wearing garish clothes, dying your hair purple, robbing banks, writing your name on subway walls....need I go on. Your ego is a fire within you which needs constant fueling. Your karmic responsibility is to master the art of fueling your ego through means which are healthful for you and productive for society.

A part of thinking that you are the best, brings with it a belief that you deserve the best. On a primary level this can manifest itself in a desire for an abundance of money, gold, jewelry, first-class tickets, and penthouse suites. Your karmic lessons will come through your ability to earn your own way in life and your willingness to work hard for the quality aspects in your life. Leo is a fire sign, which brings to you all the power and ambition you will ever need to achieve your greatest goals. Your karmic challenge will be to determine your goals aside from the demands of your ego.

Leo is also a fixed sign which means you may have difficulty adapting to change. Life is full of changes for everyone, including you. Your powerful energy may lead you toward attempting to maintain control of your life and those around you in order to minimize the possibility of change. This effort will only succeed in exhausting you and deterring you from many of your potentials. You must learn to not only adapt to change, but to initiate change and to see diversity as a friend rather than a potential enemy.

EVOLVED LEO

As you get older you will find yourself moving toward the more evolved aspects of your Leo sun sign. As you experience more of life, you will face some of the challenges brought to you through the primary stages of Leo and you will begin to master the karmic lessons of your sign. You will always have an ego. That is part of being a Leo. Also, remember, everyone on earth is dealing with the power of their ego, not only you. Therefore, you should not expect to evolve yourself to a point where you will be completely devoid of ego. That is not the karmic objective of your sign. In fact, removing ego from your personality, even if possible, would simply be an act of avoidance rather than a completion of a karmic goal. You are here to learn to deal with your ego. You need to know its needs and its strengths, to be honest with yourself concerning your wants, your potentials and the motivations behind your ambitions. No matter how barren or isolated an existence you may try to create for yourself, you will always have your ego within you. It is through harnessing the energy of this powerful force that you will be able to achieve your greatest potentials. Your ego is an energy which will propel you forward, directing you toward the fulfillment of your goals. It will give you the fuel you need to make your mark upon this world. It will, in its highest sense, bring pride into your life and a healthy love of yourself.

The fiery energy of your Leo can bring to you a commanding aura of authority and respect. Using the example of Leo the king, we are all aware of the different temperaments of people who have held power in the course of history. The use, and misuse, of power has even become part of some leaders titles: Ivan the Terrible, Peter the Great, Bloody Mary. As a Leo, you have the option of using or abusing your use of authority and power. It is almost guaranteed that you will come into power on some level in your life. Your karmic lesson does not come to you on your trip to power, but through your use of authority once you've made it to the top.   Obviously, the evolved state would see you wielding your power with benevolence and justice.

You are a creative sign with a flare for art, color, drama and splendor. As an evolved Leo, you will bring beauty to your life and our world through the bold brush of your unique creativity. You will allow yourself the freedom of your wonderful expression with a daring and brilliance which seems impossible to duplicate. Enjoy this marvelous part of your nature whether you are using it to create a work of art, to decorate your home, or to adorn your body with clothes and jewelry. You are a soul which needs to be noticed. An evolved Leo will satisfy this need with class and distinction.

REMEMBER, NO ONE IS TOTALLY PRIMARY OR EVOLVED. OUR KARMIC LESSONS ARE BEST LEARNED WHEN WE ARE DEALING WITH BOTH OF THESE ENERGIES.

DEALING WITH YOUR EGO

Your ego is the expression of yourself, the image you choose to project, to represent the true you. This image may or may not be an honest representation of the total you. I call it, wearing masks. We all wear different masks, or put forward different images of ourselves, at appropriate times. For example, the image you project while sitting in church may be quite different from the image you were projecting at a party the previous night. In church you wear the mask which shows the prim, reverent side of yourself. At parties, you don the mask of levity which represents the fun-loving aspect of you. At work, you wear your mask of efficiency and so on. You are a complex person and have accumulated many masks during your life. This is true of everyone not only Leos. But, you, as a Leo, have an important karmic responsibility to be aware of your ego's needs to don each mask at its appointed time. You must be aware of your motivations, your defenses and your vulnerabilities which have created these masks. You may not be able to expose yourself totally unmasked, who can? Yet, honesty of self-understanding and awareness is imperative for you in this lifetime.

Many Leos have fun with their masks. They enter into the world of acting where characters and dialogues become masks for which they are paid and complemented. You Leos make wonderful actors and actresses. This is because you have a need to be noticed and an equal need to hide. This is why you hear many actors says they are more comfortable in a play than they are doing a ten minute interview on TV. Interviews require exposing themselves, revealing their true ego needs. This takes true confidence, found successfully in karmically evolved Leos.

Leos who take positions of power or authority and refuse, or seem to be unable, to show the vulnerable side of themselves are examples of people who are hiding behind their ego masks. These Leos are: the teacher who maintains strict decorum in her class. No one ever knows anything about his personal life, where he lives, where he goes on vacation. His phone number is definitely unlisted. The minister who wears his white collar and black suit at all times. He never rolls up his sleeves, he never laughs at a joke or discusses anything but church and God with his parishioners. These two Leos are afraid to let any part of themselves be exposed. They fear they will be unable to maintain their reputations without the strict protection of their masks. Their egos are painfully evident and intimidating. Their insecurities are less evident, at first sight, but painfully real within them. Anyone who would try to peek behind these ego masks would be subject to their wrath...the roar of the lion. If you recognize yourself or a piece of yourself in this description this is the first step toward understanding you need to defend your fragile ego through the protective armor of a mask which puts people at arms length. The teacher and minister who are truly confident in their abilities to lead would not need to put forth such an exertion of energy in order to maintain an image of authority. As much as we all wear masks, we must recognize that some of our masks are heavier and more cumbersome than others. As a Leo, your ultimate goal is to don your lightest masks and, perhaps, dare to go naked into this world. A sentence which reveals an evolved Leo is, "*I don't know, I'll look it up*". There's no ego mask involved.

EGO NEEDS MET THROUGH ATTENTION

Leos need attention. This is a solid fact! Some ways you go about getting our attention can be anywhere from insulting to hilarious. Your first step toward understanding your karmic self is to acknowledge where you need your praise, who you need to give you attention, and how far you are willing to go to get attention.

LEO AT A PARTY

I was at a party once when one of my Leo clients came in with a hand puppet. She was the center of attention as she brought Mr. Bunny up to everyone and held conversations, cracked jokes, and mesmerized the group with her antics. She then did pantomimes of athletes bowling, in slow motion, and ice skaters skating on thin ice. With each of her new acts I marveled at the validity of astrology, the acting Leo. At this same party, there was another example of a Leo. He was most often found at the liquor table consuming enormous amounts of alcohol. His voice became louder with each drink. He bumped into furniture, knocked over the salad bowl, and yes, he really did put on a lampshade and dance the rumba. The third Leo was a fashionable latecomer. She was the date of the gentleman who was hosting the party and everyone was anxious to meet his new girlfriend. This Leo came in wearing a stylish, vibrant red dress with a black cape which she removed with gentle flair as she entered the living room. Her hair was perfectly groomed, straight blonde, shoulder length which she tossed about as she was introduced to each guest. Even the bumbling, intoxicated Leo was quiet for this entrance.

All three Leos gripped the attention of the party-goers, each with their own style, their own needs, and their individual masks. Oh, what would a party be without a Leo or two? Which Leo would you be?

LOVE IS IN THE AIR

John had been courting Sandra for seven months now and he was ready to make that final commitment. John was also a Leo who loved love and fun. He wanted his proposal to be one that both he and Sandra would remember for the rest of their lives and one which would get the attention of everyone. After all, a couple does not get engaged everyday. And they were not a plain ordinary, couple. Right now, they were the most important people in the world. They were in love and everyone should know about it. On the Fourth of July, John took Sandra to Jones Beach, Long Island, which was packed with record-breaking crowds. Good, just what John wanted. At exactly noon, as planned, a shiny red biplane flew low across the sky with a banner that read: SANDRA, WILL YOU MARRY ME? LOVE, JOHN. Everyone at the beach was looking up and ahhhing as they read the airplane's message. Then all these smiling faces were looking around for this now famous couple. There was John, on bended knee holding a diamond ring out to Sandra who, by this time, was awash with embarrassment and joy. This was a Leo marriage proposal!

PLEASE AND THANK YOU SYNDROME

Leos need to be recognized for their work whether these accomplishments are extraordinary or everyday tasks. One method of receiving compliments is by setting up the pattern by giving compliments to others. Let us look at some stereotypical role-playing in a marriage. Each partner in a relationship has his and her own responsibilities which, after time, become expected and sometimes taken for granted. A Leo in a relationship needs to periodically have praise and acknowledgment of his or her contributions to the relationship. If they have divided their relationship into definitive roles, the execution of these roles still need the reward of praise. Let us say Bob is the wage earner. His role in the relationship is to bring materialistic comfort to the union. Mary is the homemaker. Her responsibility is to maintain a comfortable, nourishing home environment for her family. Leo energy would require recognition of these roles no matter how expected they may have become.

The simplest fulfillment of Leo ego needs in this household would be the plentiful use of the expressions, *please* and *thank you*. When the family sits to enjoy the dinner that Mary has prepared, all Bob has to say is, "*Thank you Mary. You've prepared a wonderful meal for us again. I really appreciate the time and love you put into cooking this for us.*" And, as the family drives home in their new car, all Mary has to say is, *"Thank you Bob. I know you work hard to provide us with a beautiful home and now this fantastic new car. I appreciate all the energy you put into your work in order to bring us this luxury. "*

Too many times we take our loved ones for granted. After all, Bob has chosen the role of provider for his family. And Mary prefers preparing the meals every night. That is her choice. But, the Leo energy needs praise. Don't we all? In order to get praise, first you must earn it and then you must learn how to recognize someone else's merit by praising them. This exercise is simple, painless, and particularly effective.

RECOGNIZING THE MOTIVES
BEHIND YOUR ACTIONS

One of the giant steps you can take to identify your Leo ego is to examine the motives behind your actions. So many of your activities seem benevolent on the outside but can be festering with your ego needs underneath it all. To come to terms with this part of yourself will require your total honesty. You need not confess ulterior motives to anyone else. No one else is your judge. In fact, you may be quite skilled in fooling everyone all of the time, but your karmic lesson does not come to you through the applause or approval of anyone but yourself.

The PTA President: Everyone marvels at Grace's enthusiasm and energy level as she spends six out of every seven nights in committee meetings, conferences and board meetings, voluntarily giving of her time in order to improve the educational system of her school district. Grace is certainly a pillar of the community. She appears to give of herself endlessly, without monetary reward. She appears to be dedicated to the servicing of her community.
Grace's Leo karmic lesson is to be completely honest with herself. What are her true motives? How much is she doing for her community versus how much is she doing because of her ego's need for praise, power, and attention?

The Philanthropist: Irving was a self-made man. His parents were immigrants from Russia who fled the pogroms of the early 1900s and landed penniless in New York. Irving opened his button factory when he was twenty years old and by the time he was forty he was wealthy beyond anyone's expectations. He felt it was his responsibility to give back to the city which had offered him his safety and opened such wonderful opportunities for success. He decided to donate enough money to a city hospital for a wing to be opened which would house a clinic for the vast population of minorities who needed medical attention. This was a glowing Leo gesture of benevolence and kindness. Only Irving knew the measure of importance between the need he was fulfilling in the community and his own Leo need to be known to all as the successful immigrant who had made enough money to give away millions of dollars to have a new wing of a hospital...named after him.

It is when a Leo donates his time or money anonymously, with no one ever knowing, that he can feel confident that he has mastered his karmic ego lesson. Be kind to yourself though, this is not an easy lesson and may take more than one lifetime to master.

DEALING WITH POWER AND AUTHORITY

Leo is a fire sign with tremendous potential to achieve positions of power. As a Leo, your karmic tests will not concern whether or not you are able to achieve a position of power but what you do with that power once it is yours. You can be the lion who rules with a mighty roar, wielding your power through fear and intimidation. You can be the egocentric Leo, like the sun, and feel you deserve to be obeyed and served simply because you exist. This self-awareness, like all your Leo karmic tests, requires complete honesty and introspection on your part. The whole world can point out your foibles to you but your Leo ego can totally blind you to your own truths. Your ego can work as a shield protecting you from some stark realities of your inner truths.

Once in power, you must identify the needs this position is filling for you personally and you need to be conscious of your goals; what you can accomplish with this power in order to serve others.

POWER AND THE MAN OF THE CLOTH

Growing up in the city was tough on Daniel. He was small of stature and frail of health throughout his childhood and was never able to cope with the power and force that was all around him. He was a gentle child who enjoyed reading, gardening, and cooking - activities completely scorned by his street-worn peers. He became used to being laughed at, made fun of, and occasionally, beaten-up. He learned to hide from the gangs to protect himself physically, and eventually, to hide from himself his years of pent-up anger and frustration.

After graduation from high school, Daniel went to a midwestern seminary to prepare for his life as a minister. He was totally at home in the quiet, humane surroundings of school and never thought at all about his frustrating youth on the city streets. He did well in his studies, gained the respect of his fellow students and the faculty and quickly gained the self-confidence denied him in his youth. Daniel established himself as a charismatic orator and his Leo energy blossomed in the light of all this attention. With diploma in hand, Daniel entered the field of clergy with much enthusiasm.

Daniel quickly climbed up his ladder of success until he had his own church in a large suburban community outside Chicago. Now he was in the position of power, no longer the frightened, weak little boy of his childhood. He now had control and power over a whole community of people who came to him with their needs, their problems, their respect and their money. His confidence built from gratitude to assurance to over-confidence to egotism. Within ten years he became a finger-wagging, pompous Leo who ruled his congregation through intimidation and threats of damnation. He wheeled and dealed the church's finances at a whim, encouraging people to give more and more to him and his family for their personal support. Daniel become a product of the rage he had buried inside of himself from years of abuse as a child. He took the memories of those years of being powerless to his surroundings and directed that anger, under the guise of his ministry, at the people he now overpowered. His congregation became symbols of himself as a child and he became no better than the bullies who had abused him on the city streets.

Daniel was not able to maintain his position for long. The church council members began to investigate his financial dealings. He was found guilty of corruption and misdealing with the church's funds. Amidst a meeting of anger and accusations, Daniel was forced to leave his position with the church. He and his family had to start a new life and a new career.

Karmically, Daniel had already experienced two situations in his life where he had to come to terms with the power, and loss of power, of ego. His painful childhood made evident his ego need for the respect of his peers while his adult misuse of power on the pulpit showed him the full anger of his unfulfilled ego as a child. Daniel's acknowledgment of these ego needs and reactions is dependent upon his stage of karmic evolvement. His ego can blind him from seeing any fault or contribution to his problems on his part or he can use this crossroads in his life as a time to stop and reflect upon himself. It is at such times in our lives that opportunity for tremendous karmic growth comes available to us all.

Great power comes with your Leo energy. This power can be used to help others through your positions of power and authority. Your karmic lessons are learned through your use or misuse of this power. Many people in your life will look up to you and seek your advice. In these instances, the word attitude becomes significant. Your attitude toward others will be your key to understanding your evolvement. Help and guidance through unconditional love and caring must be your ultimate attitude objective. Anything less than this extent of kindness is a reflection on the soul's need for further growth.

Being in a position to help guide someone else can enable you to be a loving benefactor. The more wisdom you acquire the better equipped you are to help guide others through difficult times. This certainly can put you in a position of power and authority. Your Leo energy is, by nature, filled with kindness and positive desire to help. Leo is a benevolent sign. But, as you could see through the example of Daniel on page 114, sometimes childhood hurts and improper nourishment of your ego can bring on the tendency to misuse your power of guidance.

When someone comes to you for help, it is your karmic challenge to give the full extent of your support in a loving, benevolent manner without need for praise, acknowledgment or credit for that person's future accomplishments. As an example, I teach astrology classes. When one of my students goes on to become an accomplished astrologer or teacher, my pride must be with their success rather than needing the credit for their success. I may feel pride that I was a part of their journey but not attempt to diminish their status by taking the attention to myself. Being humble with all the true grace of humility is an important exercise for you as a Leo. Your soul knows when you are sincere. It also knows when you are full of it.

THE PAMPERED LEO

We all know that people with power can become lazy and pompous. This is also true of Leos. There may well be a part of your nature which enjoys being catered to and which feels it deserves an abundance of attention. Here is where the regality of Leo fits into your karmic growth. It's certainly alright to have people take care of you at times. It feels good to be waited on and pampered. Everyone needs that kind of attention now and then. As a Leo, you must be aware of the imaginary line you may cross over when these needs take priority in your personality.

THE BLUE-EYED ADONIS SYNDROME

Troy was always handsome, his magnetic blue eyes being his most outstanding feature. All the women in his life loved him beginning with his mother, sisters and a following of girl-friends. He also was blessed with his vibrant Leo personality which radiated with sunshine, good humor and an insatiable love of life. It was safe to say that Troy could be spoiled by the adoring women in his life, and he was accustomed to getting what he wanted. It was his charming personality which saved him from going over that imaginary line that all Leos must watch. In fact, it was because of this wonderful Leo spirit that Troy was able to handle the abundance of attention he was so used to receiving. Everyone loved him...men and women, friends and lovers. His life was blessed. It was not unusual for Troy to request and receive his favorite meals for dinner, his beer brought to him as he watched TV. He was even known to sway his teachers into giving him the higher score when his marks sat marginally between two grades. He was a natural charmer. He also had tremendous potential to be lazy, listless, parasitical and unsuccessful in life.

But, Troy was fortunate. His soul was aware of the karmic challenges this kind of adoration provided. He found it instinctively easy to give back to others the love they so willingly gave to him. He enjoyed helping others. He found pleasure in working hard and achieving success. He was not as spoiled as some may have thought. Troy took his greatest assets, his looks and charming personality, and brought them into his career choice. He is now an actor who is adored still for his blue eyes and his way with women. He is also respected by his peers for his continued devotion to his family and childhood friends and, now, to his wife and children. He has provided well financially for these important people in his life and also makes frequent visits to his home town and high school to give pep talks to the students who are interested in the arts.

Troy knows that he is adored by many people. He is aware that he thrives on this adoration. It is most probably this self-awareness which enables him to say "no" to the potential lazy side of his nature and "yes" to the benevolent side of his Leo temperament. Troy is an example to all Leos that too much love can not hurt you as long as you are willing to return it with equal devotion.

Obviously, not all Leos are able to maintain this healthy balance. If you find that you are expecting others to take care of you, wait on you, and serve your needs, then it will be to your soul's benefit to learn independence, self-sufficiency and to develop the skill of serving others. You may act like you are royalty, but even kings work actively for their subjects. The king not only sits on the throne, he also goes into battle for his country. Your subjects expect this kind of devotion back from you!

THE MIDAS TOUCH

Leos love gold. They love champagne, caviar, Porches and presidential suites. Humble tastes are not the fare of the typical Leo. And this is the way it should be. Of course not all of you Leos have the taste of Midas but many of you do. The object of your karmic lesson concerning materialism is not how much you own. It is understood that you would rather wait and save your money in order to purchase exactly what you want. For example, a Leo may choose to walk rather than own a common, inexpensive car. This Leo will wait until he has saved up enough money to buy the car of his dreams rather than any old thing just to get him around. After all, what would his image be if he was seen driving in anything other than the best? A typical Leo would much prefer to fly first-class than tourist, be picked up in a limousine rather than a taxi, stay at the best hotel rather than an economy motel. Even if a Leo enjoys camping, he wants to do it with style...at the best campsites with the finest equipment. Image, image, image!

Fulfilling such needs is proper and expected of you. Karmically you are expected to crave and own the best. Your karmic tests come to you through the possible accumulation of debt in order to satisfy your expensive tastes. Be cautious not to overextend yourself financially in order to own more than you can afford or to try to impress others through materialism. This behavior would also fall into the category of ego and ego needs. It is important that you be willing to work for what you own, live within your limitations, and learn to wait for exactly what you want. The Leo who thinks the world owes him a living has a long way to go in his evolution.

Leo is a generous sign and functions on its highest vibration when you are giving generously of yourself and your materialism to others around you. Some of our most generous people in society are the evolved Leos who give graciously while asking for no recognition in return.

LEOS NEED TO LEARN TO BE FLEXIBLE

Leo is a fixed sign which means you like things to stay the same in your life. Habits, routines, and patterns are comforting to you. As with all fixed signs, you are here to experience the karmic lesson of adapting to change. You will have a tendency to be stubborn yet you must learn to be open to change in all areas of your life. You may experience a tendency to become controlling in a situation in order to keep it from changing. People around you may not be aware of the motivations behind your actions. In fact, you may not always be aware of these complexities yourself. You can be seen as a rigid, controlling person rather than recognized as one who is afraid of change.

WHAT, ME RELOCATE?

Miriam was the executive secretary to a vice- president of a major automobile corporation in Detroit. She had achieved this status position through many years of hard work and perseverance. Miriam had worked for fifteen years at the same plant, in the same building, even on the same floor. She had followed her boss as he rose to higher and higher positions within the corporation. This kind of steady, fixed employment had earned her recognition and respect among all the other workers. Her loyalty was appreciated and, by this time, expected by her boss.

Due to the economy and reshuffling within the company, many people lost their jobs in the late 1980s which left many employees in a state of flux and fear. Miriam felt relatively safe in her position. She knew her boss would have to be fired for her to lose her job and this did not seem to be probable. One morning, Miriam was called into his office to be told that her job was not only one hundred percent protected but that, as a result of much cutting at the top of the ladder, he had been promoted to the position of first vice president and would now be in charge of their new division in Virginia. He was naturally taking her along with a substantial salary raise, and many fringe benefits to make the move an especially sweet deal to her.

Here, other workers all around Miriam were losing their jobs, willing to relocate, take pay cuts, reduced benefits, anything to ensure their position within the company. Any one of these workers would have been ecstatic to hear her news. Not Miriam. Her first instincts were to try to talk her boss out of accepting his new position. She warned him immediately of political and economic pitfalls of such a move. Her mind raced with reasons and excuses to convince him to stay in Detroit. She even plotted ways of sabotaging his promotion without any thought of how this would jeopardize both their jobs. She went home and cried. Her world was being destroyed. Miriam was being forced to change. She was no longer in control. Her loyalties to her boss wavered as her feelings of insecurity grew.

Miriam's case illustrates that what may appear to be a blessing to one person may be a difficult karmic challenge to another. This is a glaring example of how important it is for you not to judge others by your standards. Miriam realized her choice was clearly defined. She could keep her job or quit. Her willingness to move or accept change was her challenge. Her tendency to undermine her boss was now placing her karmic growth in jeopardy. Her reputation within the industry was becoming weakened, and since reputation to Leos is of utmost importance, this tenuous position shook her to an awareness of her negative actions. She ceased her efforts to control her boss and the situation entirely. Change was inevitable. Her job was changing. Her responsibilities were changing. Miriam felt she was unable to cope with all these changes and move her personal life to another state. She opted to stay in Detroit and retire from her position with the company. Some may say that Miriam "failed" her karmic test by not accepting her new position. But did not change come to Miriam no matter what her decision? She now had to adjust to the change of being unemployed. Her whole daily routine was disrupted. Her finances were in a state of adjustment.

Miriam was facing her karmic lesson of change. She had no choice. But, her fear of change had not been faced. She had been forced to accept change rather than initiate it and now she was dealing with the ripple effect that this one major change would have on many other aspects of her life. Her decisions were not over. Her test had only begun.

The karmic lesson of adapting to change may be a difficult one for you but it is a lifelong challenge which will and must be confronted over and over until you are able to roll with the changes life brings and you are able to initiate change yourself without any prodding. It is so much easier for you to lead others and advise them of their choices than it is for you to be the receiver of life's lessons. And, so, we return full circle to your ego's involvement in your life.

REMEMBER, WE STUDY WHAT WE NEED TO LEARN AND WE EXPERIENCE WHAT WE NEED IN ORDER TO GROW.

LEO MALE

The Leo male must fight an uphill battle in his youth with his karmic lessons of ego. Our society already feels that men have a problem with ego. Imagine compounding that ego with a sun sign of Leo! The unevolved Leo male can stay fixed in childlike, immature behavior longer than most men. This does not suggest that Leo men are less mature than other signs. They simply need to face their ego needs more than their brother sun signs. The class clown who captivates attention and disrupts the lesson plan is the stereotype of the Leo male. We all have stories of the boys who dunked pigtails into the ink well, climbed up the goal post on homecoming day, commandeered the high school's PA system during homeroom, and tore up the boulevard in his red convertible. Some Leo/male ego combinations can bring us fun and laughter, others can turn dangerous. The Leo male needs to learn when to turn off his pulsating ego and direct it into a steady beat of confidence without losing the child within him. Age is not always the cure-all. We have all seen the class clown, grown-up and in a business suit showing off at the water cooler at work. Age does help, but it does not guarantee maturity. Many men use their Leo energy and need for attention as a positive force in their careers. For example, Leos make great standup comics, models, performers, teachers, lawyers and salesmen. These professions allow them to make wonderful use of their ego's need for attention.

Most of our rules in life are governed by male energy. Although women have made great strides in becoming a part of the hierarchy of society's governing body, we still cloak our enforcers of rules in a male guise. Our first heavy rule-maker is associated with father. We then progress up the system through schoolmasters, bosses and judges. Sometimes the male Leo ego can feel he is above the rules, even above the law. He can attempt to buck the system and then wiggle out of the consequences with his charm and personality. The more he gets away with this, the more likely he is to continue to test the system, which can ultimately bring him a great deal of trouble. The Leo male must realize that he is not above the law. In fact, many Leo men enter into some aspect of the law as a profession. In this way, they are able to use their authoritative energy to their advantage.

Leo men are born leaders. They are meant to be in positions of authority through their careers and their private interests. The Leo karmic test comes to them as their use of power is tested. It is important for them to lead others with firmness, assurance, courage, and above all, kindness. Remember, benevolence is the true quality of the king. The Leo is able to rise to a position of power almost as easily as the king would inherit his throne. But his reputation will be determined by his own use or misuse of power. Leo men have an abundance of energy to succeed in their chosen professions and their enthusiasm, if well directed, can be beneficial to all of us.

The Leo male must recognize that he needs attention. As soon as he is comfortable with this realization, he will be able to choose wisely his directions toward achieving attention and recognition. Remember, Leo is the sign of the king. The king commands attention through his good deeds and his stance of authority. Most Leo men learn to develop this air of authority and use it effectively.

Let us not forget that Leo is a fun-loving sign. Leo men are capable of bringing much love and joy into their relationships especially to the children in their lives. After all, he has a strong childlike energy within him so he is able to get down on the floor and play at the child's level. He understands the silliness of life, the playfulness of a child's spirit. Therefore, as long as there is no feeling of jealousy or competition between him and the child, the Leo man is able to make a special contact with that child's playful soul. He is able to bring much joy into a child's life and will have that joy returned fourfold by children throughout his life.

If you are confused about what to buy your male Leo friend for his birthday, try a shiny, red convertible, or the most expensive sweater in the most expensive store in town. Labels are important to him and he will recognize the quality, or lack of quality of any gift.

LEO FEMALE

The Leo female, as a child or young woman, can be quite self-centered and demanding. She enjoys being fawned upon and well-taken care of by all people around her. If this power is given too readily to her, she will become increasingly demanding and self-centered. The negative of the Leo female energy is to be controlling, demanding and petulant. She may expect everyone to do things her way, to cater to her, pay her constant attention, buy her expensive gifts. It is important to understand that Leo is a generous sign and that Leo women can be extremely generous to others with their time and money. It is only the spoiled Leo, the pampered little girl, who becomes increasingly demanding as an adult.

Leo is a masculine energy, so women born under this sign are able to make use of their masculine traits, especially in the world of business. Their egos see no reason why they should not gain all the power and prestige of any man in their given careers. Therefore, the Leo woman will expect to be given the position and respect of a man. She will rise to managerial, supervisory positions and will demand equal pay. She will think nothing of entering a career usually dominated by men where she will make powerful use of her Leo traits of authority, strong-will, ego and self-confidence in order to compete and achieve. She also learns quickly how to dress, move and cajole herself to a position of power within any organization. Yes, the Leo female can be softly and beautifully packaged on the outside but never underestimate the fires of ambition which burn within her.

As with the Leo male, the Leo female is well equipped to be an effective, benevolent leader bestowing great kindnesses to those under her command. She is less hindered by the immature aspects of ego which helps her to succeed in the adult parts of her life but also removes her from the childlike qualities of Leo which could bring fun and merriment to her. It is therefore important that she kick up her heels occasionally with a good dance partner or get down on the floor and play with children.

If you are ever in a quandary as to what to buy your favorite Leo female for a birthday present, try a nice, thick gold bracelet. It's sure to be a hit.

LEO CHILDREN

If you are the parent of a Leo, you are fortunate to have a child who has the potential of being as bright and cheery as the morning sunshine. Leo children are able to brighten the dreariest of homes and bring charm to the dullest of lives. They enter into this world with gusto and determination along with the objective of letting you know they are here. Always remember that Leo children are here to learn to deal with the forces of their egos versus the egos of everyone around them. They bask in your attention and adoration. They love being the firstborn and will vie for the top position in your heart if they are not there already. It is your job as a parent, to feed the seemingly insatiable needs of your Leo child without giving in to their every whim.

The Leo child will act, perform, mime and woo all members of the family in order to command as much attention as possible. You, being the adult, must set limits for this child immediately while still fulfilling the Leo need to be loved. Hold your Leo child and bestow great heaps of love but also know when to hold back, particularly in terms of materialism, and when to admonish for negative behavior. Your Leo child will be seeking your attention immediately, and will continue to pursue your undivided attention as long as you allow this to go on. If the behavior is unacceptable, such as temper-tantrums, spilling things, pushing other children out of the way, standing in front of the television, banging on the piano while you are trying to converse with company or any other form of socially non-acceptable behavior, you must stop what you are doing immediately and set limits on this behavior. You must watch for that fine line of a Leo child wanting attention due to neglect and simply wanting constant attention. The child needs to know he is loved without needing to feel he is adored. Above all, never refer to your Leo child as a prince, king, or princess! Their egos already have enough royalty karmically ingrained in them without you adding to this difficulty. They do not think of these as words of endearment...they believe it!

The Leo child certainly needs a great deal of praise because, believe it or not, much of this ego inflation is based on insecurity. It is especially important that all praise be merited not simply bestowed. Since they need a great deal of your attention, be sure to please the Leo for positive action as quickly as you would scold for negative behavior.

The Leo child needs to be taken out for walks in the sunshine. They should not be kept homebound unless necessary, such as illness or poor weather conditions. Leo is a particularly social being and needs to be out in the fresh air and coming into contact with other people, of all ages.

That does not mean that he should be brought along with you to all your adult activities. If you bring him into your world he will attempt to take it over. Leo children can be exhausting and you will need your space from them at times. Yet it is important to have him around other children, not only for the socializing aspect but also for the learning lesson of sharing. The Leo child must learn to share his toys, his space, his time and his parents. Leo is a fixed sign which does not always adjust well to change and the demands of others. Nursery school, art and music lessons will help him to make the necessary adjustments in these areas.

Your Leo child also enjoys the fine arts so take him to plays, movies, museums, and dances. He will enjoy these activities as a spectator and as a participant. Let him play dress-up and pretend. His imagination will be a valuable friend throughout his life. Do not be surprised if plays are given to the entire neighborhood in your backyard. Also, be prepared to entertain his guests lavishly, his ego and pride depend on you to serve cookies and drinks of the highest quality to his friends.

He needs to be proud of his parents as much as you want to be proud of him. Do not be surprised if he admonishes you for what you are wearing or how you greet his friends or how you behave with his teachers at open-school night. Always remember that you are the parent. Leo children can be effective at confusing that fact.

It would be helpful for you to teach him to say please and thank you. Leo children need praise but they must also learn to acknowledge the actions of others. The fact that socializing is so very important to them also indicates the need for them to be polished and sophisticated in their own social skills. This learning begins at home with their parents.

Leos like nice things. They appreciate fine quality and a high price tag. You need to teach them the value of their material possessions, the skill of earning their own money, and the responsibility of providing for, and taking care of, their material desires. To be overly generous without asking them to earn it, or overly solicitous without expecting them to deserve it, would be a detriment to the building of their character.

Leo children's basic nature is to be generous to all they love, and they love with unyielding devotion. It is these traits that you wish to cultivate in their characters above all others. They are friendly, lively spirits who will brighten your lives forever.

VIRGO

August 23 - September 22

Female Energy

KARMIC LESSONS

♦ To work with the minute details of life

♦ To maintain cleanliness, neatness and organization

♦ To be of service to others

♦ To function with stability and a sense of order

PRIMARY VIRGO

Some of the greatest assets of Virgo can also lead to your downfall if you allow yourself to become consumed by your compulsive nature. Your job on earth is to keep us in touch with the rules and details of life. You bring system and order to us all through your strict adherence to the orderly process. Most of you are obsessively neat and meticulous in your manner and demand as much from yourself as you do from others. This in itself can be your undoing if you are vibrating on your primary level. If you are consumed with details to the point of not being able to think of anything else, you will lose sight of the whole picture. This will give you an obsessive nature which, besides appearing dull and pinched, will also leave you out of the mainstream of life.

The horse that pulled the milk wagon down the congested streets of Chicago at the turn of the century, wore blinders for a purpose. Those pieces of leather attached to both sides of his head, forced his eyes to stay in a forward position, only concentrating on his job which was to move the wagon forward. He would never become distracted by children playing ball on the sidewalk or cats leaping across porches. The blinders kept the horse controlled and steady on his course of work.

Your attention to detail, if totally consuming in nature, can affect you in much the same way. Your ability to focus in one direction is an asset in that it keeps you channeled in one direction without distraction, but it also robs you of the flavor and excitement of life which is going on in the outskirts of your vision. You can become quite dull and boring when you are overly intense or too absorbed with details.

Obsession is an emotional state often associated with the primary Virgo. It must be understood that sometimes this obsession brings phenomenal results which benefit our society but it may leave you alone and apart from the intricate activities of your fellowman. The scientist who secludes himself away in the jungle and dedicates his life to the meticulous search of a medical cure, is a typical Virgo type. Obviously, if he is successful in discovering a cure for a serious disease, his labor is praised. If not triumphant, he is considered to be a compulsive Virgo who has lost himself in the avalanche of details. There is often a fine line between primary and evolved with the Virgo.

Primary Virgos can become obsessed with cleanliness and order to such an extreme that they become likened to the Howard Hughes-like personality. It is important to note that Howard Hughes suffered from an Obsessive Compulsive Disorder which is an illness of physical origin. This is different from an Obsessive Compulsive Personality which may be overcome through therapy and your free will. Virgos are no more susceptible to the illness of Obsessive Compulsive Disorder than any other sign, but there may be a higher incidence of Obsessive Compulsive Personalities. Your karmic responsibility, as a Virgo, is to maintain cleanliness and neatness in our society yet, the extreme to this challenge is a mania for these traits which leaves you slave to their demands. The Virgo whose emotional well-being is dependent on his environment and personal hygiene being totally sterilized and methodical is one who is fixated in his primary stage and needs to pay attention to his compulsive needs. Many of these Virgos also become consumed with their health which can escalate into a fear of illness and death. You Virgos make outstanding caretakers in the healing field but when you allow your primary tendencies to deteriorate to hypochondria, you will be too fearful of catching something yourself and ineffective in bringing your healing skills to others. Sometimes, if left unheeded, the primary energy in a Virgo can intensify to a point of obsessive behavior that requires medical assistance. An example would be a compulsive handwasher who feels unable to break the cycle of his obligatory actions, or an office worker who becomes consumed with the position of his pens and pencils on his desk, or the homemaker who needs to vacuum the rug after someone walks on it. These are extreme Virgo traits of people who have become lost in their primary state.

There is another extreme of the primary Virgo which is sometimes referred to as the sloppy Virgo. Some of you fall into an extreme state of refusal to fit into the stereotype of the compulsively neat Virgo. You pride yourselves at being the exception to the rule by living your lives in chaos, clutter, and dirt. This rebellion does not bring you from the extreme orderliness of the primary to a place within the evolved state of Virgo.

Quite the opposite, this is yet another example of the primary of your sign. As a Virgo, you need system and order to develop yourself to your greatest potential. Any degree of extremism is an indication of trouble within your sign. Therefore, a compulsively neat Virgo is as restricted within their primary energy as a sloppy Virgo. Many times, the sloppy Virgo is an example of a person who is the product of an unhappy or chaotic emotional experience whose life did not fit neatly into the comfortable categories his Virgo would have expected for himself. A child who has experienced many changes, emotional disruptions or disappointments in life may easily grow up to be a sloppy Virgo. The key is the understanding that *system and order* play an essential role in your life and can be used as useful tools as long as you restrain yourself from extremes in either direction.

It is important for you to learn to be flexible and less demanding on yourself and others. You are working in your primary mode when you find yourself incapable of accepting change and variety in your life. The rigidity of your compulsive nature can place a great strain on you and anyone around you. You must learn that events in life are subject to change and cannot always fit into neat little categories for you. Other people in your life have their own ideas which may not always meet your standards. You are vibrating on your primary Virgo when you are unable to accept the changes brought to you by life and when your rigidity becomes a challenge in your relationships with others.

The bad press of Virgo comes from those who are fixated in their primary stages. Yet, the beneficial aspects of the Virgo may go by unheralded because they become so mundane and expected by others. Your job is not to call attention to yourself, but to function with steady forthrightness in your attempts to keep system and order in our world.

EVOLVED VIRGO

An evolved Virgo is likely to be involved in jobs that require attention to detail and being of service to others. If you are a Virgo, you may see yourself or some Virgos you know in such job categories as secretaries, office managers, doctors, nurses, watchmakers, science and math teachers, or musicians. We need people to take control of our society through order and discipline. Someone needs to keep the records and outline the discipline that maintains the efficient working of our systems in society. The evolved Virgo is the perfect sign for the job. Thanks to you, we can experience system and order in a world which would otherwise be chaotic. What boss would not want an evolved Virgo to maintain a hum of efficiency in his or her office? Who would not prefer a Virgo surgeon to perform a necessary appendectomy with their innate attention to detail and perfection? The evolved Virgo is capable of establishing and upholding order and detail in our world without becoming consumed with compulsive adherence to the demands of perfection seeking. They experience pleasure in establishing cohesiveness without becoming its slave.

As an evolved Virgo, you are able to pull back and see the whole plan before you without getting lost in the realm of details. To go back to the analogy of the milk horse, the evolved Virgo is capable of removing his blinders without the fear of being distracted from his course of action. He is capable of staying the course without fear of being diverted by outside influences. The comfort of order, structure, and solitary thought are tools which he uses to complete his goals rather than obsessions which rule his life.

Evolved Virgos are also perfect for the medical or any socially-serving fields. Looking at the medical profession, it is ideally suited to the Virgo's need for system, order and cleanliness. Surgery, in particular, is best served by those who are meticulous in their work and absorbed in the detailed accuracy of their skill. They may be introverted in nature, as surgeons are not readily known for their flamboyant bedside manner, and have no need to develop their socializing skills. Usually their patients are under anesthesia as the surgeons are performing their craft. Beyond this obvious compatibility, the evolved Virgo also has a natural sense of serving others through his diligence and need for perfection in his work. This karmic need to serve often manifests itself through career choices such as nursing, secretarial or any other job that helps others by taking care of the minute details of life for them.

The evolved Virgo is dependable and stable and capable of great caring and devotion to others. These traits will be noticed in his relationships with others both professionally and socially. A love affair with a Virgo may not be filled with excitement but it will bring you the comfort of being loved by someone who is secure, nurturing, and always there for you. Some may find this dependability too mundane for their liking while others may seek out this sign's devotion.

REMEMBER, NO ONE IS TOTALLY PRIMARY OR EVOLVED. OUR KARMIC LESSONS ARE BEST LEARNED WHEN WE ARE DEALING WITH BOTH OF THESE ENERGIES.

WORKING WITH THE MINUTE DETAILS OF LIFE

We need structure and order in our world. Someone has to pay attention to the details to make sure that everything is taken care of with efficiency and discipline. If you are a Virgo, this often thankless job belongs to you. Imagine that you are living on this new farm which has only harvested one crop and is now ready to harvest its second season. When the first crop ripened, no one knew exactly what to do. They knew that there were many fruits and vegetables ready for picking and packing, but they were not sure where to begin or how to orchestrate the whole endeavor. Crates were piled up haphazardly; some produce were lost in the melee; others rotted as they awaited their shipping to market. The harvest was not a total disaster, but did require some restructuring and system in order to be better productive. Along comes Virgo, who is ready to organize the harvesting of the second crop. She has had the advantage of having watched the mistakes of the first and is now prepared to outline a workable plan of action for her harvest. Since the Virgo is skilled at dealing with details, she is perfect for the job. She focuses squarely on the logistics of the task and sets upon her goal with precision and devotion to its outcome. The Virgo calculates exactly how many crates will be required, how many workers need to be assigned to each crop and how many days will be necessary to finish the harvest. Not a drop of energy or penny of money will be wasted in obtaining this goal. The Virgo is ideal for this job and this harvest is brought in without any mistakes and with top efficiency.

No project or endeavor can ever be completed without someone paying attention to the details necessary for its success. But this may be a lonely karmic road for the Virgo to travel especially if it becomes a life-long detour from the road more traveled by other people. As a Virgo, you may easily find yourself taking a back seat to someone else who receives the praise and recognition for work that would never have been completed without your behind-the-scenes support.

THE SERVING SECRETARY

Lois was the kind of Virgo office manager who had everything under control. She knew where everything was and how everything was supposed to be done. Everyone depended on her but no one more than her boss, Mr. Verone. He knew he never had to check after Lois. If he needed an important letter to go out, he knew it would be grammatically correct, neat and to the point. If Lois said she had done something, he knew it was done. Because of her devotion to her work, Mr. Verone was able to concentrate his energies on higher goals and soon worked himself through the corporation to the top position of senior vice-president. Lois came right along with him.

To Lois's credit, her boss was appreciative of her support and openly acknowledged the part she played in his career advancements. He lavished praise upon her and rewarded her with a generous salary and frequent bonuses. A Virgo does not have to be abused simply because she works behind the scenes. Lois loved handling the details of her office. She was far more comfortable here than she would have been in Mr. Verone's position which required public speaking, travel, and endless politicking.

THE SILENT SCIENTIST

Dr. P. was completely engrossed in the search for a cure for a disease which had taken the young life of his favorite nephew. He believed that, with steady determination and attention to data, he would be able to discover the source of the disease, and eventually its cure. He enjoyed his life as he poured over lab experiments and documented observation after observation in his logs. No fact went past him unnoticed, no statistic got lost in the process as he continued to work diligently until he successfully achieved his goal. The pharmaceutical company who funded his work immediately televised a press conference proclaiming to all the world that they now had a cure for this disease which stole childrens' lives away. They profited handsomely both professionally and financially, yet it was the Virgo perseverance of Dr. P. which truly brought this cure to all of us. Dr. P. never thought of himself as a martyr. He would have hated being in the spotlight or having the cure named after him. He was well paid for his work, honorably recognized within the scientific community, and that was enough for him. After all, he enjoyed the detail of the work and he had achieved his karmic goal. No other little child need suffer as his nephew had so many years before.

As a Virgo, you have your place in society, whether it be in your family, work or home, where you are responsible for taking care of details. This need for structure and ability to deal with the important items of life makes you a needed and, hopefully, appreciated asset. It is through this karmic behavior trait, that you bring your love and nourishment to others. You see this as a caring gesture which maintains continuity and order into life. After all, by saving your family the need to look for things, by reminding them of their dental appointments, keeping their clothes washed and pressed, and serving their dinner at six p.m. promptly, the Virgo mother has brought loving order and protection to her family.

LISTS! LISTS! LISTS!

As a Virgo, you have this wonderful ability to work within the details of this life and use that skill to your advantage. You may choose to use this skill in your profession or within your home or any endeavors of your liking. A simple example would be keeping lists. It is always to your advantage to list out for yourself what you would like to accomplish. These can be lists of short term or long term goals and they are usually kept on the refrigerator door with a magnet, never scotch taped which may leave a sticky mess. You may have a list of meals you will be serving for the week, or a list of chores you need to finish this weekend, or a list of goals you have laid out for yourself for the next year, or a list of activities for you and your family for the month. You may want to keep a pocket calendar with you at all times, detailing where you will be and what you need to do everyday. The more you keep lists, the more people will depend on you to be where you say you will be and do what you promise you will do, and the more people will depend on you to tell them what they need to do and where they need to be. Your children will depend on you to get them to the right after-school activity with all the necessary equipment rather than keep track of it themselves. Your spouse will rely on you to keep the problems of details away from him and the children and will be woefully disappointed if you mess up anywhere along the way. Not that this is a burden to you. You enjoy being in charge of the details because it is important to you that everything be done well and who better for you to depend on than yourself. You would feel uneasy if anyone else was placed in charge of this karmic assignment and would probably be keeping your own lists anyway just to make sure that they did not forget anything.

STRANGLING IN DETAILS

Beware of the pitfall of being overly involved in the realm of details to the extent of becoming lost in their web. The karmic function you play is integral and necessary, but can become a problem if you allow yourself to get caught in the web of compulsion. Rigidity is a problem for you if you try to protect yourself from the unexpected confusions of life by rigidly adhering to lists and focusing so intently on the details that you are no longer able to see the whole picture.

EDITH'S LISTS

Edith lived her life as though it were one continuous looped list. She got out of bed at the same time everyday, regardless of weekends or holidays. She attended the same mass every morning. Then she went shopping for the food she would need for the night's dinner, which was always the same according to the day of the week. Monday was always barbecued spare ribs, her children's favorite. She cleaned her house from 10 a.m. to noon, had lunch and baby-sat for her neighbor's daughter for three hours. Tuesday was wash day, Wednesday was ironing day. Dinner was always served at 6 p.m. The sound of the 6 o'clock whistle signaled her children to come in from play because dinner was on the table.

Edith's family did not need the list of her weekly activities posted on the refrigerator door, they knew her routine well by now. Still, this was a list of her own choosing by which Edith and her family lived and soon became enslaved. Everyone knew that Edith would get thrown into a tizzy if there were any deviations from her routine. They knew they would be in a lot of trouble if they were five minutes late for dinner, or if the plumbing broke and she could not do her laundry on Tuesday. Edith had become a slave to her lists. She felt this adherence to routine was bringing comfort and stability to her children but, in reality, it had become a source of discomfort and anxiety to them. Her husband was afraid to tell her he was bringing his boss home for dinner because she might have to change her menu, the kids were afraid to tell her about a class trip which might mean that she would have to go on a bus to the city instead of iron that day.

This may sound like an exaggeration, but this is a true story of a compulsive Virgo who ruled her life and her family's lives through her inability to stand apart from the details of life and look at the whole picture. All of her details were directed toward caring for her family but she became entangled in them to the point that her lists ruled her life and eventually estranged her from the loving warmth of her family. Lists can be cold. They have no sensitivity to the nuances and disturbances of life. They do not take into account the personalities of others or the sudden, unexpected surprises of life. Here we see a warm, loving woman in Edith, who wanted to give her family the best of herself so she paid strict attention to all the details necessary in providing a good home for them. In the process, Edith became lost in the attention her lists demanded of her and eventually lost sight of the human needs of her loved ones. She discovered that lists can make you mechanical if you are unable to change them when necessary.

KEEPING OUR WORLD CLEAN, NEAT AND ORGANIZED

This karmic lesson for the Virgo is akin to that of working with minute details in that compulsion can become a problem. But you must keep in mind that you karmically need to keep yourself and your environment clean, neat and organized. As we saw with the primary Virgo, some of you are sloppy and take great pride in not fitting into this category. Some of you also are perfectly neat in one area of your life and sloppy in others. Most of you will talk about one area where you kind of let it all hang out in your messiness. You never clean the inside of your car or make your bed or clean your garage. You seem to need one area of outlet in which to relax and rebel against your own tendency to be compulsively organized. This is good for you! The healthiest Virgos I ever saw were ones who had one area of sloppiness, even if they were totally clean in all other areas.

Those of you who are sloppy Virgos in most areas usually have one place in your life where you are compulsively organized. Extremism is your downfall. Balance is your goal. The bottom line is, karmically you need to pay attention to cleanliness, neatness, and organization in order to function at your highest potential. You are at peace when there is system and order around you. It does not matter whether you deny this need, as some of you do. This is your karmic responsibility, to bring neatness and order to life.

It is important that you remain attuned to the fact that you need structure and system in your life in order to achieve your highest goals. If you work in an office, it is important for you to maintain some kind of system and order in, on, and around your desk. If you are working on a project for school, you need to know where your supplies are and keep an outline of your project to help you prepare it properly. If you are keeping a house, it is helpful for you to maintain a schedule of your chores and know where all your supplies are kept, each in its place. When you find yourself in a position where there is clutter and confusion, you will not be functioning on your highest level. Chaos around you will tend to distract you and drain your energy which would be better used if directed solely toward your goal.

FINDING ORDER IN CHAOS

Jay was a carpenter known for the precision and accuracy of his work. If anyone went into a home that Jay worked on they could spot his work immediately. The miter edges of his woodworking were flawless. One would never see a seam after Jay had spackled and sanded a new wall. He was a carpenter who enjoyed giving his attention to the details of his work which included cleaning up after himself and treating his tools with respect. It is true, Jay could not be rushed nor could he be distracted; distractions annoyed him and sent him into a sullen mood.

His wife and brother begged him to start his own business instead of always working for other contractors. He had a great business sense, he was organized and an expert in his field. Why shouldn't he be looking for something bigger and better for himself? Finally, Jay, against some inner judgment and worn down by his wife's nagging, opened his own contracting business and set out to make his great financial mark. His first job was the renovation of an old house, tearing down some walls to enlarge a living room, and redesigning the kitchen. He had worked on projects similar to these many times and looked forward to his first easy challenge.

At home, Jay cleaned off his desk, ordered the appropriate forms, business cards, letterhead, sharpened his pencils and readied himself to organize the job. Everything was perfect on paper, materials were ordered, subcontractors scheduled back to back and a handsome profit loomed in his future. The first few days went smoothly, the main wall of the house came down with ease, the dumpster arrived as scheduled and clean up was simple. Then the naturally expected snags began to occur. The lumber yard was unable to deliver his entire order which would mean he would have to alter his schedule. The plumber ran into a problem and said his part of the job would take two days instead of one which meant the cabinet man would have to come a day later, which became a problem because he had another job scheduled for the next day. All of Jay's lists and careful planning were becoming useless. Worse than that, Jay was not able to concentrate on his skilled craftsmanship, which had always been his trademark. He was constantly distracted by phone calls, complaints, and disappointments.

Needless-to-say, as a dependable Virgo, Jay finished the job. His reputed perfection was still evident in the final project even though it took two weeks longer than expected. Jay closed up his new business and happily went back to his old job where he could concentrate on his work and find pleasure in his final products.

You can see from Jay's experience, that the Virgo talent for organization is best served on a smaller, narrower scale and may become uncomfortable and even nonfunctioning if put into a larger context. You will find comfort and respect by concentrating on what you do best which involves organization on a small, concise scale rather than larger, more complex situations which divert your main focus.

Jay was more comfortable concentrating on organizing his sphere of work and was distracted by having to deal with the organization and clean-up of the large project, especially when his plan of action was disrupted by unforeseen events or the undependability of others. This kind of disorganization and mess will affect Virgos in all areas of life. Some of my Virgo clients have shared their conflicts with life's instabilities:

> Neal was used to keeping his home particularly clean and uncluttered. Everything had its place. After his children came along, he could not seem to adjust to the disruption and mess. His car keys were not always where he left them and could at any time be found in the playpen, under the table or even sunk at the bottom of the toilet bowl. Why couldn't his children leave his things alone?

➤ Marie was looking forward to having an extension built on her house which would become her private, untouched room where she could enjoy her crafts. But the two months it took to build the extra room, the workmen all over her property, the noise, dirt, and dust were almost unbearable for her. She was afraid she would suffer a nervous breakdown before the room was completed.

➤ Jim was at first excited that two new workers were being added to his company until he realized that he would now have to move his desk to a smaller area which left him much less room for his workspace. He felt as though he would never be able to be as efficient and organized as he was before his system had been disrupted.

As a Virgo, cleanliness and organization are important to your composure, yet your karmic testing will come to you when you need to cope with disruption around you. Nobody's life is totally free of clutter or confusion now and again. This challenge will certainly come to you at times. You must be aware of the importance of adjusting to these stressful circumstances and be gentle with yourself and others around you while you are moving through chaos. Sometimes, you may become cranky or demanding of others while you are experiencing these stresses. Neal could have blamed his wife for the messes his children made, or Marie could have taken her frustration out on her children because her home was annoying her or Jim could have sulked at his desk and blamed his new co-workers for the bother their entry into the company had caused him. Sometimes, the Virgo will act out at the closest people around them when their routines are disrupted. This is another area where Virgos have gotten their bad press.

You can be critical of yourself and others to the point of seeking a perfection which is unrealistic. Your need for order helps you to function at your best level. When your need becomes unrealistic, or your sense of order disrupted beyond your control, you are then confronting your karmic need to adapt to change and accept the challenge to your sense of order.

FUNCTIONING WITH STABILITY
AND A SENSE OF ORDER

Virgo is considered to be a mutable sign in astrology, which means that it should be adaptable and easily adjust to change. Yet, in character, this is usually far from true as a character trait of the Virgo. As you have seen already from this chapter, you are a creature of habit who likes to live within the framework of a well-structured, concentrated approach to life. You are a hard worker who is capable of successfully accomplishing your goals by use of your assets of diligence and attention to detail. You move forward in a direct, determined manner without need for urgency or flattery nor are you easily distracted from your goal. This kind of perseverance leaves you vulnerable when an obstacle or confusion is set in your path. You enjoy walking the straight path to your goal and are not easily distracted by events on the sideline. But this does leave you vulnerable to any obstacles which appear within your actual path. Karmically, you are here to learn to change your path, re-steer your direction and adjust to alternate routes as life requires.

Over the years, many Virgo clients have told me that they consider themselves to be quite versatile and resent being labeled as fixed or rigid in their personalities. I have paid especially close attention to these people, have observed them as they adjusted to life's changes, and I have seen their ability to adjust to some difficult circumstances. I have seen a wife initiate a divorce and relocate to another state, another accept the loss of her children as they choose to live with their father, and another Virgo accept his forced retirement from a company that he had served with years of devotion. Each of these Virgos accepted their karmic challenge of adjusting to change while they continued to function within a framework of stability and a sense of order. In fact, their need for continuity became their asset rather than their demise.

Sometimes your need for order and continuity in your life helps you to cope with the challenges of change and disruption. It is like a sailboat that flips over in a stormy sea. It is built to right itself and float again upon the waves. Your unacceptance of change helps you to put yourself once again in an upright position whenever life's circumstances try to overturn you. It is the piece of yourself which you may be trying to deny that is actually the source of your survival. The karmic challenges that come with change may also be confronted with the strength of your karmic tendency to place yourself back on a steady path of continuity and routine. Each of these clients who weathered the storm of change in their lives also dove headlong into other directions which required details, organization, and steadiness of concentration. The wife who left her marriage and the mother who lost custody of her children both took the same approach. They concentrated their energy on furthering their education and advancing in their careers. The male Virgo who was forced out of his job began his own consulting company and raised large sums of money for nonprofit charitable organizations. They each mourned the loss of their previous life directions but went on quickly to form new goals which they approached with their powerful need to bring stability and order into their lives.

The karmic test comes to the Virgo who finds this kind of readjustment difficult and feels unable to place herself in an upright position after a major disruption in her life. This is the Virgo who becomes angry, perhaps even abusive, to those around her. When a Virgo is particularly critical of someone else or herself, she is displaying her discomfort. Some change or disruption in her life is causing her to feel powerless to set her life, once again, in a stable position. She is unable to accept the disruption in her life. She does not feel capable of bringing organization and a sense of order into her realm. The Virgo whose home is under repair, who feels lost and confused during the weeks of construction, may become cranky with her family, critical of the workmanship of the carpenters and generally depressed until the job is completed. Even then it may take her several weeks to get her bearings while she reorganizes her cabinets and gets herself into a new routine. The Virgo's karmic challenge comes through an acceptance of the discomfort that change brings. It also comes from an understanding of that powerful need to return to stability as quickly as possible without feeling there is justification in taking this anger out on other people or turning it inward into a state of depression. This is not always an easy challenge for the Virgo. You, as a Virgo, will be able to cite examples in your life when you were confronted with this karmic lesson and be able to examine your reaction to its uncomfortable disturbance.

BEING OF SERVICE TO OTHERS

One of the finest personality traits of Virgo, and its most powerful karmic direction, is being of service to others. Yours is a sign which is designed primarily to help others who are unable to function successfully on their own in society without the diligent aid of someone else. This is a karmic responsibility which comes easily to you. It fits perfectly into your penchant for organization, cleanliness, neatness, and attention to details. Your counterparts in Pisces, which is also a sign of service, is unlike Virgo because they tend to allow themselves to be abused. You are capable of giving of yourself in service while also demanding appropriate recognition or recompense for your actions.

There are many directions you may choose to take with this need to serve. Some examples have already been mentioned in this chapter, secretaries, office managers, nurses, doctors, social workers, scientists, homemakers, and researchers, to name a few. Your need to handle the details of life and keep your environment clean, structured and well organized will become useful tools in creating an atmosphere for others which allows them to devote themselves to the greater, larger picture. You may be serving your need to be of service to others simply by doing your job at home or at work. Or, you may choose a more obvious direction by nursing others back to health or volunteering your skills in a helping field. This innate ability you have to nurture through your stabilizing influence may be the most important karmic gift of all. How you use it or how you direct it is up to you. Many times, you will not be aware of all the energy you are giving out and, because of this possibility, you must pay attention to your actions and be careful not to allow others to use or abuse you. This can go by unnoticed by a Virgo who has poor self-esteem or who allows himself to become lost in the details and compulsions of his life. Most of you are able to graciously and consciously give of yourself in a useful and productive way in order to satisfy your karma.

GLORIA AND MIAMI

A contemporary Virgo who appears to be fulfilling her karmic responsibility is the singer, Gloria Estefan. This is a singer of Cuban descent who never forgets her roots or her people who have not had as much good fortune as she. She calls the city of Miami, Florida, her home and is always ready to support her people, her city and her state of Florida whenever they need her. She raises money for local charities, has named her group the Miami Sound Machine, and has maintained a Spanish quality in her music. Miamians love Gloria Estefan and Gloria, unashamedly, loves them back.

To prove the existence of *instant karma* and witness immediate recognition or reward, we simply have to look at the relationship between Gloria and her city. In 1990, Gloria, her husband, and her son, along with several members of her group, were involved in a serious accident. Their bus was run off the road on an icy night en route to a singing engagement. She was seriously injured, and for days, many feared her back injury would leave her totally crippled. The local newspaper, The Miami Herald, ran front page stories and headlines about Gloria for over a week. The people of Miami cried as though someone in their own family was in jeopardy, and Gloria was someone in their family. All the love and respect she had always shown them was now being offered to her through their genuine love and prayers. Many felt that Gloria's recovery was greatly enhanced by the loving outpouring of the city of Miami.

And Gloria never forgot. Two years later, when Hurricane Andrew crumpled southern Florida, Gloria Estefan was there immediately to offer help. She worked many hours physically hauling boxes of food and supplies to the frightened people. She then organized a concert and donated the profits toward the relief of her people.

With Gloria and Miami, we witness a perfect exchange of a Virgo being of service to others and an instant reward of their thanks, recognition and love. What we see here is the genuineness behind the actions. Gloria does not present her love to Miami and her Cuban ancestry because it will sell more CDs. They sense the depth of her service and the honesty of her concern, and for this, they love her back with equal intensity. Instant karma! How fortunate Gloria Estefan is to have advanced her soul through this loving karmic energy.

As a Virgo, it is important for you to look around you and recognize all the potential ways you may extend your karmic hand in service to others. It is equally important for you to acknowledge all you have done and are still doing. You may feel that you are just doing what feels best to you and may not even be aware of the service you may be rendering. If you are raising a child with love, keeping a clean, neat environment for your loved ones, working diligently on a project or taking care of the small details of life for someone else and thereby freeing them to move forward, then you are fulfilling your karmic responsibility to be of service. You may be of service to one special person, a family, a boss, or, like Gloria Estefan, to a whole city. Karmic law makes no judgment as to the notoriety of your gift or the size of your service. It is the principle upon which your soul functions. You are here to learn the concept of benefiting others through your hard, diligent work ethic. Any of us who benefit from your karma are fortunate indeed.

VIRGO MALE

Virgo is a female sign which may not always be comfortable when combined with masculine energy. Historically, the woman in society is expected to take care of the little details of life, keep the home neat and clean and pick up after her man so that he is able to get out there in that man's world without these small bothers on his mind. The Virgo male was born with a need to handle these details himself or oversee whomever he has chosen to take care of them for him. This can make him either very understanding and helpful or extremely demanding. Many times, he is a little of both. His karmic responsibility is to identify the roles he assumes in his quest for order and stability in his life and to modify any personality trait which is expressed as being excessively critical of others.

He can be demanding of his spouse if his Virgo behavior has manifested itself in a compulsive need to have a clean house, perfectly pressed seams in his trousers, and everything always in its place. The Virgo male's responsibility is to take care of his things himself, if he feels no one can do it to his liking. He can be independent and capable of taking care of himself which will make him an ideal companion. Here is a man who is able to clean his home better than anyone; cook, sew, and iron. His lawn will be impeccably tended, his flower gardens weedless. The local car wash will know him on a first name basis and his monthly bills will be paid on time.

This can also be the Virgo male who expects everyone else to take care of perfecting his environment for him precisely to his high expectations. This Virgo male can be intolerable to live with as he will never be happy with his environment or his relationship. After all, who can maintain perfection one hundred percent of the time for the critical Virgo's satisfaction? He must be cautious not to give in to extremism and inflexibility. He may tend to rant and rave when someone borrows one of his tools and then does not return it to its exact place in its original condition.

Then, there is the sloppy Virgo male who seems to love to live in squalor, or does not care if the project he was working on ever gets finished or if the car was ever washed. You wonder how he can be a Virgo when you read the books on this sign. Here we have a Virgo who has suffered pain or confusion in his childhood, has a problem with addictions or suffers from depression. The Virgo who has let himself go, is lost in low self-esteem and needs help from a professional or loving individual. He needs support to help him to organize himself and to help him believe that he is capable of success. The Virgo male functions best when his environment is uncluttered, clean and his goals carefully delineated. When he falls away from this track it is an indication of being lost in despair, mental confusion, drugs or alcohol. He needs to build, slowly and carefully, a structure around himself which enables him to fulfill his list of karmic goals.

Virgo males are often in positions of authority in their professions. Their natural desire to do a job well, along with their attention to detail, usually lifts them to a position of success. They must watch not to be overly critical of others around them on the job. If this reduces itself to nit-picking and nagging, it may offer a difficult karmic challenge to his soul. There is no such thing as perfection, not for him nor for his co-workers. Like the industrious ant, he must keep on doing the best he can without feeling disappointed in himself or others when their job falls short of perfection. It would definitely behoove him to enter a field which involves either attention to details or being of service to others. He does not usually like being in fields that are dirty or messy. He would enjoy the precision of carpentry but not necessarily the mess of cementing. He would enjoy social work but may have difficulty visiting environments of poverty or despair. He is not afraid of cleaning a mess but does not want to feel helpless in a messy situation. Other ideal professions are watch repairing, surgery, accounting, photography and banking. He needs to place himself in a position where he can confront his karmic challenges without becoming overpowered by mess or chaos.

It always helps the Virgo male to acknowledge his feminine side. He is sensitive, intuitive and has a strong need to service others by cleaning up after them. He can nurture this part of himself by devoting a portion of his time to the creative, spiritual side of life. He may choose to work in a field of art or enjoy the beauty of art as a hobby or as a spectator. Music plays an especially important role in his appreciation of life. He is able to express his creative, emotional self through his love of music and may very well be a gifted composer or talented performer.

The Virgo male is often a stable man. He is predictable in his actions and holds steady to his course. These traits may prove boring in his nature but they do ensure an aspect of dependability which cannot be refuted. The surgeon's bedside manner may not be effervescent, but who would not want a detail-minded, perfection-seeking Virgo operating on them?

VIRGO FEMALE

This is a female sign and works compatibly with the female form. However, the Virgo female must watch not to become caught in a role of servicing others. Some of the traditional female roles have been Virgo in nature. Women were the secretaries who took care of everything in the office and tended to their boss' every need in order to make their superiors look good. They were the nurturers behind the scenes who did the hard work and sat back as their bosses claimed all the credit. Women were the housekeepers who had responsibility to keep confusion to a minimum in the home so that their husbands and children could have peaceful, clean, organized environments in which to prosper, grow, and relax. She was not expected to save energy for herself to succeed in the outside world. Women were the nurses who took total care of the doctor's patients while he saw more patients in his office, played golf, and spent the copious fees he charged for his expertise.

As a Virgo female, she must recognize that she has a natural tendency to fall into one or more of these roles. That is all right as long as she is choosing the course of her life based on her desire to do so rather than succumbing to a comfortable position without regard for her own ambitions. Virgo females can be extremely ambitious and, if they allow themselves to think big, can enter comfortably into any field which may interest them. They can be found in areas of corporate business, banking, real estate, and scientific fields of medicine, psychology, and research. They also, like their male counterparts, possess an affinity to the realm of music and can find great peace for themselves within the performing, writing or appreciation of music.

In terms of their traditional female roles, they must be careful of their tendency to be critical of their spouses and children. Although this is a female sign, it is not known for its warmth or affectionate nature. The Virgo female's karmic responsibility is to bring stability and the comfort of continuity to her loved ones. If she falls victim to her compulsive nature for strict adherence to structure and rules, she will find herself absorbed in the details of her life rather than the emotions required within relationships.

The example of Edith, discussed earlier in this chapter, shows a female Virgo who became lost in her obsessions with time and cleanliness. The Virgo female is not known for her warmth. She tends to show her love through taking care of the physical aspects of her loved ones lives. She maintains order and routine through her cleaning and cooking schedules. She keeps the home, and everyone in it, clean and neat. She may even pay the bills and handle the household accounts for her spouse. Her karmic lesson is to learn how to express her love and devotion through words and touch. It is not enough for her to feed, clothe, and clean her children, she must also spend time with them. Instead of scrubbing the floors she needs to sit with them, talk with them and listen to their hearts' needs. She must be careful not to nag because they will never be as concerned with details as she is. And the more she cleans up after them, the less they will be motivated to do it themselves. A type of Virgo female may say that she does not want her spouse or children helping her with the household chores because they do not do it as well as she does. She might even complain that she would be just as likely to go over their work again anyway. This is a negative signal which she is giving out, especially to her children. They will never be as proficient at life and will never become equal to her expectations. This can be a difficult karmic awareness for the Virgo female, but an important one.

Displays of affection, words of praise, and gestures of recognition are important traits for the Virgo female to develop. She also needs to recognize her potential and be willing to take her place in society; rather this than allow her identity to be lost as someone else's assistant, wife or mother. This is a strong sign and one which is heavily relied upon by others. The Virgo female must use her assets in a positive fashion which will bring her satisfaction. She does not need much recognition other than her personal feeling of accomplishment. She must be aware that compulsive behavior or lack of system and order, as in the sloppy Virgo, is indicative of a breakdown of her positive strengths and may signal a problem on a psychological level. It may sometimes feel comfortable to hide away in a world of compulsion or disarray, but it is not a comfortable shelter for the Virgo woman and she must ready herself to move toward a more orderly sanctuary. This Virgo's karmic challenge is to recognize that neatness counts but that extremes on either side of typical structure may be indicative of a problem.

The Virgo female plays an important role in our society and must watch that she does not lose her own identity in the process.

VIRGO CHILDREN

You must realize that your child needs an environment of organization, cleanliness, and routine. You will bring her great comfort if you place her on a set feeding schedule, keep her diapers clean, and bathe her every day. It sounds routine yet it is so important to your Virgo child's feeling of comfort and security. As she gets older, she needs her own space. A place where she can keep her things, where no one else can get them. Obviously, this is not always possible, but you must recognize her need for this kind of structure and order in her life. Let us say she is in school and has started bringing home her homework assignments. You will help her if you set up a desk for her with her own calendar, pads, pencils, sharpeners, eraser, everything she feels she will need. This becomes her area for homework and this setup will help her to succeed. The Virgo child can become disoriented and waste too much of her energy if her work space is not organized. She can become consumed with the details involved in setting up for her homework rather than directing her energy toward doing her homework.

Keeping this in mind, you must be cognizant of her tendency to become overly dependent on order, routine, cleanliness, and schedules. As a parent of a Virgo child, you walk the fine line of understanding her need for these structures while also helping her not to become overly dependent on them. This is not an enviable position. You must realize that any change or disruption to her routine is hard on her. This discomfort does not go away simply because you tell her it is silly. If she gets upset because one of her siblings broke her pencils, she is reacting to an intrusion to her system and order of things. You can help her by acknowledging the impact this has on her then help her to solve this problem by replacing her pencils. It will not help for you to tell her she is acting ridiculously or that the pencils do not really matter. It is not the pencils themselves which are at issue.

You know, as an adult, that life cannot always be orderly or neatly designed. Your Virgo child will need to confront her karmic issues of accepting change and disruption to structure in her life. You will be her greatest asset if you teach her early in life that you recognize her need for order, and that you will help her sort through the times when life is not so neatly packaged. You must be attuned to her compulsive or rigid behaviors, which are indicative of insecurity or discomfort. You must also pay attention to her behavior which shows a disregard for structure and order as in the sloppy Virgo. She may be signaling you to psychological distress, abuse, low self-esteem or a tendency toward an addictive personality, usually accompanied by moodiness or depression. Of course, even the most compulsive of Virgos get pretty messy during their adolescent years. Do not get alarmed about this stage.

Your Virgo is introverted by nature. Try not to force her to enter the public eye against her consent. She needs time to be by herself and may not always be comfortable in public or with public expressions of feelings. Music is important to her and she may easily master a musical instrument. Therefore, it would be a good investment if you bought her an instrument, but do not force her to play in recitals or for the family unless she wants to perform. She may very well love to play in public, many famous musicians are Virgos, but she must not be forced. Do not be surprised if your Virgo child has some special talents. You may find her to be skilled in mathematics, sciences, music, or writing. She likes to get into things, especially areas where she finds systems, orders and rules.

Help her when the messes of life throw her into a tailspin. Give her your support without overly protecting her. The reality of life is that it is a changeable force and karmically this is what she is learning in this lifetime. She also needs to be of service to others. You will be a tremendous asset to her if you show her, through your example, and encourage her from her early life, to give of herself to others who are not as fortunate as she. With this example, it is also necessary for you to help her to define her limits so that she does not become overly worked or used by someone else's ambitions. Yours is a special child who has much to offer our world with her ability to oil our systems and smooth out our wrinkles. She is developing from the inside out. Much is going on inside of her which will show itself later in life. As her parents, you have the first contact with her inner being. Fill her with love and confidence and readiness to handle life's changes. Your rewards will be great. She is a child who does not look to turn your world inside out. She wants to fit comfortable into the already established systems of your life while including a few of her own.

LIBRA

September 23 - October 22

Male Energy

KARMIC LESSONS

- ◆ Developing independence and self-reliance

- ◆ Being true to oneself

- ◆ Education

- ◆ Learning to feel rather than intellectualize

- ◆ Beautifying the environment

PRIMARY LIBRA

It is the intrinsic nature of the Libra to be liked and socially accepted. The primary Libra nature is to be smiling and friendly in an unbridled attempt to win friends and influence people. Obviously, there is nothing wrong with being friendly, the world probably needs a lot more people-friendly individuals than it's got. The difficulty comes to you as a Libra when you allow a superficial side of yourself to govern your more sophisticated, discriminating self. Have you ever seen the doll heads on springs that people place in the back of their cars? They bob along with happy, smiling faces no matter how many bumps are in the road. This unrealistic facade can be worn by you if you are a Libra who masks any feelings of anger or frustration with a phony, sociable smile in order to be liked by others. Your karmic lesson is to be true to yourself by expressing your true thoughts and opinions even if they may contradict those of the people with whom you wish to maintain friendships.

The Libra who remains within an unhealthy or unsatisfying relationship because they are afraid of being alone, is an example of Libra vibrating on their primary level. It is true that Libra is probably the most socializing of all the signs and the one that most requires the comfort of a "marriage" relationship. This aching need within you is what forces you to confront your roles within relationships. You are here to learn about yourself through your interaction with others. Your desire to be liked is essential in fostering your eagerness to interact socially and romantically. The primary Libra lacks discriminatory behavior which must be developed in this lifetime. This is your goal. You must choose carefully who you call friend, lover, and spouse. You must learn to love yourself and, sometimes, to choose your own company above the companionship of a negative relationship.

This need to be socially accepted can propel you into friendships, love affairs and marriages which are not the best for you. The primary need to be loved and accepted can lead to unhealthy relationships which you will either stay in rather than be alone or you may join another group of Libras who jump from one relationship to the next rather than be alone. Being alone, to a primary Libra, is akin to social ostracism.

Due to the socializing aspect of Libra, you will find yourself involved in communication on many different levels. The primary Libra tends to talk endlessly on the phone, ramble without end to others about trivial aspects of their life or carry on long discourses about the weather, their clothes or gossip in general. Libra is an intellectual sign, therefore, you must educate yourself and develop your communication skills to a point of social deftness and educational skill. In other words, you can be either a social bore, which will appear as being shallow, or an intelligent conversationalist who is eagerly sought out by others.

Libra is a sign of beauty and charm. When you vibrate on your primary level you can be vain and peacockish in your behavior. Your karmic responsibility is to beautify this world but please do not assume that this will be accomplished by your own physical presence. Too much primping and strutting can be detrimental to your karmic advancement and particularly annoying to those around you. Taste, refinement and charm must be your bywords. Feathers, cheap jewelry, and flashy scarves keep you absorbed in your need for attention rather than your karmic goal of beautification. Yours is a sign which can drown in the water of shallowness when you succumb to your primary energy. The potential of your evolved state is limitless in its ability to love, understand and soften the world for the rest of us. In the Libra case, your potential to grow toward all the best you can be, is unbounded and most of you prove to be amazingly talented in your growth and evolvement.

EVOLVED LIBRA

Relationships prove to be the most difficult area of learning for most of you. Your karmic lessons may be complex and challenging where other people are concerned. Yet, it is through your relationships that you will experience your greatest growth and karmic development. An evolved Libra is comfortably independent and self-sufficient in relationships. You will know when you have mastered this lesson when you are able to rid yourself of an unhealthy alliance, when you speak your mind to your friends without fearing their rejection and when you are able to discriminate between symbiotic and sharing relationships. If you can dare to be alone without obsessing about your next relationship, you have made it!

The evolved Libra is an educated person. You have learned to enjoy the educational process whether it be formal classroom education or the school of life. The process of development is the same, you are able to open your mind to new information which becomes assimilated into your now fascinating and informational conversations. The wonderful gift of communication will befit the depth of your intelligence and people will gather around to listen to you rather than be bored with primary, petty conversations. An evolved Libra might join intellectual groups, have a few special friends rather than many shallow friendships, and find powerful comfort in a committed relationship.

REMEMBER, NO ONE IS TOTALLY PRIMARY OR EVOLVED. OUR KARMIC LESSONS ARE BEST LEARNED WHEN WE ARE DEALING WITH BOTH OF THESE ENERGIES.

WHAT IS A KARMIC RELATIONSHIP?

When we first hear the phrase, *karmic relationship,* we usually think of intense lovers who have known each other before in several past lives. They are destined to meet again in this life...bells sound, mountains move, nothing can stop them from being together. Theirs is a destined love; their fate is written in the sands of time. Many people call these lovers *soul mates.* Now, here is a term that has been as abused and overused as happily-ever-afters in fairy tales. Let us look at these terms, *karmic relationship* and *soul mates*, by   first taking a general view of all relationships.

The philosophy of karma suggests that no relationship is in our life accidentally. Each person we meet and interact with brings us an experience which has potential to further our karmic growth. Some people believe these relationships are predestined, already plotted out for us, others believe that lessons are all around us in the form of relationships and we choose our lessons as we choose our companions. It is not necessary to determine which belief is true and which is false. The basic premise is the same in both, relationships bring us lessons, experiences, and if we wish, karmic evolvement of our soul.

When we meet that someone special who sets our desires on fire, that someone who seems to agree with our outlook on life, who thinks the way we do, we tend to equate this person to our *soul mate*. We must have known him before, we have an innate familiarity. We must be destined to be together in this lifetime, it feels so right. In reality, we have numerous encounters with people with whom we have shared past lives. They are our friends, teachers, family, co-workers. It is when we mix our sexual desires with our soul's familiarity that we fool ourselves into thinking that this person is our one and only love on this earth. It is the sexual intensity that makes this overwhelmingly convincing evidence of predestined love. In truth, we have soul connections with many people in our lives with whom we have no sexual relationship yet they influence us just as powerfully in subtle ways.

Listen to the woman in line in front of you at the supermarket. She may be saying something which your soul needs to hear right now. It is no coincidence that you are working in an office with those particular co-workers, many karmic awarenesses may come to you through the interactions at work with those people. It appears to be just a fluke, a luck of the draw which puts you in contact with certain people in your life but everyone has something to teach you about yourself. Everyone is able to contribute to your evolution as a Libra. You are here to learn about yourself through relationships so you must examine all of your contacts rather than search for that karmic soul mate. All relationships are karmic in that they aid you in your karmic development. Choices are always around you. Do you choose to stay in this love relationship? Do you choose to remain at this job with these people? Will you listen to the lady on line in the supermarket? As a Libra, you will be keeping a finger on the pulse of many connections throughout your life. And, when you ask yourself if this someone special is your soul mate, dare to ask this when there is stillness in the sexual intensity and then search this relationship's potential for encouraging your karmic growth. All our relationships are karmic; some are certainly more intense and longer lasting.

WHAT IS MARRIAGE?

Libra is the sign of marriage. It is the natural ruler of the seventh house of the chart which is the house of marriage. Therefore, astrology books and horoscope columns often refer to your marriage or marriage partner. So, let us define the word marriage here since it appears to be so important to your sign.

Marriage is a man-made law. The regulations and requirements needed to be deemed "married" will vary from culture to culture, country to country, even state to state. The cosmos has no interest whatsoever in man's definition of marriage. In astrology, marriage is a relationship of the heart. It is a commitment which you make to one person, exclusive of all other relationships. If you are living with someone, sharing the bills, joining your forces in everyday activity, you are married according to the laws of nature. If an astrologer asks you if you have ever been married, you must include these long-term or live-in relationships when you give your answer. This is important for you to understand as a Libra since many of your karmic lessons will come to you through all your marriage relationships.

INDEPENDENCE AND SELF-RELIANCE IN LOVE RELATIONSHIPS

Signs which are opposite each other in astrology have similar karmic lessons. The sign opposite Libra is Aries which is also concerned with experiencing karmic growth through relationships. They may appear to take opposing positions yet the basic object is the same, to learn about themselves through their close ties. You may enjoy reading the chapter on Aries for further insight into your polar self.

Libra is a sign which feels most comfortable when in a close commitment or marriage relationship. You can sometimes feel incomplete if you are alone as though the other half of yourself can only be completed when you are married. As an adolescent you may feel it necessary to date frequently to establish your popularity and maintain long-term relationships to fulfill your need for commitment. You must keep in mind that the key word for Libra is discrimination. It is important for you to learn to be discriminating in your relationships. A primary tendency is to date, commit, and marry simply to fulfill your need to be in partnership with someone. This can lead to problems for you if you have not learned to slow down and examine the patterns of your relationships and matured enough to understand your needs within a commitment.

I was on line at the supermarket one brisk October afternoon when the lady in front of me struck up a conversation during our long wait. Her Libra identity was immediately revealed when she said that this was her birthday. She then wept softly as she confessed that this was her first time out of the house since her husband had passed away six weeks before. She talked about her loneliness and fears of being alone. Her husband had done everything for her. She had no idea how much money they had in the bank, she was ignorant of their assets, debts, or investments. She had never paid a bill or been concerned about the mechanics of their life while he was alive. She lauded praises upon this wonderful husband of hers who had sheltered her so lovingly from any worldly or material concerns, but now she was alone and frightened. This was her first step out into the world by herself. She was picking up some items at the grocery store today and she planned to explore her new world even further tomorrow by going to the bank.

As her groceries were packed, we said good bye and she tearfully headed toward the parking lot appearing very frail and unsteady with her first outing. After I paid my bill and swept up my groceries I went out to the parking lot to see this same woman wandering around the lot. I was afraid that her grief had left her dazed and went over to her asking what was wrong only to learn that she was unable to find her car. You see, her husband had bought it for her only two weeks before he died and she did not even know what make of car it was. She only knew that it was red. We eventually found her car where she had left it and she went on her way.

To me, this was a sad example of a Libra who had allowed herself to be lost in the comfort of a marriage to someone who needed to take care of her. The object of the Libra karmic lesson is to be as self-sufficient as possible within a relationship. You must learn to take full responsibility for yourself and be able to take care of yourself as though you were alone. This means that you must be able to earn your own money, balance your checking account, cook, sew, mow the lawn and repair your car. Obviously, no one is proficient in all these areas so it is your responsibility to know where to go and who to go to in order to take care of these everyday needs. If you are not handy with tools, you must join an organization like AAA and line up a good service station so that if your car breaks down you can have it taken care of without being totally dependent on your mate to help you out. You need not be a jack-of-all-trades but you must be independent enough to take care of yourself.

Your Libra need is to be with someone, to have someone significant in your life. The evolved Libra recognizes this aspect and chooses, with discrimination and not overwhelming need, to be with someone because they love them and want to be with them, not because they are afraid of being alone, or their fear of bumps in the night or inability to support themselves whether it be emotionally or materially. You must know within yourself that you choose to be with this person simply because you want to share your life with a significant other, not because you are afraid to be without someone.

We all marry for different reasons. An experienced astrologer can look at a person's chart to see their personal reasons for marrying. We may assume that the overwhelming reason in our society is love, but this is surely not the case. Many people marry because they have an oppressive family life and need to get away. In past years, a woman was discouraged from leaving her childhood family unless she was entering into a marriage. She was not encouraged to get her own apartment or travel or even develop a serious career. Many women of these generations and cultures will marry simply to get out of the house.

In modern times, the economy is restrictive of people leaving the nest and setting up their own independent lives so they tend to either stay home with Mom and Dad well into their 20s and 30s or until they marry (or live with) someone for financial reasons. Men and women who have experienced divorce or death of a spouse may wish to remarry for reasons of loneliness, finances, protection, or help with their children. If love happens to come along, that is great. Some people even delude themselves into thinking that this is love rather than admit their true motivations. As a Libra, you must be painfully honest with yourself concerning your motivations and actions within your relationships. Your karmic path will be testing you for this honesty throughout your life. You do not have to admit your truths to anyone but yourself, but you must never try to deceive yourself either. In other words, there will be no karmic judgment on you if you marry for security as long as you are honest with yourself concerning your motivations. And, while you are in this relationship, once you are aware that your motivation is based on your insecurity, it is important for you to begin to develop yourself to a higher state of security through your own resources rather than remaining dependent on your spouse. You will then be able to establish a mature, healthy bond which will be increasingly satisfying for the both of you.

The motivations behind, and the dynamics of, your closest relationships will show you which issues you need to be working on within yourself. They will appear to be issues between you and your significant other, but they will really be, very personally, your issues and indications of your Libra karmic directions.

One final suggestion, you must be cautious not to become so absorbed in finding a relationship that you become obsessed. This is usually an indication that you are afraid to address your own issues.

PEOPLE RUNNING TOWARD LOVE

When Louisa was 13 years old she could think of nothing but boys. She dressed in her twenty year old sister's clothes, wore make up and had her hair frosted in an attempt to look older. All she talked about was who she was dating, who she would date next and who she would marry. Her Libra goals were set firmly on finding a husband, marriage being the end purpose of her ambitions. Most of her fellow students found her shallow and boring with little to talk of beyond movie stars' weddings and who was dating whom.

Georgia is a forty year old Libra who was married and divorced young. She has spent the past twenty years as a single woman focused solely on remarriage. She spends her free time involved in activities that would attract men. She skis in the winter, bicycles in the summer and frequents singles bars on weekends. Georgia is an attractive woman who could easily find a man, but her anxiety and intensity frighten away any perspective men. She appears to them as a desperate woman who cannot live without a man. Interestingly, it is because of this desperate need on her part to be within a relationship that she is alone. Her aura signals men to run for their lives but she cannot see that part of herself. She continues to look for a husband, while in reality, she becomes more and more alone.

Ralph has been unhappy in his marriage for many years. He loves his home, his security and the habits of marriage itself, but he does not love his wife. He had felt this way for many years but had not been willing to give up the comforts of marriage by leaving his wife. He eventually got involved with one of the secretaries in his office. She was divorced with two small children, had her own small house and most importantly, was lonely without a stable relationship in her life. They began seeing each other and eventually fell in love. Ralph left his wife, after his new relationship was well established, and immediately married his new love. There was no way Ralph could leave his first wife without having another woman in his life. It was necessary for him to maintain his Libra need for a steady relationship by sliding from one marriage directly into another.

Karmically, all of these Libras were in need of developing their independence and individuality before they were ready to experience a fulfilling relationship yet they were running headlong into love without first establishing their own awareness of self. As a Libra, sometimes time alone is your greatest gift.

THE SOCIALIZING LIBRA

Even as a youngster, socializing was important to you. Libras need to be liked at all ages and by all people. Birthday parties and celebrations are splendid opportunities for you to meet with old friends and nurture new acquaintances. Parties, entertainment, social gatherings are ideal situations for you to mingle and recharge your sociable temperaments.

Probably, the greatest insult to a Libra is to not be invited to a social event! Keeping this in mind, you must not allow yourself to fall into the abyss of social madness. As much as it is important for you to be liked and invited places, you must maintain your integrity to your true self. You must not allow yourself to be like that little doll in the back windows of cars who nods and smiles like a bouncing zombie. It is important for you to choose your friends wisely, people who share your opinions and outlook on life and, certainly, be careful never to compromise your standards or beliefs in order to be accepted by a group or individual person. As a Libra, you can expect to be tested in this area as part of your karmic journey on this earth.

You have the ability to be charming, attractive and socially acceptable just as you are, without having to conform or compromise yourself in any capacity. You need to be able to know without a doubt that people choose to be with you because they like you not because you have the ability to please them or because you are easy company. The more you grow, karmically, the more you mature, the easier this lesson will become for you. Being aware of this Libra lesson, you may now see other Libras in a different light as you eye them in socializing situations.

FOLLOW THE LEADER

A particular fraternity was the "in" group on campus and all
the members were fully aware of their social appeal. As the
year progressed, the frat members became increasingly
absorbed in themselves and soon began testing their power.
One by one, they began to break the school rules, and as
they got away with each infraction, they added another and
another until they felt omnipotent. They began to throw wild
parties, alcohol and drugs became staples in their cabinets.
Female students began to complain of sexual abuses in the
frat house, professors murmured under their breath as grade
averages slid down as quickly as the frat's popularity
increased. Several of the members were uneasy with this new
image and lifestyle but they were too weak to respond.

Andrew, a Libra, was one of those who was
becoming disenchanted with his fraternity. He wished his
group would tone down but instead he found them recklessly
pressing their power from one escapade to the next. His
Libra nature wanted to be a part of this popular fraternity
and he found it impossible to stand up against the men he
considered his brothers even though he was disliking them
more and was feeling little pleasure in their weekend funfests.

Andrew was now in the midst of his own personal
karmic test of being true to himself at the expense of his
popularity. His final test came during hell week of frat hazing,
which, being against school policy, had been banished for
years. The frat members were truly feeling their might on
campus at this point. Up until now, their simple hazing of
degradation and demoralization seemed harmless to Andrew,
and he went along with the group, feeling very much a part
of the social scene. His test came on the final night of hazing
when they forced one of the pledges to drink a bottle of rum
and then put him in a car trunk, drove him to a wooded area,
and left him to his own devices to get himself back. Now
Andrew voiced his objections, and to his amazement, many
other frat members joined with him fighting those who turned
out to be a minority within the fraternity. Consequently,
Andrew and the majority of the frat members called a halt to
any further hazing.

Andrew realized that he had taken a gamble on his
social stand but it had paid off. He was also aware that even

if he had not received the backing from his fellow members, he had to make his stand at that point regardless of its social consequences. He became a respected leader of his frat after that night but, more importantly, he became an evolved Libra in the lessons of social consciousness. Some people are much older before they are ready to accept this challenge. Some do not seem to learn it at all.

SMILE THOUGH YOUR HEART IS ACHING

Marlene was one of those Libras who was always smiling and pleasant, no matter what was going on in her life. She was a ray of sunshine in everyone's day so, naturally, she was extremely popular in her small Midwest community. If you asked Marlene how she was she always replied, *"Oh, wonderful!"* with a radiant smile. Now, we know nobody's life is *always* wonderful every day of the year. Still, Marlene industriously insisted that hers was perfectly marvelous, every minute of every day.

Truth was that Marlene's life was falling down all around her. Her husband's small health food business was failing rapidly. His creditors were losing patience, had long ago refused him credit, and his store would probably not be open much longer.

Her youngest son was developing a behavioral problem which she finally acknowledged when he tried to set the laundry room in their apartment complex on fire. He had become increasingly angry over the years but now his temper was out of control. She was no longer able to take him with her to her friends' homes or on social outings. She was embarrassed by his antisocial behavior.

Yet, on the verge of bankruptcy and feeling a failure as a mother, she continued to smile prettily for the camera of life in order to feel socially accepted. She was taught, by her parents, that little girls are to be pleasant and polite, a lesson easily assumed by the Libra child. Now, as an adult, she felt convinced that she would lose social standing and credibility if anyone was to know of the disasters in her life. By refusing to acknowledge the problems in her life, Marlene had cut herself off from any possible support systems. Her need to be liked and to have social approval could have brought disastrous results. It is a tremendous strain to always be pleasant, to continually wear a smile and be camera-ready for society. Marlene was forced to confront her issues when the school system contacted her concerning her son's antisocial behavior. They suggested counseling and support groups which helped her to break through her self-made barriers. In time she learned that it was alright to admit that her life was not always perfect. She accepted the difficulties in her family and saw herself as more *socially normal* rather than *socially friendly.*

Not all Libras are this fortunate. The noted poem by E.A. Robinson gives us an example of a Libra who was unable to satisfactorily confront his socializing karma.

RICHARD CORY

Whenever Richard Cory went down town,
We people on the pavement looked at him:
He was a gentleman from sole to crown,
Clean favored, and imperially slim.

And he was always quietly arrayed,
And he was always human when he talked;
But still he fluttered pulses when he said,
"Good-morning", and he glittered when he walked.

And he was rich - yes, richer than a king-
And admirably schooled in every grace:
In fine, we thought that he was everything
To make us wish that we were in his place.

So on we worked, and waited for the light,
And went without the meat, and cursed the bread;
And Richard Cory, one calm summer night,
Went home and put a bullet through his head.

To be an evolved Libra, you must be honest about your feelings with yourself and with others. You need to choose your friends with discrimination and not be adverse to changing your allegiances in friendships and groups as you change and grow.

To remain stagnate socially can be intolerable to an evolved Libra soul. As you grow and mature, you experience changes in your personal philosophies and social needs. It is imperative that you voice any discontent or disapproval you may feel within a relationship or group rather than acquiesce out of fear of being disliked or rejected. You need not be afraid of isolation or social ostracizing. You are a social being and will always be able to find like-minded people to befriend.

THE KARMIC RESPONSIBILITY OF EDUCATION

Libra is an air sign which means you are concerned with intellect, communication, and education. In keeping with the socializing aspect of your sign, you will naturally develop your communication talents. You enjoy talking, laughing, singing, dancing - all forms of communication. Your karmic lessons will come to you through your development of your mind. You are here to learn, to learn through formal schooling, socializing, and the world of literature. You are here to communicate, to pass knowledge from one source to another in the course of your social activities.

The Libra home needs to be filled with books, magazines and newspapers, the telephone ringing with call waiting and message machine cranking away. Yours is a cerebral world which ingests knowledge and then disseminates information throughout your environment. You are the farmer of knowledge in our society. You are able to seed our world with thoughts, create beautiful bouquets of wisdom and spread your seeds from one group to another through your charismatic appeal. Obviously, karma requires that you take full responsibility for the communication you sow. You will require a sound education, either formal or self-taught and an obligation to verify your facts before you pass them on to someone else. You must also develop a maturity which brings you from idle gossip to quality communication.

Many Libras, in their need to be sociable, love to talk for talk's sake. They can go on and on about their hair, children, favorite laundry detergent or beloved soap stars with no regard to the quality or depth of their conversation. To talk simply to be part of a social circle, is the primary tendency of Libra. If you find yourself doing this, as we all do at times, you karmically need to look at the amount or lack of amount of intellectual stimulation in your life. Your potentials are limitless, therefore it is important for you to reach for your highest goals on a mental level.

One suggestion is to surround yourself with people who you feel are more learned than yourself. People who you can learn from, people who can guide you toward your highest self. This does not suggest intellectual snobbishness as your goal. As a Libra, your karmic goal is to embrace the skills of communication and education and to use these talents to improve the world around you. You will accomplish this by continuously increasing your knowledge and then by sharing this learning with others. From its simplest to most complex form, this is what communication is all about.

In order to truly comprehend the intellectual aspect of a matter you must also be able to *feel* its significance. The Libra quality within you is readily capable of understanding on a mental level, therefore you need to train yourself to comprehend an issue on a feeling level as well. We have all heard of teachers who are experts in their fields but who are unable to successfully teach their expertise to their students. One reason may be that they are not attuned to the needs of their students. They are not able to *feel* their students fears or confusions. A successful teacher must not only know his subject but also be attuned to his student's needs.

You must be willing to learn in this lifetime but also be able to understand the emotional messages behind your learning. To be book-smart is not enough. You need to be able to relate to and apply your knowledge to everyday events.

BOOKS + EXPERIENCE = EXCELLENCE

Vivian was a typical Libra who loved to learn. She excelled in her undergraduate work at UCLA and decided to continue on with her Masters program majoring in psychology.   She found no difficulty maintaining a perfect 4.0 average and truly enjoyed her years of study. After graduation, she continued her education by increasing her accreditation acquirements and also pursued less formal avenues of study such as metaphysics and astrology, while partaking of countless seminars and workshops of "how-to" orientation. Finally her knowledge was all put into place.   She was able to put out her shingle, at long last, as a bonafide, certified psychotherapist.

The degrees on her wall verified her credibility as a psychotherapist. That, along with her reputation as a gifted public speaker, brought many new clients to her practice. As expected, Vivian had all the intellectual tools necessary from her studies, but it took years for her to be able to move away from the therapists clichés of *"I hear you"*, *"would you like to share that with me?"* and   *"I'm sure that really pushed your buttons"*. She was so skilled at intellectualizing her own feelings that she found it difficult to be able to *feel* her client's needs and expectations. It was only after Vivian began experiencing pain in her own life that she was able to understand the emotional needs of her clients.

She understood the passions of her clients after she herself became sexually obsessed with someone other than her husband. She was better able to help others with their feelings of guilt and grief as she watched her husband succumb slowly and steadily to pancreatic cancer and experienced his loss when he died. All of the textbook learning she had accumulated did not prepare her to be an effective counselor without the firsthand experience that life brought to her. Vivian had to be taught to feel through suffering pain. Her natural Libra instincts were to intellectualize the human condition.

The Libra mind is eager to learn. Karmically you must remember that not all lessons will come to you through books. Life will be your greatest teacher.

LIBRA MALE

The Libra male needs to be in a partnership. He may concentrate this energy on business and/or love partnerships. Let us look at the business partnership first. His natural instincts will be to join with one or two other people in his business dealings. Since this is a natural instinct, it is one which should be encouraged. The karmic lessons will come to him through his handling of these relationships. Anyone who has ever been involved in a partnership will tell you that it is as important and complex as a marriage. He must choose his partners with care and with an interest in establishing long-term commitments. As with a marriage, communication is fundamental. A Libra must have frequent business meetings with his associates to establish open relationships and clarity of thought. He will do best to state clearly his expectations, objectives and job roles within the partnership and then have frequent meetings to discuss any changes necessary in these areas along with any problems which may come up. The karmic lessons will come to the Libra male through his functioning within business partnerships rather than his decision of whether or not to enter into the partnership. Most Libra men I have seen in my practice have established long-term business relationships which have matured to the highest levels of commitment and loyalty. They may have gone through several alliances before they found that special one, but, once a successful partnership has been established, it becomes an integrated part of their lives which goes beyond the confines of business.

If this sounds like marriage, it is not far in its comparison. The Libra male feels just as strong a need to be in a committed personal relationship. Remember, this does not necessarily mean "marriage" in its legal sense. He needs to feel secure and comfortable within a long-term, committed relationship which may or may not require the sanction of state or church. Popularity is important, being liked, being loved, being with someone. If good judgment is used, a Libra male can form a successful long-term commitment filled with love, loyalty and happiness. The greatest stumbling block is when the need to be in a relationship becomes stronger than the need to discriminate. He must learn to take his time before entering into a "marriage" and be willing to develop his own independence rather than run from one relationship to the next. If he sees himself already looking for relationship #2 as relationship #1 begins to flounder, then he is running from being alone more than he is looking for love. He may need a good friend or loving family member to gently point this out to him. If he is unable to listen, you must recognize that this is his karmic lesson to learn and he may not be ready just now. We all take our time in confronting our issues but they will be presented to us continually until we are ready.

Sometimes the Libra male has difficulty letting go of one particular person even after the relationship has long passed. Even if he remarries he may still be comparing the new with the old. This becomes a significant problem if these emotions manifest themselves in obsessions and anger. If a Libra's self-identity is too closely entwined with the personality of someone else, it will be difficult for him to establish his own instincts for survival when that relationship dies. He then becomes angry and obsessed with that lost love, for he feels that a piece of himself has been taken away. This indicates one of the dangers the Libra experiences when he fails to maintain his own identity within a relationship. I have a client who moved immediately on to his next long term commitment after the end of his marriage but he never again trusted women or let go of his anger toward his ex-wife. Every connection in the Libra's life is here to teach him something about himself, therefore anger placed on someone else very often indicates an anger at oneself. This is not always an easy karmic lesson.

Libra is ruled by the planet Venus which brings a strong female vibration to the sign. This female energy manifests itself in the form of art, creativity and a sensitivity to the colors and textures of your environment. Many men feel more comfortable directing their Libra energies toward business rather than the arts or they combine business and art within their careers. It is important for the Libra male to be aware of his need to dress and groom himself well, and to create a pleasant atmosphere of color and design in his environment. Many Libra men are comfortable in careers or hobbies often associated with the more feminine of our society. Some traditional fields are hairdressers, interior decorators, artists and librarians. Society has often made Libra men ashamed of these important needs within their sign. We must remember that, in nature, it is the male of the species who most often looks the prettiest and struts his wares to attract the female. Yet, in many human cultures, it is considered vain or feminine for the male to follow this same custom.

The Libra male must learn to be comfortable within his own feminine side. He must develop a strong enough sense of his masculinity and self-identity that he is able to pay homage to his need for beauty and pleasant surroundings without feeling threatened. Karmically, he is here to love himself without depending upon the love of others and to be true to all aspects of himself without first gaining the approval of others. He then will develop his great talents for beauty, art, color and design which far exceed most other signs.

LIBRA FEMALE

The first and foremost message to the Libra female is not to marry or commit yourself to a relationship too early in life although the pressures of society are often great in this direction. The Libra female is sure to hear: *"You're such a pretty little girl, do you have a boyfriend?"* and *"Now that you're eighteen, you must be ready to get married."* and *"Don't worry that your marriage didn't work, an outgoing woman like you will meet someone else right away."* Society's pressures are strong for the female Libra to settle down and commit herself to a relationship right away. Some might say that these pressures are true for every female, but we must remember that the tendency of the Libra is to rush too quickly into love for the sake of being with someone which can be fueled by society's expectations.

Once in a relationship, it is imperative for the Libra female to establish and maintain her own identity and independence. She must be especially cautious not to be taken care of by her partner to the extent that she loses her feeling of self or her self-reliance. She must not be intimidated by activities usually classified within the male domain such as mechanics, banking and investing. She must be able to maintain her home and property, balance her checkbook and make viable decisions in the partnership's financial investments. She must be able to look herself in the mirror and assert that she is in this relationship or marriage because she loves her mate, not because she is afraid to, or unable to, be on her own. She must know that she chooses to "marry" because she wants to, not because of her fears or the pressures of family or society.

Many people think that Libras are unable to make decisions, especially female Libras. This can be a device to hold you in your place if you are not careful. Libra women are intelligent women capable of higher reasoning and advanced education. Why then would they be unable or incapable of decent decision making? This is a fallacy which can easily undermine the Libra's self-confidence. The Libra female must have confidence in her decision-making ability, which in fact is superior to most, in order to maintain her needed position of self-confidence. She must not allow others around her to use these points of sensitivity to keep her controlled or in a subservient position. The key to the Libra female's self-confidence in this area is education. She needs to educate herself through formal schooling, reading, and group activity in order to prove to herself her intellectual and decision making aptitudes.

The groups the Libra female is drawn to may establish her progress or lack of progress in her intellectual growth. Being homebound with young children, for example, may cause a halt in one's intellectual stimulation for a while. Many Libra women find themselves standing by their backyard fences talking about diapers and laundry detergents during this phase of their life. This can be particularly hard on them. Remember, the Libra needs to socialize, to fit in with the group. Therefore, talking with other women who also are homebound with young families is satisfying the Libra's need to fit in, and talking about detergents is far better than not talking with anyone at all! Still, the Libra woman must also be attuned to her desire to advance her learning and communication skills and may do well to consider planning a night or two a week out of the house meeting with people of different interests or taking a class in something totally unrelated to children, home, and family. Remember, the more you learn, the better you communicate. The better you communicate, the more diversity you bring into your life. Intellectual stimulation is an important karmic objective for you, and it will increase your awareness of yourself as an individual which, in turn, will help you to become an even better person for yourself and your loved ones.

LIBRA CHILDREN

As an infant, your Libra child is learning from your voice, your tone, your facial expressions, and body language. He is here to study life through all modes of communication which will begin with his interaction with his family. Never underestimate the extent to which your child understands and absorbs his surroundings. Knowing this, many parents expecting a Libra child will talk to him and play music in order to stimulate his mind even before his birth.

It is certainly important not to talk down to a Libra child. This does not imply that you should not bill and coo to him as an infant. These are soothing forms of communication which offer a loving expression, which he needs and enjoys. But, it is also important for you to be aware of the wonderful extent of his mental capabilities. Do not be afraid of using three and four syllable words to your child instead of limiting his vocabulary to child-like expressions. Your Libra child is bright and is willing and able to absorb not only words, but also the textures and hues of his environment. He is sensitive to sounds, sights and colors. Keep this in mind when you are decorating his room. You need to stay away from loud noises and wild designs. Peace and harmony are his friends rather than flamboyance and brattle.

Since your Libra child needs to learn the skills of communication, it would be advisable to enroll him in a preschool program as soon as possible. He needs to be able to play with friends and socialize with neighbors at an early age. An important lesson to teach him is to deal honestly with his feelings within relationships. He will be watching you closely to see how you deal with your socializing issues. If he hears you talking about how much you dislike Uncle Louie and then sees you smiling and friendly with Uncle Louie at the next dinner party, you have reinforced his tendency to be nice at all times in order to be liked and to keep the peace. We all know the complexities of social interaction are not easily comprehended by a child, but your Libra may be well ahead of his years in this area. Diplomacy will be the key to his success. Phoniness will be his downfall.

Do not ever forget the Libra child's birthday! Not only does he need recognition for his special day, he also needs a party, cake, hats and presents, the party being the most important ingredient. As he gets older, hold on to that telephone. Most Libras as teenagers seem to have a phone growing out of their ear. Certainly, you want to keep tabs on who he chooses as friends because friends will always have a strong influence on him throughout his life. You will have some say in this area, although your input may become limited as he grows older. To be overly controlling may pull him out of the necessary socializing experiences he needs yet you may have to assert yourself if you see him falling into the wrong crowd. One way to handle this is to encourage his friends to meet at your house, which will help you to maintain an awareness of the quality of his relationships and observe his skills of interacting with others. Then you have to learn the most difficult lesson of parenting...let him go. Do not restrict his social interactions with too many rules or with an overbearing spirit. He is here to socialize, so teach him manners, grace and ease and then let him make his own way in his relationships. Do not be too quick to blame other people around him for mishaps in his friendships, but be there to help him if he needs your support and advice.

Your Libra child has a special love of the fine arts, beauty, and the harmony of nature. He would enjoy music and art, having a say in the decorating of his room, wearing fine clothes, choosing his hair style and visiting art galleries and museums. Teach him to appreciate fine music and notable works of art. Do not think he is too young to understand. His Libra energy picks up on the quality of art and beauty at a very young age. If he shows talent in any of these areas, you might want to encourage him through classes or lessons in the area of his interest.

Some people have difficulty understanding the feminine directions of this sign when they have a male Libra child. They feel they would rather have their son playing ball than taking painting lessons. Your Libra son is able to find pleasure in both. Try not to direct him away from his sensitive nature. This would only prove to teach him to hide a part of himself from you and others.

Allow communication to be open and forthright within your family unit while stressing the importance of learning, book reading, and schooling. Your Libra child will be advantaged if you include him in some of your adult conversations concerning politics, the arts, and personal relationships. You are his first teacher, but you are far from being his last. The most precious gift you can give him is the ability to maintain an open mind so he may include other views and philosophies beyond what he experiences with you. This will help to encourage his independence.

Your Libra child needs to be equipped to cope with life on his own before he will be able to establish a healthy long-term relationship or "marriage". You can help him by allowing him to be self-sufficient and independent from an early age. If he is overly dependent on you or if he witnesses a union based on dependency between his parents he will tend to mimic that pattern in his own adult relationships. He will be watching you and all adults to observe how you interact. He is able to easily pick up on the subtleties and nuances in relationships which he will easily incorporate into his own personality.

Always remember that your Libra child has chosen you as his parent because he is in need of the lessons you will bring him simply by being yourself. Be true to who you are and observant of his special Libra needs, and he will have all the tools he needs as an adult.

Many Libras are gifted children either in the arts, the world of academics or through their communication skills. Take pleasure in watching your little package open as he matures; he may very well hold a special gift within.

SCORPIO

October 23 - November 21

Female Energy

KARMIC LESSONS

♦ To deal with death and abandonment issues

♦ To be comfortable with deep emotions

♦ Sexuality and sexual experiences

♦ Integrity with other people's money

♦ The occult

PRIMARY SCORPIO

Scorpio is a sign which requires quiet and alone time. As a Scorpio, you are naturally a private person, but an excessive need for privacy which manifests itself in an overly withdrawn personality, may be indicative of a problem. Your thoughts may be intense and create a brooding character which isolates you from the mainstream of society. This is an indication of a personality disorder which may be your Scorpian primary energy manifesting its force.

This intense personality may be coupled with extreme compulsive behavior traits which require a strong need to be in control at all times. All Scorpios need to feel in control of their lives. This is why you are secretive by nature and keep your vulnerabilities to yourself. If you have been abused or betrayed by others you may attempt to protect yourself from further hurt by creating controlling and compulsive behavior patterns. The more you need to maintain control of your life and your destiny, the more likely was the experience of abuse or mistrust in your early life. An excess of compulsive behavior will handicap your advancement to a more evolved level of your Scorpio energy.

The Scorpio who is sexually overactive and can perhaps be classified as sexually addicted, is one who is vibrating on his primary level. Much will be learned by this soul through her sexual experiences but moderation and responsibility for her actions needs to be the ultimate goal. Sometimes the primary Scorpio will act out in rages of jealousy and vengefulness when her intense emotions and sexual energy is wounded. This primary reaction must be examined closely in order to foster emotional growth and positive relationships.

Since this is a psychic sign, the Scorpio who is lost in her primary energy may tend to misuse her power of the occult. The Scorpio who threatens people with black magic or uses the occult to inflict physical, emotional, or monetary harm on another, is certainly abusing her special powers.

It is easy to find reasons for the Scorpio who has difficulty rising above her primary level. This is a complex sign and needs to be explained carefully in this chapter. Although her growth to her evolved status is difficult, it is still necessary and expected of her by the universe.

EVOLVED SCORPIO

The evolved Scorpio still requires her quiet time and privacy, but is able to use this time to look into herself and discover her inner truths. If you are an evolved Scorpio, you are interested in exploring your subconscious through all forms of introspection including psychology. You may even choose to study and work within this field.

An evolved Scorpio is also filled with intense emotions but is able to let go of past hurts and emotional injuries. She removes herself from the hindrances of jealousy and revenge and allows herself to forgive and forget. This does not indicate that she is denying her feelings but that she has chosen to look at them with introspection and then cast them away rather than allow them to fester within her soul. An evolved Scorpio will still experience death and abandonment in her life but will not fear these losses in future relationships. She is accepting of death and sees it as a natural transformation of a life force.

The evolved Scorpio has a healthy sex drive and uses this force to express the fullest extent of her intense feelings. She usually takes care to establish a wholesome sexual pattern in her relationships which add strength and stability to them.

If she chooses to enter the field of the occult, she will do so with the utmost integrity and stability of purpose. Many of the leaders in the field of metaphysics and the occult are evolved Scorpios who are channeling their innate psychic powers toward the betterment of mankind. They are not concerned with making a lot of money at someone else's expense. Their purposes are far more concerned with improving other peoples' lives and bringing others closer to their own inner truths.

The evolved Scorpio can play a powerful role in mankind's evolution and will do so with little need for praise or recognition. The negative reputation of the Scorpio comes from those who vibrate on their primary level and, often, the evolved Scorpio moves through life unnoticed.

REMEMBER, NO ONE IS TOTALLY PRIMARY OR EVOLVED. OUR KARMIC LESSONS ARE BEST LEARNED WHEN WE ARE DEALING WITH BOTH OF THESE ENERGIES.

BAD PRESS OF THE SCORPIO

Scorpio is one of the most difficult signs to interpret due to the complex emotional issues surrounding it even before the person's birth. This is also a sign which is widely misunderstood by the general population. In a sense, it has been subjected to *bad press*. When dating or making the rounds of the single bars, Scorpios can often receive negative reactions when they expose their signs to perspective amours.

One of my students once gave me a cartoon of an employment manager behind his desk, interviewing a perspective employee. The caption read: *"Oh, we certainly don't discriminate against race, nationality, or sexual orientation...we just don't hire Scorpios."* This chapter is devoted to explaining to you the motivations behind these stigmas and the true, complex issues that you Scorpios are working on in this lifetime. You are courageous, strong souls sailing upon a lifetime of emotional complexity with deep-seated issues of love, sex and abandonment.

DEATH AND ABANDONMENT

Scorpio, in astrological study, is the natural ruler of the eighth house of the chart. This eighth house deals with death; not your death, but the concept of death as it relates to all living matter. We all must come to terms with our own mortality. But first we must come to an understanding of the mortality of others around us; here today, gone tomorrow. The loss, sorrow, and questions of eternity are thoughts for all humans to ponder. Yet you, as a Scorpio, have a special interest in this area.

Quite often, the Scorpio's mother has experienced a loss of someone either directly before her pregnancy or during it. She is immersed in a feeling of loss and abandonment. You see, whenever we experience the loss of a loved one we are likely to feel abandoned. Even if that special someone happened to die, which we know logically was not a conscious desire on their part to leave us, we still experience a loss akin to abandonment. All logic dissipates in a wash of our emotions.

The mother of the Scorpio is in the process of experiencing abandonment issues while she is pregnant. It is interesting to note that sometimes there are additional issues going on for this Scorpio's mother. The timing of the pregnancy may not be convenient. Money may be tight, perhaps she's not married, she's pregnant with her twelfth child, her husband is out of work. She is unhappy.

As she travels through this pregnancy, she alternates between her feelings of frustration and her joy of perspective motherhood. She cries for help, *"Why am I pregnant now? The timing is terrible! I don't want this baby, not now!"* And then she feels guilty, *"No, I didn't mean that. Oh, please, let everything be all right with this baby. I really do want it!"* Back to, *"Why am I pregnant now? I can't handle this now."*

There you are, this Scorpio soul, in embryo, feeling the loss, mourning, fear, confusion of your mother and you pick up on these emotions. You, even before birth, start to wonder if you are really wanted. The abandonment your mother is experiencing starts to be imprinted on your soul. Your mother may be feeling abandoned by a person, by fate or by her necessary support systems. Yours is such a psychically sensitive sign, that you easily absorb these fears and emotions. Are you wanted? Will you be abandoned? A Scorpio becomes fearful of loss almost immediately upon entering this world.

Not all mothers of Scorpios can relate immediately to this conflict they were experiencing during their pregnancy, some do not allow themselves to admit these emotions to their children. Allow room for forgetfulness on her part while also realizing that your mother may very well be a part of that small minority who cannot identify with such conflicts. Yours may very well have been a totally blissful event in your parents lives. But for the majority of Scorpios this was not the case, and it is important to realize that there is a powerful karmic purpose behind the intense emotions surrounding your birth.

Let us start with the karmic lesson of death as a form of abandonment. All Scorpios will experience a variety of deaths around them. Sometimes these deaths come early in your life. For others, the deaths have bizarre circumstances or powerful impacts. You are here to learn to live with death and, eventually, learn not to fear death but to view it as a transitional concept and a continuation of life from one form to another. Most Scorpios are not afraid of their own deaths nor are they afraid to be in the same room with death. They work comfortably in jobs which involve death such as medical, hospice, funeral work, life insurance, seances. Their lives are touched by a death which usually triggers their abandonment issues.

SUDDEN LOSS

Claire was only ten years old when her father was killed by a drunk motorist. It was a sunny Saturday afternoon. Her father was mowing the front lawn and had a craving for pink lemonade. He got in his car, went to the local supermarket and never came back. A drunk driver ran a stop sign, stuck his car and killed him immediately. Claire never saw her father again. She kept waiting for him to walk in their front door with a can of frozen pink lemonade. Everyone explained to her that he had been killed and that he'd never be back, that she'd never see him again. She, logically, knew that her father's death was not his fault; she knew, intellectually, that he had not meant to leave her. Still, she felt abandoned by him, and would continue to fear abandonment when the people she loved were out of her sight.

DEPRIVATION

Jimmy lived an isolated, loveless life with his parents. His father was a migrant worker who was now picking apples in the mountain orchards of New Paltz, New York. His mother was an Irish immigrant who spent most of her days pining for her early life in her homeland. The only attention and love he received was from his grandmother who would lift him up to her ample lap and rock him against her cushioned breast while she softly told him what a grand boy she thought he was and what a special man she knew he would be. Grandma gave Jimmy the nurturing he needed to survive and, when she died, he felt as though his own breath had been taken from him. He felt all the abandonment he had always felt at the lack of love his parents provided. He felt frightened, on the edge of death himself. Perhaps it was safer to dwell in relationships of isolation than suffer the pain of losing such a special love. Yet, how could he have survived without Grandma's love? How would he survive now even though he was no longer a little boy? Which example of love should he mimic in his adult relationships?

DOUBLE LOSS

Annie's mother was taken to the hospital in the middle of the night. During the next few days, her father and uncles spoke only in hushed words, something about her kidneys not functioning properly. But Annie was 16 years old and this was the 1960s. Parents don't die. They go to the hospital, get fixed up and come back home. So she went about her business complaining about her schoolwork, sneaking out to see her friends after lights-out, wondering when the boy of her dreams would realize she existed, until one day her father came home to tell her that her mother had died. Annie couldn't, no wouldn't, believe it. She went through the funeral as though it wasn't real. Surely her mother would come back. Annie was only 16 years old. Mothers weren't supposed to die yet.

Then Annie watched her father grieve and become a broken man. He leaned on her to keep him fed and care for their home. The depth of his sorrow kept Annie from feeling her own loss. Six weeks after her mother's death, Annie heard her father calling her from his bedroom. She rushed in to find him in the midst of a massive heart attack. Within minutes, her father died in her arms. Annie was 16 years old, it was the middle of the 1960s and she was alone. Within six weeks her whole life had been changed. How could they both have abandoned her like that? What was to become of her?

Fortunately, not all Scorpios have to experience such dramatic and emotionally costly losses in their lives. But, those Scorpios who do experience these emotional losses, are forced to deal with their fear of abandonment. If the Scorpio child feels the mother's ambiguous attitudes toward the pregnancy, she will enter this life wondering if she is truly wanted. Will her mother eventually decide to leave? Does she belong to this family? Many Scorpio children fill the homes of foster parents and orphanages.

It is with equal emotional depth that the Scorpio child who has lost a significant loved one early in life becomes distrustful of future relationships.

ABANDONMENT THROUGH
DIVORCE OR BREAK-UP

A significant number of Scorpios lose loved ones through a rift in a relationship. While it is true that people of all signs are likely to experience these kinds of losses, the karmic lessons involving abandonment are far stronger for Scorpios. They must confront these challenges and come to terms with their psychological ramifications.

Tim's mother was fourteen years old when he was born. He never knew his father. All he got out of his uncle one time was that his father belonged to a street gang, was young and showed no interest in his son. He refused to offer any financial support nor did he show any desire to get to know Tim. Tim was abandoned before birth by his father. No matter how much love and attention he received from his mother and maternal family, his emotions were consumed with his anger and betrayal of his father.

Sometimes the Scorpio's abandonment comes later in life:

Alice fell in love and married her childhood sweetheart. They were consumed with each others' love through their four years of high school and married the year after graduation. They loved hard, they laughed hard, they worked hard. Intensity was the byword of their love.

Ten years into the marriage, Paul fell out of love with Alice and filed for a divorce. It happens every day. Statistics bear the numbers. To Paul, it was a time to move on. To Alice, this was the ultimate abandonment. She had put all of herself into this marriage. She now was left with mistrust, loss and her intense anger.

Scorpios tend to react to abandonment by displaying a need to control. In fact, control issues are as equally prevalent in the Scorpio's personality as their abandonment issues. Very often, there can be seen a connection between both experiences.

ABANDONMENT AND CONTROL

Let's start with our initial example of the perspective mother who is pregnant with a Scorpio child. She's vacillating between wanting this child, and feeling overwhelmed by her own troubles. She rages with guilt and frustration for nine months. When that Scorpio child is born, this mother may now become the "best" little mother in the world. She'll tell everyone how excited she is about this baby. Why, isn't he the best or cutest or smartest baby you ever saw? And she's going to be the best parent anyone's ever known. She can become doting, smothering, overly protective. God forbid something ever happened to this child when she had once wished she hadn't been pregnant with him. She could never live with the guilt.

With this attitude, a parent can easily become overly protective and controlling. The motivation behind this intense caring may certainly be guilt but the message to the Scorpio child is oppression.

This duality of psychological dynamics can work both ways. If a child has experienced abandonment, she may then become overly possessive of a parent. She may fear the loss of her parent through death, divorce or the rivalry of another sibling or stepparent. The Scorpio energy in a relationship can create an emotionally intense struggle of power, control, manipulation and symbiosis which mimics love but is, in reality, based on fear of loss. The karmic lesson of the Scorpio is to come to terms with her fear of abandonment and to be able to identify, and eventually, discard her complex defense mechanisms. These patterns quite often begin in childhood although they may become evident through adult experiences.

IS LOVE FOREVER?

Lois's Scorpio needs in love were comfortably fulfilled in her marriage to Bill. They did everything together, which was natural since they had the same interests. In fact, they experienced everything with great intensity. Their marriage was fully culminated when they found out that Lois was pregnant for, as close as their relationship was, they were thrilled to add children to their union.

During the middle of Lois's pregnancy, her parents finally, yet suddenly divorced. Their marriage was always "on the rocks". As a little girl, Lois used to listen to their heated arguments with childlike fear of her world being turned upside down if Daddy should ever truly leave as he so often threatened. But they had made it through all those turbulent years. They were older now. Why were they divorcing? Her fears were no less now that she was an adult and mother-to-be herself. To compound matters, her father moved to California, a thousand miles away from her. Her worse fears came true, her father left her, just as her mother had always said he would. He abandoned them both.

Lois mourned the loss of her childhood. She retreated into her own childlike needs which distracted her attention from her pregnancy. How could the happiest time of her life be so completely shattered? This is not the way she had pictured her first pregnancy. Why was she pregnant now?

Lois and Bill's daughter, Rebecca, was born two days before Lois' birthday and the Scorpio energy increased within the family. Nine years later, Bill was killed in a motorcycle accident. Once again, Lois was abandoned by an important man in her life. This time, Lois and Rebecca experienced the loss together. They became inseparable; living in fear that something would happen to one of them. They each inflamed the other's fear of loss and abandonment until an unhealthy, totally symbiotic relationship developed between them. To the outside world, theirs may have seemed to be an extraordinarily close, loving mother-daughter relationship. In reality it was one fraught with fear, laden with control, and embedded with guilt.

The psychological issues which emerge from relationships like these may take years of introspection. Uncovering an acute desire for healthy future relationships, initiates the healing process.

Both these women had difficulty dating. They were unable to go out on a date in order to have a good time. Each relationship had to have meaning and long-term potential for them. They were so leery of loss that dating a man for one or two nights and then moving on to another man was too much like a break-up or abandonment to them. They called themselves *one-man-women* while, in reality, they were women who lived in fear of loss.

This is one of the reasons Scorpios have gotten their bad name. The Scorpio loves hard and totally. When they fall in love they do so with tremendous intensity and control. Therefore, if the person of their desires decides to call off the relationship, the Scorpio screams foul. *"That's not in the rules. We said we loved each other. Why, that means forever...that's what commitment and love is all about."* The Scorpio has trouble letting go and moving on.

Karmically, if you were born under the sign of Scorpio, your life lesson is to identify your needs within a relationship as they pertain to your childhood and past experiences. You need to become in tune with your fears of loss, abandonment and your issues of control. The negative Scorpio action is to hold on through jealousy, possessiveness or vindictive behavior. This is where most of the "bad press" of Scorpio was initiated. The Scorpio who rages with anger, vindictiveness, and possessiveness over the loss of a relationship is a Scorpio who is reacting blindly to her fear of loss and abandonment. She can cause great misery to herself and those she loves by destroying that which she cannot have for herself. This becomes a karmic test of the use of power and acceptance of her loss of power.

KARMIC USE OF POWER AND CONTROL

Power becomes a part of the Scorpio's life usually as early as childhood. Your karmic responsibility is to identify the issues of power and control in your life and then come to terms with your use of these very same powers in your adulthood.

Most Scorpios experience a relationship in their early life with someone who is extremely controlling. They may witness a battle of wills between their parents, or between their mother and her mother or, perhaps, between siblings. The lines of battle are drawn early and clearly and the Scorpio learns how to play by these rules of power and control.

DEFINING FAMILY ROLES OF TWO SCORPIOS

Mary's mother, June, was obviously unhappy in her marriage to Mary's stepfather, Al who, over the years, had proven to be a dependable, loving parent. Mary felt secure in her relationship with Al, but, it was evident that he was not as successful in pleasing her mother.

Al was a hard worker whose long hours in the shop kept him from spending as much time at home as June would have liked. She nagged, filled her life with neediness, and feigned illness in order to win his attention. And there were times these ploys worked but, eventually, Al would return to the shop to put in even longer hours to make up for the time he had lost. After all, time was money. Al was secure in his role as wage earner and provider of his family. Each saw his role differently. June needed a husband with which to share her time, to fill her emotional needs. Al provided food and shelter as a witness of his love. The more he gave of his love, his way, the less June felt loved. This battle of control waged furiously within this marriage with Mary in the middle of these two people she loved. Eventually, June began looking toward her daughter, Mary, for the fulfillment of her neediness. The dynamics of a controlling, symbiotic relationship emerged. June became an overly protective parent. She hovered over Mary constantly watching, monitoring and orchestrating her every move. Mary was expected to fill in the gaps left by her mother's unfulfilled marriage. Mary became her constant companion. They went to the movies together. They ate dinner together. They shopped together. June always knew what was going on in Mary's school and was involved in the PTA, class projects, homework assignments and school trips. What appeared to be a loving, close relationships was truly an oppressive situation for Mary with far too much responsibility put on her to be her mother's companion, daughter, friend, and spouse.

As Mary grew older, she tried to break away, as all adolescents do, but was then controlled by her mother through her skilled use of guilt. *"Look at all I've done for you and now you no longer need me. You simply want to cast me aside like an old dog. Of course you want to see that movie with your friends, Dear. It's just that I was looking forward to seeing it too. Too bad all my friends have husbands who take them to the movies. I guess I'll watch the summer reruns tonight, alone."*

These dynamics continued to grow into increasingly complex issues which could only be sorted out with the help of a skilled professional therapist and many years of hard work for both women. Interestingly, the karmic lesson was brought to June through her relationship with her daughter rather than her husband, as would seem likely. Each relationship in our life brings with it a purpose and a karmic lesson.

We must listen to our soul's whispers to understand and learn from one another. The karmic lesson of the Scorpio is to remain aware of the use of control within relationships and to take responsibility for your emotional actions. What may appear to be a loving, close relationship may actually be emotionally unhealthy for all involved.

THE SCORPIO GUILT TRIP

The Scorpio child is raised on guilt. She experiences it in some form, either through her reaction in embryo to her mother's mixed feelings concerning her birth, or as a means to control the love and attention of family members or by observing the power of other people in her environment. The message of guilt is there and she absorbs this emotion easily.

If you are a Scorpio or if you are in a relationship with one, it is important for you to be fully aware of the use of guilt and its effect. I refer to Scorpio guilt as a way to control or manipulate someone by getting them by their emotional short-hairs. It can be a down and dirty technique used to manipulate and undermine another person's will. You must force yourself to be conscious of this dynamic within the relationship because it often is covered with the guise of devotion, friendship and love.

Because most Scorpios are raised with guilt around them, they become experts at inflicting guilt. They incorporate this trait so neatly into their personalities that they have difficulty seeing it for what it is. Remember, karmic growth comes only with your willingness to face yourself and dig beneath your psychological surface.

A formula to remember is:

GUILT = RESENTMENT = ANGER

Obviously, these emotions can be volatile in nature. They can undermine the healthiest of relationships. The following case is an exaggerated example of manipulation through guilt.

> Joey's Mom is sitting in the living room looking out the front window as he pops in his head and announces:
>
> *"I'm going to the movies with the guys, Mom. I'll see you later, okay?"*
>
> *"Oh....now? You're going out now?"* She responds in what Joey likes to call her "little-girl" voice.
>
> *"Yeah, it starts in ten minutes. Is that okay?"*

"Well......", she answers with a heavy pause, *"I was kind of hoping someone would be home tonight."*

"Why, Mom, is something wrong?"

"Well, I've been having some chest pain. But, you know, I'll be all right. You go and have a good time." Her voice suddenly taking on a very brave tone.

"Mom, if you're really sick, I'll stay home with you. I'm not going to leave you alone."

"No, no Joey. You're young. You should be out with your friends. Just do me a favor. Put the phone over here close to me before you leave. I'm sure I'll be able to dial 911 if the pain really gets bad. You be a good boy now, and go on and have a good time."

Mom has just given Joey a clear message that she wants him to stay home but she won't take the responsibility of asking him to keep her company. She probably is not experiencing any chest pain, but it was easier for her to say that then to ask him to spend the night with her. She used guilt to speak her needs. In the process, she left Joey with no safe decision. If he goes to the movies now he will be worried, it will ruin his evening, he will resent her actions, and he will be angry. If Joey stays home, he will experience these same emotions, and additionally, he will miss the movie.

Straight forward communication is a must for a relationship with a Scorpio.

An evolved Scorpio is often quiet and intense but they use this time in order to look within themselves and touch upon their own fears of loss and abandonment. They are able to acknowledge that these emotions may motivate them to control people through guilt in order to keep them within the relationship. These evolved Scorpios usually involve themselves in psychotherapy and subsequently may make fine psychotherapists.

An evolved Scorpio must be able to look at his past, take from these experiences what he needs in order to grow emotionally, and then be willing to let go of that past in order to move into his future. This process takes time and a willingness to look within. It is easy to blame others for our unhappiness; it is more difficult, yet far more rewarding, to forgive them.

SCORPIO SEXUALITY

I was at a restaurant the other day and could not help but overhear the conversation near me. Two women were having cocktails and, as they say, feeling no pain when a couple sat down at the table across from them. It became obvious that these women had only a passing acquaintance with the woman but were interested in flirting with her man. Some bantering began between them until eventually one of the martini ladies asked the gentleman his sign. Before his reply of Scorpio was fully out of his mouth, these women were up and over to him with lustful anticipation. His date did not stand a chance.

What is this magic of sexuality in the Scorpios? It seems like a fine trait. After all, wouldn't everyone like to be sexually attractive? Wouldn't we all like to be like honey to the bees? But let's get back to the title of the book, *Karma and Your Sun Sign,* and look at the karmic issues surrounding the Scorpio's sexuality.

We all need to deal with our sexuality. We must discover our individual sexual needs, learn to adapt to the rules, mores, and codes of conduct of our society. This is certainly a responsibility of all sun signs. Still, we must remember that sexuality is the karmic lesson of the Scorpio, therefore, a Scorpio's lessons may be more complex, difficult, or testing to their character.

Keep in mind that Scorpios have strong needs to be loved and possessed within a relationship. Their sexuality is a significantly important method used in the expression of their emotions. With feelings of love, they need to express to their partner with total completeness the depths of that love. So often they have been hurt by others which keeps them from expressing themselves verbally. They fear the vulnerability of their emotions. Their emotional internal signal says, *don't say it, show it.* All these deep feelings trigger the pleasure response of the Scorpio's sexuality. The sexual act is safe for them. It becomes the outlet for their feelings without having to say a word.

Obviously, if karma is playing a role in all this, the Scorpio must pay heed to his sexual conduct and the use of his sexual magnetism. While in a relationship, the Scorpio needs a healthy sexual involvement with his partner. If problems arise, they must be worked at or the relationship will become unbalanced and unsatisfying for the Scorpio. Nothing is too kinky or unconventional for a Scorpio, as long as both he and his partner agree on the rules.

Sex is power. Scorpios have power issues stemming from their early lives. Many will encounter their sexual karmic testing through their use, or misuse of sexual power.

A Scorpio woman, who knows that she can have all the partners she wants, must be aware of her responsibility toward these people's emotions as she skips through her relationships. Her anger toward her father, brother, or past lover may fuel her sexuality which then becomes a weapon she uses to hurt all lovers. When you see a Scorpio woman who sleeps with many partners but does not form any commitment to one, you may be watching an angry soul who feels she needs to punish others for the hurts brought upon her by a single experience in her past. This is a typical emotional action of a prostitute or even a sex addict.

Naturally, this repressed anger syndrome is not exclusive to Scorpio women. We see it as frighteningly strong in charts of men who also bed with many partners. This anger is also evident in sex addicts and rapists. The psychological connection of sex and repressed hurt is particularly strong in the Scorpios who use their sexual power to control, manipulate or misuse their partners. Of course, sexual misconduct is not exclusively a Scorpio phenomenon but it is the karmic responsibility of the Scorpio to face their difficulties honestly and to take the initiative in correcting any sexual misconducts.

It is important to note that *"sexual misconduct"* may not be defined by the rules of the governing forces or religious communities. Sexual misconduct is any act which creates a misuse of sexual power without the well-being and consideration of the partner's desires. This would also include the well-being and consideration of anyone else who may be witness to the sexual act.

Some Scorpios suffer sexual abuse through the sexual misconduct of adults, relatives, angry partners or rapists. This then becomes a karmic experience for them. It does not mean that they karmically *deserve* sexual mistreatment, as many people tend to justify difficult experiences. This kind of sexual experience places the Scorpio in a position where he or she must face all the Scorpian issues of power, abandonment and sexuality. They are forced to confront the power of someone else by being overpowered themselves. They feel abandoned by those around them who they feel should have been there to protect them. Sometimes, they feel abandoned by the system, the courts, who may not protect their rights by refusing to condemn the offender. These Scorpios must come to terms with their experiences not only on a physical and emotional level, but also on a soul level. These lessons are sometimes tragically difficult to understand and may require the Scorpio to seek the help of professionals.

Statistics show that people who have been abused may often become the abusers themselves. This would then become an additional karmic challenge for a Scorpio. There would be, not only, the moral issue involved pertaining to the laws of society, there would be an additional lesson of karmic consequences of any abusive actions taken by a Scorpio.

Most Scorpios have simpler, more traditional lessons coming to them through their sexuality. They must come to terms with their sexual actions, motivations, and consequences. If you are a Scorpio, you must take responsibility for your sexuality in this lifetime.

SCORPIO - THE SIGN OF WITCHES AND THE OCCULT

All the water signs, Cancer, Pisces, and Scorpio, have an exceptional psychic sensitivity and each has it's own direction within the psychic realm. Scorpios celebrate their birthday around our greatest satire of witchcraft and the occult, Halloween. It is not by coincidence that we associate Scorpios with death, cemeteries, goblins and witches brews.

Your Scorpio psychic sensitivities bring you in close contact with those souls who have already passed over. You make natural mediums which means you are able to play the middle role or medium connecting this world with the world of the dead. Your natural talents in this area may be yet another reason why people feel uncomfortable around Scorpios.

The karmic testing will come when you make conscious use of your psychic talents. You will need to confront the challenge of using your special abilities to either help or frighten people. Again, this becomes an issue of power, most specifically your use or misuse of your psychic power. Most Scorpios have mastered their talents in previous lifetimes and have been born into this lifetime with a psychic remembrance of much they have learned before. Powers of the occult come easily to them. The more closely they are attuned to the mysterious powers of the occult, the stronger their karmic lessons will be concerning their use of these powers. Psychic sensitivity must always be used in service to mankind and individuals, never as a tool of manipulation or control. A classic example of Scorpio power is hypnotism.

THE PSYCHIC THERAPIST

As a child, Roy had special abilities to sense people, situations and dangers. He had many dreams which warned him of impending accidents for his family, led him to lost objects, and connected him with relatives who had died even before he was born. He observed quickly the reactions of others when they learned of his powers. Some were frightened by him, others revered him. He learned that he could use this psychic energy to get what he wanted and to earn great sums of money.

As an adult, he decided to put his talents to use in a profession, but he wanted to work under a more socially acceptable and professional umbrella. After considerable searching, Roy decided that hypnotism would be the modality he would choose. He became a professional hypnotist and spent many years helping people break nasty habits of smoking and nail-biting. He then dabbled in past-life regression, bringing people back to their past-life experiences in order to help them better understand any psychological difficulties they may be experiencing in this life. While under hypnotism, his clients were totally dependent on him to guide them through their past-life experiences of emotional and physical pain. They needed him to guide them safely back to the reality of their present lives, to help them learn to deal more effectively with their lives now by understanding their past-lives.

Roy's feelings of power increased with the neediness and adoration of his clients until he slowly began to step over the parameters of his professional integrity. He started by sexually abusing a young beautiful secretary who was being treated for a sexual disorder, probably past-life initiated. At first, Roy convinced himself that he was helping her through the use of his hypnotism and sexual therapy. After this case, he again, sexually raped a housewife who needed his hypnotherapy to overcome her fear of flying. He could not justify his sexual relationship with her in terms of therapy but he was now overwhelmed by his power when beautiful women were "under his spell" of hypnotherapy. This sexual misconduct continued for many years until Roy was caught and prosecuted for his misuse of professional power. He had more than man's laws to deal with in this case. Roy also had been given a fine-tuned Scorpio power of delving into people's psyche and he had unquestionably abused this power. Karmically, Roy has to deal with the karmic consequences of his misuse of psychic Scorpio energy which may require far more difficult actions on his part than the punishment of man's legal institutions.

It is through the Scorpio misuse of their occult powers that so much of the evil reputation of Scorpio has developed, but I must note that most Scorpios I have known have offered an abundance of positive assistance to people in need. I have known Scorpio psychics who have devoted their entire lives to helping people come to terms with death, loss, fear of spirit world, and endless guidance with relationships.

I see our world and spirit world existing side by side with only a glasslike wall separating them. The light is on to us in our world simply because we are here and the room next door is impossible for us to see into because we are blinded by our own light which makes their world seem dark. The Scorpios very often sit quite closely to that glasslike wall. They are positioned so that they can use the soft glow of this world in order to gaze slightly into the darkness of the next room. There are certain spirits who are also hovering closely to the wall on their side hoping someone will look in on them. They see us easily because they are comfortable with the light of our world, having recently left it themselves. They see our suffering and mourning. They wish to convey messages to us, messages of their well-being and warning of dangers they see for us. These spirits dwell close to the glass wall because they are not ready to journey any further away from this world yet. They are adjusting to their new surroundings and need to still keep our world within their sight until they feel strong enough to continue their journey into the other world. Scorpios play a wonderful role in helping these spirits to convey their messages to us. The Scorpio is able to place his ear upon the wall and hear the whispers of the souls who have passed over. These whispers may come in dreams, seances or in waking states to those who have highly developed psychic energies. These Scorpios play an important role to all of us in the healing of psychic wounds, and our acceptance of loss through death. This can be the glory of the Scorpio on its highest level.

SCORPIO MALE

The sign of Scorpio is ruled by the planet Pluto. Certain positioning of Pluto in a chart can indicate an overbearing parent, usually a mother. With this consideration, the Scorpio male may begin his life with a complex mother/son relationship which, in turn, can create an emotional confusion in his adult, female relationships. Keep in mind that the Scorpio male, as with all Scorpios, is dealing with a fear of loss and abandonment issues in his early life. He looks toward his mother to take care of him and always be there for him yet, he may get more than he bargains for when his mother is overbearing, overly protective and creates a symbiotic neediness within him. He then finds himself in a power-play relationship from which it may require great effort on his part to break away with any kind of healthy relationship left to them. All too commonly, the Scorpio male's karmic lessons take him to a love/hate relationship with his mother which may become extended into his female relationships as an adult. He must learn to understand the complex psychological dynamics in his mother/son relationship, which will not be easy for him. He tends to hold his thoughts guardedly within which has become his learned pattern of protection. He packs his hurts, memories, and fears neatly into his subconscious where they color and taint his attitudes toward women, in general. If you have an emotional relationship with a Scorpio male, look at his relationship with his mother and you will be able to look into the mirror and see your future.

Men are taught to deal with power, to be the power brokers of our society. This seems an ideal compatibility with the Scorpio karmic lessons of power and control. As a male, the Scorpio has to watch out not to create an explosive combination of male and Scorpio power. He must keep in mind that it is not the gaining of power at issue, it is the use or misuse of power that tests his Scorpio's valor. In business dealings, his powerful determination and skill of strategy will be invaluable traits while his inclination toward stubbornness and revenge may eventually seal his downfall. The misuse of power will spell trouble for the Scorpio. He cannot avoid avenues of power and responsibility, these are areas where a Scorpio must dwell. His karmic lessons will come to him as he works through his power/control issues with people and business.

It is common to see Scorpio men in fields which require the handling of other people's money such as real estate, insurance, the stock market and the IRS. Once again, the integrity issue of use and misuse of power must be considered. He may feel important telling his friends how he invested a million dollars for a client today but he must take responsibility for his client's money as though it were his own. Much of the world's power involves money so, once again, the Scorpio will confront his major karmic issues if he works in a money field.

In terms of sexuality, we are all aware of the different standards for men and women. Men are expected to be free sexually and more active than women. Scorpio men have an exceptionally intense sexual appetite along with a karmic responsibility not to misuse their sexuality. Women are drawn to the sensuality of Scorpio men, their warmth and intense natures. Keep that in mind guys, women love water signs. They sense your emotional intensity and vulnerability. This means that your karmic testing will come to you through the way you handle your sexual relationships. You may be attracted to unusual sexual desires, some bizarre some unconventional from free love to homosexuality. The guidelines will be the same no matter what directions you choose, you must avoid sexual misconduct as defined earlier in the chapter, and must acknowledge your emotional involvement in relationships. Water signs are here to deal with their emotions and this is a part of your karma. A Scorpio man who is mature within his karmic journey is able to love one person with intensity and passion and not have a need to control or possess that person.

Another important facet of the Scorpio energy is the phenomenal psychic power of the sign. Society allows women to feel comfortable with their intuition but not men. As a Scorpio male, you must learn to develop your psychic energies and to use them in any and every aspect of your life. You walk with great spirit protection and guidance through this life and you are able to tap into this side of yourself whenever you wish. You will be able to effectively sense the energies of people around you which you can use to judge characters of others from work to personal relationships. What a wonderful asset for you. This is definitely coming from the feminine or passive side of your nature which society does not encourage in men, but you must realize that this is a legitimate part of your nature and it is to your advantage to develop and use your psychic powers. Learn to trust your emotional reactions and needs. Acknowledge your psychic link with the spirit world for they are clamoring to help you in your journey through life. As much as you may need time alone now and then, you are never alone completely. Your psychic connections are profound and can be used to aid yourself and to benefit others and situations around you. This is a powerful tool for you to use and develop even though it may mean having to lean toward your feminine energy. Do not be afraid.

If you have unresolved anger toward your mother or women in general, you may also dislike your own feminine side. This then becomes an issue for you to resolve. The benefits of healing this rift would be especially helpful to you as a Scorpio male.

SCORPIO FEMALE

Sometimes the most complex relationships can be found between mothers and daughters, and how especially true this is for Scorpio females! Your first role model as a little girl is your mother. You see her as representative of what you need to be like when you grow up. She shows you how to be a woman and how to interact with men. Unfortunately, most Scorpio females have complex emotional issues with their mothers which include abandonment, control, manipulation and guilt, among others. It is very easy for jealousy and competition to enter into these mother/daughter relationships even though they often wear the disguise of extreme closeness and compatibility. The issues within these relationships are complex and heavily cloaked in years of emotional complexities and often, secrets. It is important for you to look carefully at your relationship with your mother and examine what role you played in the dynamics between your mother and your father. Was there any jealousy? Did you feel manipulated by your mother? Do you call her because you feel guilty or because you want to talk to her?

It may take many years to cut the apron strings. Scorpio women who feel restricted in their mother/daughter relationships often flounder within these psychological boundaries until they are between 38 and 40 years of age. There is a great breaking-away planetary transit which occurs at that time in your life which will help you to assert your individuality and discover the woman within you apart from being your mother's daughter.

Your karmic lesson is to beware of perpetuating this cycle of control and manipulation in your relationships with men and especially with your own children. A natural barometer for you will be the emotion of guilt. When guilt rears it venomous head, you will know that you are facing an issue of great importance to you. Let your feelings of guilt lead you toward focusing on vital issues rather than immobilizing you as it did when you were a little girl.

In our society, men are conditioned to assume the control positions for all to see, whereas women are told to wield their power behind the throne. As much as our world is striving to break these role-playing patterns, the subconscious messages to this effect are still being taught to children. We have a long way to go before parental conditioning goes through all the necessary changes. As a Scorpio female, you could have watched your mother get what she wanted from your father through all sorts of devious, secretive means. The message of *"Don't tell your father"* is one you may have heard frequently while growing up. You were being taught that women stick together and men are the natural enemy. You could have also seen that the more power Mom gained, the more Dad seemed to need her. These are the subtle yet powerful messages the Scorpio female absorbs as a child.

All Scorpios are here to deal with their karmic lessons of power and control. Yours are not always upfront and easy to label but they are equally powerful and intense. It is important for you to identify your power issues as they relate exclusively to your upbringing. As a woman, you are most likely to seek counseling or psychotherapy in your quest for self-understanding and this would be an advantageous approach to fulfilling your karmic lessons. Do not be afraid of introspection. Above all, do not try to control or manipulate your therapist!

Your sexuality is an important issue because you are a Scorpio woman. You will learn early that you can use your sexual appeal to control, manipulate and get what you want out of life. Whenever there is a control issue in your life you must look at how you use that energy. Some men and women will be drawn to you because of your sexual aura and you will be able to sense this power at an early age. Some Scorpio woman spend a lifetime attracting men whether they remain single or choose marriage. Therefore, you must take responsibility for infidelities in your life. You may be attracted to pornography or prostitution, much as a man would be, which comes from your ability to detach your emotions from the sexual act. From another perspective though, when you are emotionally involved, you must have a healthy, strong sexual aspect within the relationship. Sex is important to you because it is an effective way for you to express your intense feelings. Often, sexual compatibility will have to be worked on by you and your partner. Simply because you need sexual satisfaction does not mean it will always be there for you. Karmically, you must take responsibility for your sexuality and the use of your powerful sexual energy. You must be cautious not to abuse your innate ability to attract a sexual partner. This lesson is usually a lot more fun to work on than your relationship with your mother!

SCORPIO CHILDREN

Your Scorpio child came into this life with many complex and intense issues on a karmic level. You will not be able to "save" her from these lessons, nor should you try. Your help to her will come through giving her freely of your love and nourishment without manipulation, control or guilt. Her relationships with her mother, grandmother and sisters will be significant. All Scorpio children, whether they be male or female, are here to absorb their early lessons from the women in their lives. This is a water sign which means it must deal with emotions. Their emotional lessons will come primarily through their mothers in their early lives since women traditionally hold the rights to emotions within the family unit.

Remember, your child entered into this world wondering if she was truly wanted at this time. She felt an ambivalence at the time of her birth and will be especially sensitive to the emotional reactions of those around her. As an infant, she will be able to feel your moods, she is attuned to your emotions even as you hold her in your arms. This sensitivity is effective no matter who is holding her, Mom, Dad, siblings or grandparents. If you are arguing, the Scorpio baby is attuned to your mood and will be ingesting your anger which will add to her insecurities.

She will not express her reaction by crying, she will hold it in, store it away in her subconscious. Scorpio children very seldom openly express their fears, they do not know how. They are like squirrels storing away their fears like nuts which they will feed upon in their later relationships. It takes great responsibility as a parent to raise a Scorpio child. You need to be especially aware of the psychological and emotional dynamics of your family unit. Be as clear as possible in your demands and expectations. Do not use guilt or tricks to gain control. Your Scorpio child will be adversely affected by subtle manipulation and positively affected by straight talk and open communication.

Your Scorpio child needs to have some control in her life. Allow her to make her own decisions with only your guidance, not your interference. Since she is here to learn about control issues, you will serve her well by encouraging her to take responsibility for someone or something other than herself such as younger siblings or a pet. You will want to encourage her sense of loyalty without promoting her sense of possessiveness.

As with all children born under water signs, your Scorpio child needs a great deal of loving, hugging and affection. She needs to be shown that she is wanted and that you will always be there for her without giving her a sense of being smothered by your love. She may encounter death, separation and abandonment early in life. You must not feel that you must protect her from these hurts. They are part of her karmic lessons. Just be aware of her need for special consideration during these times. Many Scorpios tend to retreat or withdraw during these emotional times, which may be healthy for her to a certain extent, but she also needs your comfort and reassurance that you are still there for her. Examples of difficult times would be the death of a loved one or pet, divorce or separation. If you have several children, you may find the Scorpio giving you the least difficulty at this time. It is natural for parents to attend to the children who are the most vocal or problematic and ignore those who are quietly dealing with the situation. Watch out for this with your Scorpio child. She may need your attention even if she does not ask for it. Change in itself is difficult for a Scorpio when it involves moving, changing schools or adding a new brother or sister into the family. She likes things to stay the same which is a rule the game of life does not always follow. Give her extra consideration during any changes or adjustments in her life.

She is possessive of people, pets and possessions. Keep this in mind when she suffers a loss in any of these areas. You can teach her about the guidelines of possessiveness by monitoring your own behavior in this area. If she sees excessive jealous or possessive behavior around her she will easy fall into this pattern in her own personality.

She will be particularly attuned to the psychological dynamics between your family members. A Scorpio is a naturally quiet observer of human relations who is absorbing the nuances and actions behind the words within your family relationships. Be especially cautious of involving her in power plays such as, "*don't tell your father what we're doing*". Or, "*go ahead and do it, I'll handle your father*".   She picks up easily on this kind of behavior and you may find her becoming very skilled at an early age in manipulating you, her parents.

Your Scorpio child feels and reacts strongly to the use of guilt so you want to pay particular attention to your misuse of this emotion in getting her to do what you want. The straightforward approach is always the healthiest for all of you in this family.

Your child is here to learn about her sexuality and take responsibility for her behavior. As a young child, it is important for you to protect her from any abuses sexually by other people. This can be done by maintaining an open channel of communication especially concerning sex. This openness will come in handy as she gets older. It will enable her to come to you and openly discuss her feelings in this area. Do not expect her to be very talkative though. Scorpio is a secretive sign and she will always guard her privacy.

She may become sexually active earlier than you would like, so do not put off that discussion of sex too long. She needs to know how to protect herself and be taught what her responsibilities are to her partners. Sex must not be a dirty word in this family.

As you can see, these are adult issues with which a Scorpio child must deal at a tender age. Help her through these lessons by preparing her and walking through with her rather than trying to shield her from them. If someone dies, talk to her about death, take her to the wake, answer her questions. Help her to be comfortable with death rather than view it as a secretive, mysterious issue. This attitude is important on your part concerning all areas of her learning. Your Scorpio child is wise karmically and will eventually have much to teach you. Listen to her wisdom as a child before she becomes clouded by the confusion of adults. She is not a fragile being at all. She is strong, one of the strongest signs in our Zodiac. You need not fear for her. You only need to love her as she needs to be loved, with touching, comforting and stability with strong acknowledgment of her need for alone time and privacy of her thoughts.

SAGITTARIUS

November 22 - December 21

Male Energy

KARMIC LESSONS

◆ Education/Teaching

◆ Spirituality

◆ Physical Fitness

Sagittarius is the most multifaceted of all the signs. There are so very many directions that you can go toward with this energy that you will need many lifetimes to experience and complete them all. This is a sign filled with excitement and adventure with both physical and intellectual stimulation that can have you hopping from one activity to another throughout your life. As with all the signs, Sagittarius has its own primary energy which you need to approach with caution but, in general, this is a sign of wonderful optimism and boundless opportunity.

PRIMARY SAGITTARIUS

Extremism is certainly one of the major problem areas of this sign. As with the other fire signs, (Aries and Leo), Sagittarius can give you a super abundance of enthusiasm and vibrancy which can plunge you into behavior traits of brashness, loudness, and overzealousness. You must remind yourself that you are not the only person on this earth with awarenesses, philosophical beliefs and superior intelligence. Your ideas may be truly wonderful but they may only be suitable for you, not everyone else within your reach. The overzealous preacher is not always admired by the masses. The pompous professor is not necessarily a worthy teacher. You will be vibrating on your primary level when you find yourself increasing the volume of your voice to a level beyond the sensitivities of the human ear. If you need to be boisterous in order to be listened to, you may need to tone down your teachings along with your voice.

As a Sagittarius, a naturally adventurous sign, you will enjoy many exciting adventures on this earth from conventional traveling to hang gliding. You have a powerful drive to explore the wonderment of this world which will lead you to many out-of-the-ordinary experiences. In a primary sense, this can put you off the conventional mill of life and onto a

by Joan Kilgen

ARIES	MARCH 21 - APRIL 19
TAURUS	APRIL 20 - MAY 20
GEMINI	MAY 21 - JUNE 20
CANCER	JUNE 21 - JULY 22
LEO	JULY 23 - AUGUST 22
VIRGO	AUGUST 23 - SEPTEMBER 22
LIBRA	SEPTEMBER 23 - OCTOBER22
SCORPIO	OCTOBER 23 - NOVEMBER 21
SAGITTARIUS	NOVEMBER 22 - DECEMBER22
CAPRICORN	DECEMBER 22 - JANUARY 19
AQUARIUS	JANUARY 20 - FEBRUARY 18
PISCES	FEBRUARY 19 - MARCH 20

Ask for *Karma and your Sun Sign* at your local book store. Available through New Leaf Distributors, 401 Thornton Road, Lithia Springs, Georgia 30057, 1-800-326-2665 and Sunrise Press, P. O. Box 271, Sayville, New York 11782, (516)567-9126.

Perfect as gifts for

- ◆ Birthdays
- ◆ Chanukah
- ◆ Anniversaries
- ◆ Christmas
- ◆ Graduation

road of carefree exploration, far away from everyday responsibilities. This choice is yours to make, but will cause trouble for your soul if you make promises of responsibility to others and then break those vows as you dash off to the next adventure.

EVOLVED SAGITTARIUS

Moderation is the key to your success. Self-awareness is the keyhole to your future. Keep aware of the multifaceted talents of your sign. Remember, you will have many lifetimes to work through each of your potentials as a Sagittarius. You do not have to do it all at once. Yours is a fun sign, so take pleasure in your potentials, enjoy the adventure this life will bring you while maintaining awareness of your karmic lessons.

As an evolved Sagittarian, you will educate yourself with as much of life's experiences as possible. You may decide to gain this education through the established schools and universities, or through reading, travel, communication with others, or by walking the streets of life. Your karmic involvement does not specify how you get this education, only that you find it in your own way. This makes you a natural teacher which, as an evolved Sagittarian, will prepare you to be an outstanding educator. Your wisdom and knowledge will become a great asset to us all.

An evolved Sagittarian is capable of vibrating on the highest of spiritual levels. Your sensitivity to the spiritual and philosophical realms of man's consciousness far surpasses mundane reasoning. You are capable of becoming a great leader in spiritual and intellectual realms. Your writings and teachings can be a powerful influence on many people.

The evolved Sagittarian is also attuned to the body which houses his mind and soul. You, as an evolved Sagittarian, will be aware of the importance of exercise, nutrition, and proper maintenance of your body. In fact, you may excel in sports or other activities you may chose in order to exercise your body.

Keep in mind that this is a sign of body, mind, and soul which, when vibrating on the evolved level, is capable of reaching great heights in any or all of these categories.

REMEMBER, NO ONE IS TOTALLY PRIMARY OR EVOLVED. OUR KARMIC LESSONS ARE BEST LEARNED WHEN WE ARE DEALING WITH BOTH OF THESE ENERGIES.

UNDERSTANDING THE SAGITTARIAN FIRE SIGN

In order to fully comprehend the power of this sign, you must acknowledge the omnipotent power of its element, fire. Sagittarius is the last of the fire signs, Aries and Leo preceding it. Even though they are each fire signs, they are dramatically different in their use of this powerful energy.

Picture yourself in front of a fireplace on a cold, New England night. You bring in the logs, arrange them in the hearth with a hardy layer of kindling, and light them in preparation for much needed warmth. As that fire blazes at its height of intensity you can feel its power, heat, and potential danger. This is descriptive of the Aries use of fire. As the fire becomes controlled and reaches its stage of steady glow to the point where you can relax and enjoy its comforting warmth, you are experiencing the fiery energy of Leo.

It is after the fire has burned away its anger and exhausted its fuel that you are left with the hot, gray, smoldering remains which continue to bring you warmth, although less intensely. It is at this stage of a fire that you will tend to be mesmerized by the wispy funnels of smoke rising from the ashes. Your body relaxes and you are able to reach a meditative, philosophical state of consciousness. It is at this stage that you enter into the Sagittarian power of fire. It is through this level of consciousness that you are able to cross over into the abstract realms of philosophy, religion, and education.

THE PERPETUAL STUDENT AND
THE ARDENT TEACHER

Sagittarius is the natural sign of the teacher. But, in order to teach, you first must become the student. Simply put, your karmic responsibility is to learn as much as you possibly can in this lifetime and then to teach what you have learned to others. In fact, many of you actually become teachers professionally. The sign opposite to Sagittarius is Gemini and you may find a piece of yourself in that sign as well. Gemini is the child where Sagittarius is the adult, yet one sign builds upon the other. Sag's usually feel much more mature and intelligent than their Gemini cousins, yet one is not far removed from the other.

The teaching profession is perfect for you since it allows you to incorporate many of the Sagittarian needs under one umbrella. In order to be an effective teacher you must also enjoy the process of learning. A successful teacher is one who is knowledgeable of his subject, willing to continue his education process by attending classes, workshops and other learning experiences throughout his life, and is able to adjust his curriculum at a moment's notice. All these qualities can be found in a mature, evolved Sagittarian teacher. In fact, the style of a Sagittarian's teaching may very well indicate the level of his evolvement.

THREE LEVELS OF TEACHERS

Raymond Forbes, Ph.D., was a man of diminutive stature, limited in physical dexterity and popularity with his peers during his early years. His greatest asset, by far, was his love of books and ability to learn. Naturally, Dr. Forbes strove for academic achievement as he went on to teach at a local university. He chose a college which was relatively new, thereby creating opportunity for himself to begin his career without the obstruction of an already entrenched faculty hierarchy.

Freshman students who walked into his required English 101 class were greeted with an opening line of: *"Fifty percent of you will fail this class. There will be no As given here. I don't believe any freshman is capable of earning anything above a B grade. If you wish to drop this class you may leave now, and I would advise most of you to take that action."* Naturally there was usually a mass exit at this point. The rest of the students who opted to stay were left to search their minds, was he a man who would strive to teach them with the same high quality he was demanding of them, or was he an egomaniac who would use his power to torture them through the semester? The ultimate power would lay in the hands of Dr. Forbes. He was, it turned out, an ambitious man who would demand excellence from his students in order to propel his career, and if students learned well in the meantime, so be it.

As if to solidify his reputation for future classes, the posted grades of English 101 read ten Fs, four Ds, seven Cs and one B+. Everyone was now duly warned of Dr. Forbes stance as a teacher.

Within ten years, Dr. Forbes was named chairman of the English Department. The University was maturing and gaining status within the academic community. The standards were considered high, the curriculum rugged and the English department in particular highly regarded. Dr. Forbes no longer teaches English 101. He does not need to teach a class he never liked in the first place. He still has no room for mediocrity found in freshman classes where students still function at a high school level. He considers himself a scholastic superior equipped solely to teach the advanced and gifted student. The fiery ego of his Sagittarian energy has propelled him into the highest levels of academe where he is now sheltered from the childhood taunts of inferiority complexes and insecurities.

Sagittarian karmic lessons are woven all through Dr. Forbes' academic career. He entered into this lifetime with an above-average Sagittarian intelligence which he choose to use, or misuse, in compensation for his lack of physical and social skills. He planned a career for himself which put him into a position of power as a teacher, power he always felt lacking in his youth. He allowed no one to question his teachings or authority; therefore, his karmic goal was to learn to question himself. This kind of soul-searching may not necessarily be visible to others although we may see products of its results through the change in his behavior. When a Sagittarian puts himself into a position of power which closes off the opinions or advice of others, it is then his responsibility to question whether his actions are intellectually or emotionally motivated. Remember, it may appear to be safe on the top but it can also be very lonely and may tend to isolate one from one's own truths.

The strong intellectual and learning prowess given to most Sagittarians is a gift which needs to be appreciated, nurtured and shared. We all have varied degrees of intellectual capacity, and Sagittarians are no exception in their diversity. We are all here on earth to learn as much as we possibly can, but Sagittarians are here to be karmically challenged in the handling of their teaching and learning responsibilities.

Sometimes intelligence can be used as a tool or even as a weapon to gain leverage over someone else. This intellectual bullying can be as damaging as physical bullying and carries with it an equal degree of consequence. Dr. Forbes was not only damaging the esteem and confidence of his students, he was also tarnishing his own potential for karmic growth. They say a mind is a terrible thing to waste, it is also a terrible thing to abuse. For, with the mind, there is always a symbiotic connection to a persons emotions and a portal into their spirit. To damage someone's mental confidence is to place in danger their self-esteem, future progress, and emotional potential. Just as Dr. Forbes was emotionally damaged by derogatory references to his physical prowess when he was young, his students may be equally damaged by his intellectual abuses to them in a classroom setting.

Power is available to the Sagittarian in his intellectual capacity. The karmic lesson will come through the use or misuse of this power.

At the opposite end of the spectrum of education is the Sagittarian teacher who is filled with the enthusiasm and adventure of the learning process and cannot wait to pass their love of learning on to their students. We have all had teachers like this in our lives. These are the ones we tend to remember with fondness. These are the teachers we credit with the successes in our lives. Remember, you do not need to be a schoolroom teacher in order to influence others with your teaching skills. All Sagittarians are teachers in some capacity. Yet, it is within the classroom setting that many of you choose to put to use your karmic skills.

Sue was as ardent student throughout her college experience. She was raised with a Jewish, middle income, suburban background which stressed the importance of education and its correlation with success. Is was natural for her Sagittarian love of learning and the nurturing of her upbringing to lead her to the teaching profession. After college, she found her first high school teaching job in a lower socioeconomic area of New York City. These children hardly knew how to read. Their minds were focused predominantly on survival on the streets, sex, and drugs. Unlike Sue's experience, they were not raised in homes which emphasized the value of education. School was something they had to put up with until they were of age to quit and get a job. Their futures never strayed further than the several blocks radius of their ghetto community or the prospect of immediate money. They had not been taught, like Sue, that education would buy them a better future, that education could purchase them a ticket out of the ghetto. School was more of a prison to them; time they had to put in until they could get out.

All Sue's enthusiasm as a first-year teacher and her love of learning put together could not break through their intellectual lethargy. She knew some of them were gifted, she saw that most of them were capable of learning way beyond their own expectations, but she seemed to be unable to capture their curiosity or arouse their interest in learning. Still, Sue put her time in, she filled the day with stimulating class plans, she kept teaching and slowly she began to gain their trust.

One morning her class came in upset about a killing during the night just outside of their school. They were unable to get themselves into the lesson she had chosen to teach, so Sue decided to drop her plans for the day. She had them put their desks into a circle and let them talk out their feelings about the shooting. Soon their conversation became animated and went from the shooting to neighborhood events, to politics, to their feelings of despair. Sue listened and offered only guidance in keeping the discussion orderly. Soon Sue realized she was being taught that day. She learned to listen to their needs. She learned to direct her teaching methods toward their backgrounds and to encourage them according to their needs. This circle discussion became a weekly part of their schedule and preplanned lessons were often thrown out in order to address current events or the student's specific needs at the time.

Through the years, Sue became more and more effective in her teaching methods. By meeting her students halfway, she became successful in teaching them a fundamental love of learning. Many of her students found she was right when she promised them that education could open many doors for their future. Here was a Sagittarian teacher who helped many of her students leave the ghetto through the power of higher education, yet she would never leave herself. Sue still teaches high school English in the same school she started in twenty-five years ago. Sometimes she says that she feels like she's bailing out a sinking boat with a Dixie cup but she knows this is where she belongs. Every child whose mind she touches is a success to her. She is an idealistic Sagittarian with her feet firmly planted in the harsh realities of life.

Many people think of Sagittarians as airheads whose minds are filled with facts but who have difficulty placing their intellectualizing capacity toward a tangible use. Sue was a Sagittarian teacher who found it easy to relate the philosophy of education to the practicality of every day life. We can all identify with Sue, we need not be teachers by profession. Please keep in mind that as a Sagittarian you are naturally a teacher. You do not have to have this label printed across a pay stub. As a Sagittarian you will naturally find yourself in teaching positions throughout your life. You also have the ability to take what you have learned and use it to benefit others simply by sharing your knowledge and experience. Sue shows us the example of sharing with love and joy to help others benefit themselves through advancement.

As I have journeyed through my own studies of astrology, I have come across other astrology teachers who had wonderful knowledge to share, and were more than willing to do so, as long as they had a paying student. But they had limits to how much they were willing to give if they saw that a student may be close to becoming a rival astrologer. Soon, the teaching ended and the doors of communication closed. Teaching was powerful to them when they had the superiority of knowledge, and threatening to them when the student came close to equaling them.

Whether it be in the world of the abstract or the material world of business, teaching can be a tool with many edges and several uses. As a Sagittarian, you must always be attuned to the motivations behind your use of the power of knowledge. It may help to remember that your mind will never be emptied of its contents no matter how much of it you give out to others. As you teach, a piece of you becomes a part of someone else's consciousness which, in turn, continues to be shared with countless others. Therefore, your mind becomes your immortality, the quality of your giving becomes your legacy, your thoughts become tangible. An idea may be sparked in your mind. You may choose possessively to leave it there or you may decide to share it with others, the choice is yours. Your idea may die with you or it may pass from mind to mind until someone puts their mind to work on it and puts your idea into reality. The idealistic Sagittarian teacher is one who is not dictatorial or possessive of their knowledge but one who enjoys the spark of intelligence and the sharing of information in order to help others.

Another Sagittarian teacher is the one who learns his ABCs through life's experiences and chooses to pass on those lessons to his students. This kind of teacher must always keep in mind that what may feel right to him may not be appropriate to the needs of his students. With that awareness in mind, he is able to give his students the invaluable gift of learning the lessons that life has to offer through everyday experiences. These teachers seem to defy the traditional rules of teaching, they follow the lead of their instincts and, like the other two Sagittarian examples of teachers, have a love of learning which they pass on to others.

Carlo could not remember when he first became addicted to heroin. The closest he could figure was when he was about ten years of age. Everyone in his neighborhood took drugs. It was as natural a stage of development to them as joining intramural sports was to his suburban peers living twenty miles south of his inner city. As natural as it was to take drugs, was dealing drugs and stealing money for more drugs. By seventeen years of age, Carlo was arrested for the sixth time and sentenced to five years in an upstate prison.

What to do with all this time on his hands! Taking the natural Sagittarian route, Carlo directed himself to the prison library and found himself reading everything from dime store novels to the classics. He also spent a lot of time watching TV and joining any and every kind of group discussion made available to him. As time went on, he realized he had something to sell now, his experience as a criminal. He put together a talk on what it was like to grow up in his neighborhood, and he, along with a group of his fellow inmates, petitioned the warden to allow them to give their talks to kids who might be looking to get themselves into trouble just as they had. Their lectures became famous. Students were bused to the prison to hear the horror stories of Carlo and the other inmates and of what could happen to them if they wound up in prison. Prison life was detailed to the point of horror, with no exaggeration, in order to teach these youngsters the facts of life according to their upbringing and environment.

He also put together a curriculum on how to protect your house from burglary. He found himself on national TV talkshows telling people of the methods which he used to rob them and how they could best safeguard themselves against other criminals like himself.

Was Carlo a reformed criminal who was trying to right his wrongs in life? We don't know. He was certainly a confined Sagittarian who needed to share his education with others. Life and drugs had been his educators, the slums had been his college, and so he choose to teach what he knew. Carlo displayed a strong Sagittarian need to fulfill his karmic destiny of teaching what he had learned. Perhaps, as with all teachers, Carlo also learned more than he taught.

To all Sagittarians on their karmic quest for knowledge, comes the awareness that you always learn more as you teach others. And so, whether you are a teacher or a student, you will always be the recipient of learning. This is, by far, the strongest karmic advantage of the Sagittarian. In the evolved stage, you will always be actively educating yourself through compulsory education, the accumulation of university degrees or self-chosen education. The more you educate yourself the more you have to give out to others in the form of teaching. Remember, this teaching can be in the form of salaried employment with teacher written across your paystub, or through your everyday experiences of passing information on to others. Your university of learning may be a formal school of study with semiannual tuition requirements, or the school of life found anywhere from close to home to far away in distant lands.

THE TRAVELING SAGITTARIAN

Travel is an essential need of all Sagittarians, which fits wonderfully within the yearly schedules of American teachers. Notice that the same people who love to travel also choose the teaching profession with all those lovely holidays designed perfectly for world travel. An evolved Sagittarian sees travel as another educational experience for karmic growth and evolvement.

Usually when we think about our karmic lessons in life, we associate them with struggle and difficult challenges. So, how can your karmic lessons be associated with world cruises and weekend getaways? As a Sagittarian, you will play the role of the liaison between different nations and various peoples. We are all here on the earth, together, yet with many differences and it will be your karmic role to blend the common seeds of differing cultures. As you travel, you learn, and as you learn, you bring your knowledge back home to others. Most Sagittarians have a love of foreign languages. They bring the appreciation of foreign art and culture into their lives and thereby into the lives of those around them. It is not at all uncommon for you to marry someone of a different culture, background or religion from which you were raised. Aquarians also enjoy relationships with those who are different from themselves, but their motivation is more of a shock value, giving society a jolt. Your motivation is the intellectual interest in differing cultures and people and the adventure which can be found through these travels and relationship experiences.

I am sitting on a porch in Key West, Florida right now as I'm writing this chapter. As I look around, I'm reminded that few of the trees and plants which I see are native to the Keys. They were brought here by pirates and explorers from all the different lands they traveled. They would find something interesting in their travels and bring it home to show to others. Soon, this vegetation became totally accepted and a part of this land.

This is your karmic responsibility as a traveler of our world. You must bring home your experiences and learning from your travels so we may all incorporate a piece of each other into our own cultures. You show us that we can all live together in respectful harmony, that our similarities are far more common than our differences. You also keep us aware of the fascination of our differences. Vive la differance!

Besides the intellectual aspect of travel, you also need the sense of adventure it brings. Your karmic contribution to our society is to nurture our instinctive need for adventure and inquisitiveness found in our neighbors' backyard. You have a responsibility to yourself to maintain a youthful sense of adventure within your nature. Even the smallest amount of attention put into this part of your life will bring you a quality of youthfulness throughout your years.

SAGITTARIAN CONTRIBUTIONS
TO LITERATURE

Sagittarian-like adventures have been the makings of such stories as *Raiders of the Lost Arc, Gulliver's Travels* and *Quantum Leap*. It is through these tales that we can escape to foreign lands and eavesdrop on the lifestyles of other cultures.

It has been said that all of us have a book within us bursting to come out onto the written page. As a Sagittarian, you truly have the gift of writing and the skill to get it published. This does not mean that all of you will become writers. Remember, you will have many lifetimes as a Sagittarian. You need not try to do it all at once. But, should you choose to follow the course of writing, you do have a karmic responsibility toward the integrity and honesty of your work. Some people get behind a keyboard and feel that they are the ultimate authority on whatever they are writing simply because they have put their thoughts on paper. Keep in mind, you are the teacher of the zodiac and you have karmic responsibility toward the integrity of your writings.

Some of you may choose to work within the publishing field in capacities other than authoring the great novel. The greatest tool for teaching is the written word and any involvement on your part may be beneficial to all.

SPIRITUALITY

Equally important as your academic education is the development of your spirituality. Our western civilization has a tendency to place spirituality as one of our lowest priorities. How often have you heard someone say, *"If I don't stay out too late on Saturday night and if I don't party too much, I'll go to church on Sunday morning."?* But you certainly don't hear many people say, *"If I don't stay out too late on Sunday night and if I don't party too much, I'll go to work on Monday."* We tend to take our materialistic responsibilities far more seriously than spiritual needs.

As a Sagittarian, you are here to question, probe and explore your spiritual truths. Religion, spirituality and morality are significant aspects of your character. Many of you feel comfortable in conventional, traditional religions, others of you feel trapped by the religious choices of your childhood. The truths you search for are for you alone and cannot be forced on you by others. Nor should you attempt to force your beliefs on others. These truths must be measured and sewn carefully for each individual. One size does not fit all.

A NEW AGE CATHOLIC

Ian was raised in a strict Irish Catholic upbringing, the fourth of seven children. The whole family followed the Roman Catholic religion faithfully. As a child, Ian had no alternative. He was taught that his religion was the right religion. In fact, Ian never knew any other alternative existed until he was in the sixth grade and a Protestant family moved on the block. He sensed they were different because they didn't go to confession with the other kids on Saturday afternoon. Not only was Ian taught that his was the only religion of significance, he was also instructed never to question its doctrines. The church and its priests and nuns were authorities to be feared and obeyed without question. Even his parents seemed a bit nervous when the priest was coming over for dinner. The whole family went to mass at least once a week, confession on Saturday, no meat on Friday (this rule was still in effect when Ian was a boy). Everyone in his neighborhood thought of the church as the center of their life. Instead of asking what section of the city you came from, people would ask in which parish you lived.

Being a typical Sagittarian boy, Ian enjoyed the pomp and circumstance of Catholicism and the comfort its moral structure brought into his life. He sometimes wondered why some of these rules existed and he often questioned some of the laws of the church which seemed not to make sense. *"After all"*, questioned the healthy youngster, *"how can newborn babies not automatically go to heaven? What would happen to his soul if he had thoughts of sexual craving for Betsy Lou whose breasts seem to be growing faster than those of the other girls in class?"*

Ian became friendly with Tom from that lone Protestant family down the block and wanted to go to his small church on Sunday but was told by the priest that this would be a sin. He must only attend Catholic mass. His Sagittarian curiosity was truly piqued with this rule. Still, he was afraid to question or rebel against his whole world.

When Ian graduated from high school he was accepted to many colleges. His father wanted him to attend a Catholic University since he had always attended parochial schools, but Ian decided to take his degree at the State University which now blew open the doors of opportunity to meet people of diverse backgrounds.

At first Ian continued to go to mass every Sunday and practice his religion as he always had. He also found himself exposed to countless other people with beliefs that differed from his own upbringing. Ian spent many late nights questioning and listening to the views of his new friends. Finally, one Sunday, he was ready to go to church with one of his new Baptist friends. He just had to see what this was all about. Would he get struck down by God? What would happen if his mother ever found out? Still, he had to go. And what a difference he found. No sedate parishioners sitting primly in their pews repeating the ageless Latin chants of Catholicism. Why these people were up and down, singing, handclapping, interrupting the sermon with Amens and Yeah Lords. This was fun...and a bit scary. Could these people all be going to hell?

Ian's interest in religion intensified as he searched from religion to religion to discover the truths of God which best suited him. He sought out information from his new Jewish friends, he read about Buddhism, Zen, Latter-Day Saints. He finally settled on a New Age circle that met once a week and talked about metaphysics, spirituality, and the power of meditation.

There were many times Ian questioned his childhood beliefs and found himself angry at the church for discouraging his curiosity to explore other creeds. He wondered if they tried to control their believers by keeping them in the dark. Surely all these new friends he had made could not be mortal sinners. They believed just as powerfully in their religions as he believed in his.

Ian eventually drifted back to Catholicism as the nucleus of his belief system. It was here that he formed his basic morality, which he found to be a positive base on which to build. He wove many aspects of other beliefs into the fabric of his childhood religion until he was fully satisfied with the spiritual aspect of his life. This search for his personal truth took many years but there was such pleasure to be found in the quest and so very necessary for his Sagittarian soul.

Not all Sagittarians need to concentrate as heavily on the religious choice as Ian did, but you do need to search for your spirituality. There is no judgment, astrologically, as to what eventual conclusion is best for you. Your karmic responsibility is to initiate the search itself and to leave yourself open to many possible conclusions. A word or two of caution is required at this point. Be wary of following gurus or spiritual groups blindly. Remember, you are a natural inquisitor and need to question your soul's direction. To follow a belief or cult impulsively is denying your karmic quest. You will know when you have found your spiritual truth because you will then be living it, not talking it.

Be careful not to preach your beliefs to others in a condescending or judgmental tone. If you find yourself forcing your convictions on others, you have strayed far from your karmic lesson of spirituality. Many religions believe strongly that their responsibility is to convert others in order to save their souls, such as modern born-again sects or missionaries. As a Sagittarian, you must be cautious to maintain a position of teaching, not forcing. Always remember, what is truth to you may not be truth to someone else. You are here to nurture spirituality, not religious dogma. This is a difficult test for many Sagittarians.

SAGITTARIUS THE ATHLETE

We have explored your need to develop yourself intellectually and spiritually. Now let us examine your karmic responsibility to keep yourself physically fit. Are you beginning to understand why you will need many lifetimes as a Sagittarian to accomplish all of this? Be patient, all the time necessary is there for you!

It is important for you to keep yourself balanced by paying attention to the physical part of your being. You need to think of your body as a part of you which needs to be well taken care of since it houses your intellectual and spiritual self. Athletics are healthy for you. They offer an outlet for your fiery energy and bring all areas of yourself into alignment. An accomplished athlete has a well developed body, an intense concentration, and is usually not adverse to praying for a win.

Sports get you out there with people too. Nothing is healthier for you than a Saturday softball game or Tuesday night bowling match with your friends. People are a great source of learning for you in all capacities.

Animals may also play an important role in your life and many Sagittarians enjoy athletic activities such as horseback riding. Tennis is also a popular sport with your sign.

Karmically, you will create inner balance by developing the athletic part of yourself. It can become too easy to concentrate on one facet of your development while neglecting the other parts of yourself. Think of how often we stereotype intellectuals as inept athletes. The egghead is always picked last for the volleyball team. Not so with you Sagittarians. You are able to balance it all.

Even being a spectator is healthy for you. Watching a sport, whether it be on TV or at a stadium, will also help you to maintain a balance within. As you can see, some karmic lessons are easier to handle than others!

MALE SAGITTARIAN

The sign of Sagittarius has a fiery element which can produce great enthusiasm but also an inclination toward extremism. Couple this with the well-documented male ego and it can lead to trouble. You must be aware of tendencies on your part to exaggerate whether you are referring to your past achievements or future promises. A great part of you believes you can fulfill all your optimistic promises, but you need to keep yourself grounded and curtail your goals. Many handy clichés come into play here. Careful not to "bite off more than you can chew", not to "promise more than you can deliver". If you promise someone you can complete a job in three days, will it really take you five? If everyone is placing a five dollar bet on the football game, do you really have to bet ten?

Sagittarians are wonderfully gifted storytellers, just be sure that your embellishments do not infringe upon the world of reality. Moderation and good sense may become your most needed allies.

Gambling may often become a problem to Sagittarians of both sexes. First there is this cockeyed optimism that makes you truly believe you will win. Then comes the attraction to long-odds bets, if you're going to win, why not win big? This affinity to gambling may not be restricted solely to the race track or gambling casinos. It may also extend itself to business deals and get-rich-quick schemes.

Education is the key to your success. It is important for you to advance yourself scholastically as much as possible, according to your circumstances. But classroom education is not your sole source of knowledge. Be a reader! Use your library, subscribe to magazines. Be a listener! Surround yourself with intelligent people, join workshops, attend seminars. And, you must always be willing to give generously of yourself by teaching others what you have learned. Your intellectual achievements will always be a source of pride for you as long as you maintain a standard of moral integrity.

When you are a student, you may be interested in joining clubs, striving for the honor roll and running for class office. Your academic achievements will serve to bolster your ego as well as enhance your future success. Some suggested studies for you would be education, political science, and philosophy.

You may find yourself with some special talent for sports which will be beneficial to you in many ways. Most Sagittarians have the ability to achieve in both the athletic and scholastic areas. Whether sports be your focal point or simply an outlet for a Saturday afternoon, athletic activity is healthy for you both physically and emotionally. You need to kick the ball around or jog or lift weights. You need the camaraderie of other people. Group or team sports come highly recommended to you. It is also healthy for you to get together with your friends and watch a game on TV or at the stadium. Games and sports bring balance into your life.

Our society expects you, as a male, to concentrate your energies on the material and physical parts of your life. You may not be encouraged to probe your spirituality but karmically, you must question your beliefs. Some may find it through an established church or religion, others through philosophical quests, still others discover it within nature. Many a Sagittarian has touched upon his spiritual self while camping or hiking through the wilds of nature. Remember, the judgment is not there to find THE truth rather the obligation to search for YOUR truths.

As a Sagittarian you may want to explore the possible fields of a teacher, airline pilot, athlete, clergyman, forest ranger, philosopher or foot-free adventurer. Whichever you choose, education is the essential key to your success.

SAGITTARIAN FEMALE

The sign of Sagittarius brings with it a strong masculine flavor. It is important for you to encourage this aspect of your personality. Therefore, it would not be unusual for you to be a bit of a tomboy as a child. You are comfortable doing "boys" things such as camping in the woods, learning how to shoot a gun, traveling across America on a motorcycle, or being the star pitcher of your softball team. Adventure is important to you and you will minimize your experiences if you sit daintily in starched dresses simply looking out the window at life. You must be an active participant in the action of the world. You need not worry about losing your femininity by being physically active. Sagittarian woman often maintain a particularly sensual feminine mystique within their muscular bodies and sporty attire.

You need to be communing with nature and with your friends so it behooves you to join groups who share your interests. You are fun-loving and so the best side of your nature comes out when you are actively involved in some activity with other people. But, you are not to find your pleasure simply with people. You also have a great love of animals, particularly horses and dogs. This probably comes from your ease with nature, for it seems that you are able to understand the animal world and they share a kinship with you. You are both the hunter and the protector.

Education is the key to your success, as it is with all Sagittarians. Your elementary and secondary education will be the cornerstone for your future and college will advance you further. Once you find a study that fascinates you, advancement and achievement will come easily. Many Sagittarians become perpetual students, earning one degree after another simply for the fun of learning. Most of you though, find one or two major areas of interest and then absorb as much information in these areas as possible. You are gifted in the learning and teaching areas and can have great confidence in yourself. Keep in mind, you do not know everything. Be willing to listen and learn from others.

Areas of interest for possible careers are similar to those for Sagittarian males, teaching, writing, publishing, the ministry, and athletics. You need not shy away from traditionally male-oriented careers in such fields as medicine and law. Both of these fields may hold promising futures for you. You are a strong sign and you must always believe in your own strength.

You, too, need to give time and attention to the spiritual side of your nature. As a female, you are encouraged in this direction more than your Sagittarian brothers. You may find your truths within traditional beliefs or among the wanderings of your body and mind. Do not ever be afraid to question dogmatic doctrines or to put your beliefs to the test. You are an adventurous soul both physically and spiritually. If you should decided to enter into a traditional religion, do not fear your desires to attain positions hereto achieved only by men. You have the ability to be a leader in your spiritual realm, always keeping in mind that what is best for you may not be appropriate for someone else. Your Sagittarian enthusiasm can sometimes get the best of you.

SAGITTARIAN CHILDREN

As soon as your Sagittarian child is born, start a college tuition bank account but do not think you will be spending it only on traditional educational systems. Your Sagittarian child will need to touch upon all kinds of educational experiences. Starting as a child, he will benefit from playschools, preschools, and Headstart programs. Yours is a sociable, intelligent child who enjoys much stimulation around him. It is important to read to him and to show him the books. Let him touch them, keep them in his room, and play with them. Encourage him to design his own books, write his own words and draw his own pictures. Read to him about foreign lands and people of different cultures. Bring him pictures of animals and trees and nature.

The greatest gift you can give your Sagittarian child is the benefit of understanding that his family and his life is not representative of the rest of the world. Show him that there is wonderment and adventure in exploring places and cultures outside of his own. As he grows older, include him in your adult conversations especially as they refer to philosophy, religion, and politics. One thing parents tend to do with their children is to indoctrinate them with their beliefs. You were born a Catholic, you are a Catholic. You were born a Republican, you are a Republican. Allow, and yes, even encourage, your child to question all such matters and help him to establish his own beliefs. You may be very surprised to see him grow up quite comfortable in the family tradition, but he needs to be able to draw those conclusions for himself.

It is important to raise your child with some kind of belief system of spiritual guidance. He needs religious training in his youth. It is the dogma that inhibits his growth not spirituality. If you sense he is becoming pompous or dogmatic himself as he grows up, it may be your parental responsibility to bring this flaw to his attention.

Yours is a child who loves adventure. He needs to learn about and touch nature, so camping and fishing and hunting trips may be perfect for him. Remember, although I use the pronoun, him, these kinds of outings are equally important for female Sagittarian children. Sit your child down in the dirt, show him the beauty of leaves, grass, and bugs. Show him the adventure of nature and the power behind it.

Do not raise him to be afraid. Do not overprotect him. He needs to explore life and cannot stand to be fenced in. Of course, it is your responsibility, as a parent, to protect him from harm but do not forbid him from experiencing adventure.

When you travel, bring him with you. He is able to soak up the newness of different cultures easily. In fact, many Sagittarian children have a knack for learning foreign languages. You may consider enrolling him in a foreign language study at an early age.

Your Sagittarian will also benefit from group sports at a very young age. He is a perfect candidate for Little League baseball, football, soccer, or bowling teams. This does not mean that he is guaranteed to be the star of these teams. He benefits from the physical activity and the camaraderie of sports without necessarily having to be the star player.

Your Sagittarian can be quite a chatterbox, so you will need to encourage his verbal enthusiasm while teaching him that there is a time and place for quiet and listening. He may also be plagued with unbridled optimism and self-confidence that can put him in jeopardy. Too much of anything can be bad at times. This will be a fine line for you to walk, as parents, to ground him at times without destroying his enthusiasm and self-confidence.

One of the most difficult lessons you will experience will be to let him go. You must let him go his own way; to follow his own beliefs, to explore his own territory. He could come to you after high school and say he wants some of that tuition fund you have been saving so he can take a year off and travel across Europe. Well, what about college? What about his medical degree? Your Sagittarian child will also find his traveling to be an education, perhaps one more worthwhile for him now than college. When I suggested that you save for his education, I had mentioned that it may not always be the education you planned for him.

If he comes home with a different religious belief than you raised him in, or with a spouse from a foreign country, or a career choice you never pictured him in, then realize that you have raised him perfectly in the spirit of Sagittarius. He is the explorer of the zodiac. He will explore on many levels, intellectually, physically and spiritually. He will bring back many souvenirs from his varied travels which, if you are willing to be open, will also benefit your life. He can bring wonderment to all. The greatest assistance you can give him would be to raise him in an open, intellectual, inquisitive, loving family environment encouraging him to find his truths in his journey through life, and showing him that the loving arms of his family are always open to welcome him home.

CAPRICORN

December 22 - January 19

Female Energy

KARMIC LESSONS

◆ Dealing with authority

◆ Keeping with traditions and rules

◆ The use of power and being in charge

◆ Maintaining organization and stability

◆ Being attuned to emotions

◆ Dealing with burdensome karmic responsibilities

A favorite expression of the hippie generation of the 1960s was *"heavy karma, man!"* We saw from Chapter Two of this book that karma does not have to be a burden but, without fail, if we put the word "heavy" in front of it, we are most certainly implying the kind of karma that symbolizes hard work and responsibility. The sign of Capricorn carries the suggestion of someone who has chosen to wear the yoke of heavy karma throughout this lifetime. The extent toward which you handle these karmic lessons depends upon how long you allow yourself to remain in the primary stage of your sign. Capricorn is one sign that suffers the most in its primary or immature stage while, conversely, can lead to overwhelming success and good fortune when you allow yourself to advance to your evolved state.

PRIMARY CAPRICORN

Capricorn karmic lessons will come to you when you are young and will continue throughout your life. Some Capricorns are instinctively aware of their potential for early lessons and try to avoid their inevitable karma by fleeing from any form of responsibility. They feel that *heavy karma* can be avoided by sidestepping any *heavy responsibilities*.

Capricorn, when used in its highest form, is a sign of great authority and industriousness. Therefore, when we see a Capricorn avoiding responsibility, giving in to lay-back or lazy tendencies, we are aware of a Capricorn who is afraid of confronting her lessons through the taking on of hard work.

It is a misconception that avoiding responsibilities will lead to an avoidance of your life lessons. They will need to be confronted regardless of your desire to hide from them. Reality has shown that the more you move toward your lessons the easier they become. Trying to avoid them will not work, they will always outrun you. In the case of Capricorn, responsibilities and obligations in this life will benefit you, not only on a soul level, but also in the immediate gratification of material reward. You are vibrating on your primary level when you feel yourself afraid of responsibility and trying to shirk it.

Capricorn is a sign of tradition and rules but a Capricorn who is fixed in her primary level may become overly rigid and controlling of her world by demonstrating unyielding adherence to the rules, laws or traditions of her times. She may be excessively strict with herself and others, and may portray a facade of a hard, cold disciplinarian who wields great authority and power. In reality, she is a Capricorn who is vibrating on a primary level of her sign and is afraid of facing the world of change and free will. She finds comfort in the stability of sameness and tries to find shelter in the walls of tradition which will inevitably become the bars of her prison. What is frightening is that these people often are found in positions of power where they are able to use their authority to intimidate others. This can break not only their spirits, but those upon whom they inflict their rules. Rules and tradition will be discussed at length later in this chapter where we will see how they can be used or misused by mankind. What needs to be understood is that the person who wields the power may not be vibrating on her highest level karmically. This is of great concern to all those born under the sign of Capricorn since they are the keepers of the laws.

The primary Capricorn must also come to terms with emotions. Many astrology books show Capricorns as cold, ruthless people who are out to conquer the material world through any means available to them. They are depicted as social climbers and status seekers. When a Capricorn behaves in this fashion, they are vibrating on an exceptionally low primary energy. I must emphasis that this personality direction is not one which is commonly followed by Capricorns. But they do sometimes bury themselves in the material world in order to hide from their own sensitive emotional states.

The opposite of Capricorn, in astrology, is Cancer, probably the most emotional of all the signs. Since we tend to cross over to our polar signs, the Capricorn is a far more emotional sign than it is ruthless and callous. The cold exterior worn by the primary Capricorn is an indication of her fear of reaching into her own recesses of emotional vulnerability and anxieties. Rules, discipline, and sternness are mere defenses to keep others and themselves away from the fears and hurts which they have stored away in the niches of their subconscious. The Capricorn who appears to be without feeling, is the one who is lost in her primary stage as a result of many pains and emotional hurts experienced in her early life.

The primary Capricorn will also react to crisis with addictions and depression. Most people associate these struggles with the water signs of Cancer, Scorpio, and Pisces, but research has found that this earth sign of Capricorn must also deal with these emotional pains. When a Capricorn is vibrating on her primary level, she may find herself immersed in the rapids of depression and addiction. Her challenge is to find her passage to high ground where she can observe her inner self without fear of failure or recrimination. These low states of mental health may be used as escapes from the work and responsibility which need to be confronted in order to obtain karmic growth.

EVOLVED CAPRICORN

Your age need not be a factor in your ability to vibrate on an evolved energy level. By accepting your responsibilities and by being unafraid of maintaining structure and order in your life, you are securing your evolved station as a Capricorn. The motivations behind your actions are the keys to your karmic position. If you are assuming your responsibilities with dignity and purpose in hopes of bettering yourself and your environment or securing stability around you, you are vibrating on your evolved Capricorn level. Your karmic lessons will come to you through responsibilities which sometimes wear a price tag of restrictions. You will discover early in life that the harsher restrictions will come to you through the avoidance of your lessons rather than by confronting them.

You evolved Capricorns are able to distinguish between obligations which are truly yours and those which other people may try to heap upon you in order to lessen their own load. This discrimination takes some learning. The final result will be an ability to accept karmic challenges while passing back to others the duties which truly belong to them. You cannot help another by taking over their karmic lessons. You will serve them better as a teacher by showing them, through your example, how to face their lessons and assume their responsibilities. An evolved Capricorn is skilled at perceiving the difference.

It is at this stage that the Capricorn displays her talents as a leader and teacher. Our world needs people to follow the traditions, document the rules, and teach the old-fashioned way. The evolved Capricorn has the innate ability to preserve the traditions and pass them on to others. This brings stability into her life and the world. It is here that she is able to make positive use of her sense of discipline. She is able to teach this structure to those around her if it is used as a source of order rather than a misuse of her power. The evolved Capricorn has no desire to pervert power and authority though the misuse of her ego. The rules of life are second nature to her and she uses them to structure her teachings.

We see evolved Capricorns as hard workers who are not afraid to roll up their sleeves and get themselves involved in the business of hard work. A true leader is someone who will never ask one of their subordinates to do something which they would not do themselves. This is especially true of an evolved Capricorn. Because of this acceptance of life's travail, they are greatly respected and admired as leaders in our society.

Family and responsibility to relationships is paramount in the morals of an evolved Capricorn. They are probably the most loyal of all signs. When they take on the commitment of marriage, children, partnership or friendship, they do so with full awareness of their duties in that relationship. Their loyalty and devotion can be totally selfless and magnanimous and will easily bear the test of time.

Depression and excessively serious thought may also be the burden of the evolved Capricorn, but she has learned how to have fun along with assuming her difficult responsibilities. All work and no play can truly make Capricorn a dull sign. The evolved Capricorn is aware of this need for balance and will forbid herself to fall into the trap of workaholism by planning ample time for family fun, vacation, exercise and spiritual retreats. This balance will help her come to terms with her darker side and face her fears, which could become the object of her depression.

REMEMBER, NO ONE IS TOTALLY PRIMARY OR EVOLVED. OUR KARMIC LESSONS ARE BEST LEARNED WHEN WE ARE DEALING WITH BOTH OF THESE ENERGIES.

DEALING WITH AUTHORITY

The first people of authority in a Capricorn's life are her parents or the person in charge of raising her. Since dealing with authority is one of Capricorn's karmic lessons, her relationship with her parents and her elders in general, will have great influence on her ability to deal with all forms of authority as an adult. There is a tendency for the Capricorn child to experience a stinginess, strictness or restriction in her life which she sees as coming from one of the people in authority in the early years. Sometimes there is a strict parent who dictates many severe rules within the household. This rigid atmosphere teaches the Capricorn to conceal her emotional needs while it also dulls all her creative senses. She is taught that she must follow blindly the rules of her world, an attitude she will bring with her into her adult world. Many a Charles Dickens' story is based on this Capricorn kind of world.

Other Capricorn children are raised within a different kind of restriction such as poverty, hardship or health limitations. A Capricorn who is eldest of a large, poor family very often feels the weight of her karmic responsibilities quite early in life. We will see this Capricorn nurturing her siblings, baby-sitting, earning money for the family, and in many ways assuming the role of the parent not only for her siblings but also for her parents. The Capricorn feels born into adulthood skipping through childhood completely. In order to see how a Capricorn child will adapt to authority it is important to observe how she interacts with the adults in her childhood.

A PROTECTIVE CAPRICORN DAUGHTER

Maureen was only 16 years old when she gave birth to her Capricorn daughter, Kaitlynn. Her mother's youthful inexperience with adulthood was instinctively sensed by Kaitlynn who, even as an infant, assumed an easygoing, well scheduled manner. When Kaitlynn was three years old, her mother, now better equipped to handle motherhood, was pregnant again. By this time, she and Kaitlynn had already established their relationship of care and concern.

In this case, it was Kaitlynn who felt a tremendous responsibility toward her young mother. She knew how upset her mother would get if she had left a mess, or if Daddy was late for dinner, or the colored laundry got mistakenly mixed with the whites. So Kaitlynn became a caretaker. She observed her mother closely, noticing her dark moods or tears. Kaitlynn's first experience with authority was a poor one since her mother was still grappling with her own loss of childhood and the early onset of motherhood. Maureen's age combined with weakness perhaps made Kaitlynn feel responsible for her mother's unhappiness. She sensed she had to take care of her mother.

One snowy day, Maureen was carrying Kaitlynn, resting her on her growing womb as she carefully inched her way down the snow-covered driveway toward the car. Kaitlynn felt her mother's tension and instinctively became protective. She patted Maureen's back with her little hand and soothed, *"Don't worry Mommy, I got you"*.

Kaitlynn's first experience with authority taught her to be a caretaker, to take on responsibility for others. It was also part of her own need to protect herself from their fears and their rage. This was quite a heavy responsibility for a little girl.

Sometimes a Capricorn experiences a parent or teacher who is excessively strict as his first example of authority.

THE CAPRICORN'S BROKEN SPIRIT

Danny's father believed in rules in order to keep his family safe and together. Everyone had to be up by 6:30 a.m., even on weekends. The chores were evenly divided among them down to the youngest child and there was never an exception or excuse for breaking this routine. In one sense, Danny felt secure in his father's world. He always knew what was expected of him just as he never had to question what he was allowed or not allowed to do. The rules were strict, simple, to the point, and unchangeable. As Danny grew older, he found his family life restricting and unfair. He resented being unable to make his own decisions and his own mistakes. His father's world became intolerable. His life at home became dull and, eventually, he too lost his luster and enthusiasm. He loved his father because he was taught to love him. He hated his father because he was unable to break from his bonds without guilt or fear of reprisal.

Danny learned from his childhood that the person in authority held all the power and that power can easily be used to control others. He also learned that it was natural to experience a love/hate relationship with authority but that to resist was futile. His spirit was broken at an early age.

As these children entered their new domain of schooling and socializing, they saw their teachers as extensions of their parents' authority. Kaitlynn instinctively sought to please her teachers, doing as she was told, cautious of their moods and needs. She became a good little girl at school. No trouble at all. Danny, on the other hand, saw the school system as an extension of the restrictive rules he had experienced with his father. He became sullen and, even more disturbing, he became agitated when he was given choices or introduced to creativity such as music and art classes. He wanted the comfort of the rules which had always bound him, yet he resented both the restrictions and choices of school. Danny became a passive/aggressive personality by missing classes due to "illnesses" and submitting his homework assignments late.

These personality traits will follow the Capricorns into their business world, long-term relationships, and eventually, their own patterns as parents.

We all must deal with authority throughout our lives. This is a necessary structure of society which keeps us functioning within the rules. Capricorn's lessons involve attitudes toward authority and the eventuality of becoming that authority figure. As a Capricorn, you are gifted in assuming responsible, authoritative roles in our world. We look toward you to fill the role of teacher, police officer, judge, corporate president, and clergy. No matter what your working or social position may be, we look toward you to set the pace of authority for us. We also watch how you deal with the authority around you, for no matter how high up the ladder you may be, there will always be someone to whom even you must answer. Some of the bad-press of Capricorn comes from those who are ruthless in their quest for power and status through their position of authority. The karmic lesson for you is not whether you achieve a position of power but rather how you use or misuse that power once you have achieved it.

History has shown us kings, czars, and emperors who have raged ruthless war in their quest for power. We have seen presidents in our own history who have flung great political clout in order to gain their positions, all of them winning the love and approval of the people who were unaware of their scheming and conniving means used to reach their goals. The karmic test of the Capricorn is the validity of the methods used in achieving positions of authority and then the practical use of power once the position of authority has been achieved.

Most of us are not kings or presidents. We are made up of common folk, with simple goals. Do not mistake the level of authority achieved with the amount of karmic lessons involved. The karmic objectives and tests of an office manager in a small, midwest business are as important and as difficult as those of world leaders. If you are a Capricorn, you must always examine the motives behind your actions (a glance back to your childhood relationships will assist you) and maintain a awareness of the repercussions of your actions as a Capricorn who now wields power.

We need people to take responsibility and maintain authority to establish peaceable order for the masses. It is through the mismanagement of authority that chaos is born. As a Capricorn, you must not be fearful of your karmic challenge. You were born to take control. These lessons can not be avoided. And no one can tell you how well you are doing except your own inner voice.

TRADITION AND RULES

Traditional customs of our society, our religion, and our family bring comfort to all. We enjoy the repetitions of our customs for holidays, special events, and Hallmark occasions. In fact, we find satisfaction in the rhythm and repetition of traditions. They bring with them a sense of order, rules, and familiarity which solidify our units of family, fellow countrymen, and co-workers.

Each family has its own unique traditions for celebrating birthdays, holidays, and special events. Social groups such as schools, governments, and businesses also establish their traditions through alumni homecomings, reunions, independence day celebrations, inaugurations, and company picnics. It reassures us that life continues without our need for new thought through the repetition of the same events year after year, century after century.

Capricorns are the keepers of these traditions. You are responsible for maintaining their continuity and making sure that they are not subject to change by the whims of a few individuals or cultural swings. Because of this gravitation toward tradition and rules, you find yourself seeking the familiar, and sometimes, fearing the new. As a child you craved traditional values of family and home. You were most comfortable with the "typical" family of father setting the rules, mother nurturing the family, one brother, one sister and the traditional number of pets. Love of family and respect of your elders is a natural reaction of a young Capricorn. After all, it is the elders in our society who are the holders of the ancient laws and customs. They are the keeper of traditions for, by maintaining the traditions of one's era, one is able to leave one's mark upon the world. In many Native American cultures, the elders who told the stories and passed down the mores of the tribe to the young were most revered by the group. Your Capricorn karmic responsibility is to maintain and sustain the traditions of your family and culture. You understand the power held in the force of stability and establishment. You will find your success and strive within the boundaries of tradition, sense and order. This responsibility will seem boring and dull to many other signs of the Zodiac, but it is comforting to you.

CARRYING THE FAMILY NAME

Arthur was the third child of a family of six. His parents had immigrated from Germany at the turn of the 19th century and settled in a small rural town to raise their family. What they lacked in education they made up for with values of hard work and perfection. His father became a skilled carpenter who found plenty of work in construction as his new country grew with each wave of added immigrants.

Arthur respected his parents' work ethic. He appreciated his father's approach to carpentry which was to do your best work at all times because your good name was valued more than the weekly paycheck. He listened to his parents' stories about the old-country and enjoyed the holiday traditions they brought with them. They were a hard working family but Arthur found comfort in the family unity as they worked together to survive.

As the six children grew up, many of them went their separate ways. They did not want to stay in this small, rural town. His two sisters married city-men and moved away to start their own families. His oldest brother joined the Navy and decided to make it his career. Soon, only Arthur and his younger brother, Hans, were home with Mom and Dad. He could see that Hans was twitching through his adolescence, waiting for the time when he would be old enough to move away from this stodgy town and old-fashioned parents. So, as the nursery rhyme goes, soon there was one.

Arthur served his apprenticeship and perfected his father's craft of carpentry and soon their business read, Wurther and Son. He married a local girl, raised a family, cared for both his parents through their old age and maintained the family traditions with his own children. Arthur's brothers and sisters would have felt burdened or stifled by this existence yet it brought great contentment and happiness to him. He was foregoing his individuality to maintain the lifestyle dictated by his parents. Arthur, as a Capricorn, was comfortable in these traditions and felt it was important to carry them on for his next generation.

Not all Capricorns are as traditionally minded or disciplined as Arthur, but there are many of you out there who find the sustaining of tradition a great source of pleasure. As with all karmic responsibilities, attitude is everything. The feelings and attitudes behind your actions have a far greater impact on your soul than the actions themselves.

You realize that tradition and rules are necessary. As much as we need people to break free of the old in order to explore the new, we also need the structures of the past to regulate us and protect us from extremism. Sometimes the explanation of Capricorn's karmic direction seems so cut and dry, yet this is exactly what you keepers of tradition need. This does not mean that you are unable to move with change. Many innovative people in our society have created great changes in our cultures. Still, they will continue to work within the structures with which they feel most comfortable and enjoy their chosen traditions.

A NONTRADITIONAL LIFESTYLE

Nora knew she was a lesbian from the onset of her teenage years. Being a Capricorn, she tried hard to fight these feelings and follow the guidelines set out to her by society. But her need to be honest with herself surpassed her desire to be socially accepted. She openly lived her life as lesbian, was active in the gay and lesbian social groups, and worked hard at organizing demonstrations to counterattack the bias of society.

Nora may have appeared to be a nonconformist. In reality, she took all of her Capricorn skills with her. She organized groups giving them the structural basis of constitutions and by-laws; she sought to educated the establishment by speaking in schools, at church meetings, and to parents of gays and lesbians. She also fell in love and maintained a long-term relationship with one woman. They bought a house together in the suburbs where she worked hard at her job and rose up the corporate ladder. She was not afraid of her Capricorn karmic lessons. She used these traits to promote her cause and establish a safe environment for herself and her lover.

The key to these two examples is sincerity of feeling and moderation. You are struggling with your karmic lessons when you are either afraid of responsibility and the rules of society or if you are overly strict and puritanical in your beliefs. Authority, rules and tradition can also be used as weapons. Many a frightened Capricorn has hidden behind the skirts of mother tradition.

Other Capricorns take their role of caretakers too seriously and become overly concerned and protective of their family and loved ones. This trait is usually found early in the Capricorn's personality as with the following example.

THE LITTLE HELPER

Robin was the oldest of five children but not by many years. Her siblings were spaced no more than 16 months apart. Still she felt much older and terribly responsible for her younger brothers and sisters. While her parents never felt that they put any additional responsibility on Robin, she took that responsibility upon herself. By the time she was seven years old, she was bringing clean diapers to her mother, keeping a keen eye on everyone as they played on the swing set, and helping to bathe whichever child was placed in the tub with her at night. Her childhood was seldom one of playing and mischief. She devoted her early life to the challenge of being the good little girl at home. She went on to become the good little student, the industrious employee, and the devoted wife and mother of her own children.

Where did Robin's childhood go? Many a Capricorn will look back on their early life and find that it was filled with work and responsibility with little time given to play.

WHOSE RESPONSIBILITY IS IT ANYWAY?

It is understood that you Capricorns are here to assume some serious duties in this life. This is your karmic direction. Therefore, it is imperative that you learn how to discriminate between your responsibilities and those that may be put on you for the convenience of other people in your life. Since you readily accept responsibility and duty, people tend to place, too willingly, a great share of work on your shoulders.

> ➤ The good little child who eagerly helps mommy and daddy, who never makes trouble and does as he is told, will be given the chore of starting the dinner and watching his brothers and sisters. His parents can count on him.

> ➤ The industrious student will be given the more difficult assignments and tasks. Often neglected by the teacher, because he is not a discipline problem, he can easily be lost in a chaotic classroom situation.

> ➤ The hard worker who gets her assignments in on time, comes up with the best ideas, and works in a consistent manner may easily find her co-workers and bosses depending on her to make them look good. Other people will take credit for this Capricorn's hard work.

> ➤ At home, the need to structure and organize, which is inherent in the Capricorn may find her taking on more than her share of the family duties for her immediate and extended family.

Your karmic responsibility is to learn to discriminate between the lessons and obligations which are karmically yours and those which are thrown upon you by others. Most Capricorns find this to be a long hard lesson but one which comes eventually through a combination of your weariness and maturity.

Let us take the examples of Robin and Kaitlynn. As children, they fell into caretaking roles, and in so doing, they began to assume responsibilities way beyond what is expected of children. Their parents may have begun to take these helpful behaviors for granted because it was easy to do so. Once this pattern was established as their children's first childhood example of authoritative direction, they continued to live up to their "good girl" image by assuming some of the responsibilities of their friends, lovers, children, and co-workers. This is where weariness sets in.

An excellent method of detecting too much responsibility in your life is by observing your posture! It is a simple technique and it works. Pay attention to your body as you sit, stand and walk. If you slump down in your chair, if your shoulders are rounded, your head tilted down, you are carrying the world on your shoulders. Your karmic responsibilities will not wear you down! They will make you feel good about yourself. Only the weight of others will bring you weariness, poor posture, and eventually, ill health.

Do not be afraid of hard work and responsibility. They cannot hurt you. The inability to discriminate can be your downfall. You are a hard working, responsible person. Do not allow others to take advantage of this wonderful asset. And do not be hard on yourself when they do. All Capricorns experience times when they give too much of themselves and overwork themselves because they know they can do it right. A job has got to be done and it is easy for you to feel that no one else can do it better than you. As true as this may be, you still need to share the work with others. You are a boss, a manager, by nature. A good manager knows how to delegate responsibility! Allow yourself to relax. Take a vacation. Don't be so hard on yourself.

WHO SAYS CAPRICORNS AREN'T EMOTIONAL?

Because of your karmic lessons discussed so far in this chapter, you may appear to be a serious, responsible person who goes about the business of life in a disciplined, organized fashion without emotional reactions or needs. This reputation of being devoid of emotion and callous is without foundation or truth. You are a person of tremendous defenses built over the years to protect yourself from the vulnerability of your intense feelings. You were the child who was expected to take on the adult traits of responsibility, seriousness, and discipline. You may not have been encouraged to laugh, be silly or behave in a childlike manner. Your rewards came to you when you were mature rather than youthful. This does not mean that you are without feeling. Quite the contrary, you are filled with intense emotion which you have been taught to contain rather than display.

I see Capricorn's emotional state very much like the furnace that warms a Cape Cod house on a cold winter's day. When we walk into this warm house we see no evidence of the power that has heated it protectively against the severity of nature's winter. All we see are radiators or baseboard vents along the walls. They do not look puissant enough to heat an entire house, so we walk downstairs. Here we find a box in the center of the basement. Could this furnace be containing enough power to fight the winter elements? It looks innocuous enough. So we open its door where we see and hear a raging fire of energy. This is characteristic of your Capricorn emotions. Indeed, you do have a blazing fire of emotions inside of you which you tend to keep carefully contained just as powerfully as the furnace has contained its fire within the bounds of its galvanized steel casing. People in your life must be aware of the intensity of your feelings and your vulnerability. You must learn to be able to open yourself up, particularly in your closest relationships so that people can feel and see the power of your love.

You may tend to equate your love with protecting. Many Capricorns feel that if they work hard, protect, provide for, and support their loved ones they have automatically displayed the true extent of their love. After all, what greater love can be given than your loyalty and support? You must come to realize that your lovers, spouses, children, friends, family and co-workers will also need your verbal and physical expression of love. It is important for you to learn how to express yourself in other ways beside your hard work and carefully controlled "adult" behavior. You must tell people that you love and need them in your life. You must flatter and praise when it is deserved. You must learn to laugh and cry with others, not within the self-made protection of aloneness. Some Capricorns seek professional help in learning this karmic lesson, and in doing so, allow themselves to enjoy the child within them later in life.

Simply because you were given or assumed heavy burdens in the early part of your life, does not imply that you need to be serious and emotionally self-protective throughout your life. You will find that it is alright to be frightened, confused, unsure, insecure or needy at times. We all are. You cannot always be the adult or parent who takes care of everyone else when they experience their difficult times. You must recognize that you too are vulnerable and that you will be loved and respected in spite of your vulnerabilities. To your surprise, you may find your relationships entering a stage of greater depth and pleasure once you have faced this karmic lesson.

An evolved Capricorn is able to kick up her heels and have fun. For you to enter this phase of maturity, you must be able to work less and laugh more. Your family and friends need you to share their fun and pleasures just as much as they need your material support.

ADDICTIONS AND DEPRESSION

Astrologers have long observed Capricorn's karmic challenge of depression and alcoholism. These tests are usually associated with the water signs, particularly Pisces, yet it is found often in the personalities of Capricorns who have "successfully" repressed their emotions.

THE WEIGHT IS TOO HEAVY

Jerry became the caretaker for his mother and younger sisters after his father was drafted and sent to Vietnam. His Dad's parting words to his five-year-old son were, *"You're the man of the house now, Jerry, until I come home in a year. Take good care of your Mom and sisters for me"*. Naturally, being a Capricorn, Jerry took his father's confidence in him seriously. His age limited how much he could really do, but did not stop him from feeling guilty and responsible for his mother's financial worries and tears of loneliness. The fact that his father's promise of one year away extended to three as he re-enlisted for additional tours of action, added to Jerry's burden. Jerry did not play with his friends after school; he came up with all sorts of interesting ways of making money - selling juice, cookies, and even worms to local fishermen. He became a sullen and serious boy, easy for his mother to handle but aged beyond his years.

After Jerry's father returned from the war, Jerry was replaced as head of the household with a sincere thank you and handshake, but he did not know how to be a child anymore. He felt displaced, not fitting in comfortably with his family or his schoolmates. He simply became a quiet boy who did as he was told and became an accomplished student. Everyone in the family was so proud of him. When Jerry entered his freshman year in college something broke inside of him. He became much more quiet, withdrawn and, finally, seriously depressed. He was hospitalized and required therapy and medication before he was able to resume his studies.

In Jerry's case, his breakdown was his first step toward help. He was forced to face his angers, frustrations, and fears through intensive therapy. He had to confront his karmic lessons of dealing with emotions through his depression. Some Capricorns try to hide from their feelings with alcohol abuse.

GOOD BOY - BAD BOY

Mike was an upcoming junior executive in a large, growing corporation. He had always gained attention through his achievements whether it was in the classroom or the soccer field. He had all the necessary Capricorn skills of hard work, organization, and ambition. What was happening, without his awareness, was that Mike's life was not balanced. He had chosen a wife who looked like the perfect, corporate-executive's wife, he joined the right sailing club, wore the appropriate wardrobe. His sights were set on success.

Mike's parents were both alcoholics, and throughout his childhood, Mike strove to be the successful son in his effort to gain his parents attention and respect. As an adult, he found it important to win the admiration of his bosses, which he set about to do with careful and deliberate planning.

The tension was high every day. Even his weekends and days off were geared around image and status in his quest for love and esteem. As you would surmise, Mike failed to look toward the people who truly loved him. He found little satisfaction in the love of his wife or his other family members who had always loved him. His parents died, in a haze of their alcoholic making without ever giving him the attention and praise he had sought from them. At that point, Mike worked even harder at becoming the successful executive. He worked longer and longer hours, planned more and more strategic parties, and scheduled a profusion of power lunches. The more he closed himself off from his own emotions, the further he moved from his loved ones, and ironically, the more he himself began to drink. At first it was social drinking but soon the social occasions became so frequent that Mike was drinking everyday starting at lunch through the evening, seven days a week.

Alcohol deadened his feelings of loneliness and disappointment. He did not have to confront his feelings of loss with the death of his parents, or the grieving for his marriage which was dying without his nurturing. The circumstance that caused him to wake up was the loss of a major promotion within the corporation. His immediate supervisor called him into his office to confront Mike with his drinking problem. Mike had now become all that he had despised about his own parents. In order to hide from his own emotions, he had tried to keep himself busy with work and his goals of success. His alcoholism revealed the breakdown of this plan.

Depression and alcoholism are an indication that the Capricorn is not confronting his karmic issues concerning his deep emotions. The emotions are there. They are real and they cannot be denied forever. Sometimes the very breakdown itself becomes a gift to the Capricorn by allowing her to pass through her own defense mechanisms and enter into her emotional neediness. It is virtually impossible to hide from your emotions forever.

CAPRICORN MALE

The Capricorn male must look toward his relationship with his father in order to understand himself. Even if the father is absent or distant, he still carries a powerful impact on the Capricorn son. He must pay attention to the dynamics of this relationship and be willing to examine it closely in order to understand himself fully as a man. Since society does not always encourage males to get in touch with their feelings, it is a natural tendency for the Capricorn to deny his emotions. This self-examination may become a formidable task for them, yet, a necessary one.

His father represents his first encounter with authority. It is through examining this relationship that the Capricorn male will identify his needs and relationships with all people who hold positions of authority throughout his life. There are some Capricorn men who claim that exceptionally strong women in their childhood took over this authoritative role. The impact will be the same. Whomever the Capricorn identifies as his first person of authority will symbolize his future relationships with authority.

Although Capricorn is considered a female sign in astrology, it symbolizes many traits which our society bestows upon its male citizens. The ethic of hard work, responsibility for protecting and providing for loved ones, and the need for status and recognition are traits easily assumed by men. The male is expected to earn a living, provide the home and protect his family. Even modern society with its equal expectations of women continues to judge a man's worth by what he does and how well he provides. Society is also less concerned with a man's emotional state than with his bank account. These pressures place an added burden on the Capricorn male even though, at first glance, they appear to be compatible. This is why many Capricorn men come to terms with their relationships with authority and their emotional complexities later in life.

The Capricorn male's karmic responsibility is to be sensitive to his own motivations and emotional needs. If he is avoiding responsibility, or on the other extreme, obsessed with his power, then he must challenge himself by looking toward his childhood in order to determine who he has been trying to please since he was a little boy. He also needs to pay great attention to how he deals with power and authority once he has achieved this position as an adult. His karmic test is not whether he achieves power but how he uses it.

Most Capricorn males are career oriented and many enjoy being self-employed. They have a need to be the boss, therefore they should avoid a family business where they are not a blood relation. This could limit their advancement in the business. On the other hand, a Capricorn male could enjoy establishing his own family-run operation which secures his family's future for generations to come.

Since rules and tradition are important to him, the Capricorn male may demand strict adherence to his rules and traditions which the rest of his family may feel are outdated. He can, therefore, become overly strict or controlling of his family unit. He must recognize that he has a gift of bringing the comfort of structure and order to his home and work but that, if carried too far, this can become a power trip for him which will alienate his loved ones and co-workers. He may be the boss but he may not always be right.

As he gets older, it would be wise for him to look into the mirror and see who he sees. He may find himself to be the mirror image of the person he liked the least in his childhood. If he has come to terms with his inner self, he will find a composite of the personality traits he has most admired in all those who were influential in his development. The Capricorn male is a strong man who has much to offer us in terms of consistency and solidarity of principles.

CAPRICORN FEMALE

The Capricorn female has been taught, from an early age, to accept life's responsibilities and live within its restrictions. She may have felt deprived on some level; deprived of affection, praise, money or freedom. She was taught to live within the limitations of her environment and to sustain an essence of loyalty and duty to family through tradition. This has long been a female role in our civilization. The woman is often the holder of traditions and the central force within the family unit, therefore, the Capricorn female can feel comfortable with this role.

She also has a distinct advantage over her male counterpart because she is "allowed" by society to feel and express her emotions. Her obligation to her karmic quest is to explore her relationships with those of authority in her early life and determine the effect these associations have on her behavior as an adult. It is not uncommon for a Capricorn female to have suffered the oppression of severe discipline, deprivation and oppressive obligations as a child. The little girl who is placed in charge of her siblings and household chores, who never feels satisfied by the affections of an emotionally distant parent, or who finds herself parenting her parents at a young age is typical of many Capricorn females. She is taught the lesson of solidifier and supporter either through personalities or circumstances around her. Her natural instincts are to take on responsibilities and so she wears her mantle of obligation with pride and strength.

She must establish an awareness of her relationship with her father, because this will directly correlate with her future relationships with men. It is common for Capricorn women who have been repressed in their early life to marry men who continue this pattern of restriction. She needs, and deserves, praise for the hardworking woman she truly is. In reality, the Capricorn female is able to maintain a relationship, raise a family, care for her home, and achieve positions of prestige within her career. She deserves a spouse who rewards her for these traits rather than one who feels threatened by her or relies too heavily upon her.

All Capricorns must be cautious not to take on the duties and responsibilities of others, and this is particularly true of the Capricorn female. There will always be people around her who will try to take advantage of her strength. Many women of all signs of the zodiac have difficulty drawing the line in their care-taking but this is a significant karmic lesson for the Capricorn female. She must learn to pull herself away from situations in her life so she may be better able to examine them from afar. This is a technique which is suitably used by many Capricorn women. It enables them to view their life with detachment from their intense emotions.

Capricorn is a sign of big business and strong ambitions which will not go unheeded by the Capricorn female. Whatever she decides is her career, she will pursue her strong need to succeed. If she feels that her family and home are her career, she will set out to be the most successful wife and mother you ever saw. You will probably find her organizing community functions, presiding over the PTA, and any other area she feels relates to her family's well-being.

The Capricorn woman who goes out into the job market has potential for brilliant success in the career of her choosing. She must not be afraid of fields which are traditionally associated with men such as banking, medicine, government or law. But, whatever field she chooses, she will strive to move up the ranks to the top position. Even women who enter traditional female fields are driven to achieve. Teachers will become principals, nurses will become hospital administrators. It is through these positions that the Capricorn female will meet her karmic tests of the use and misuse of their power. The Capricorn boss can be tough and not always the most popular. Getting the job done well, with a positive reflection on their character, will be far more important than winning a popularity contest. They must always stay attuned to their subordinates and co-workers if they are to grow karmically.

Capricorn women are wonderfully equipped to partake in the role of nurturer and career woman. The world is open to her, especially now. They have great potential to lead our society through their strict adherence to tradition and rules and their ability to demand as much from themselves as they expect of others. This may very well be the optimum time for them.

THE CAPRICORN CHILD

Your Capricorn child came into this life with a soul's awareness of the seriousness business of her karmic lessons. You may even sense a sadness or quietness in her newborn nature. What she needs, more than anything, is to be held and loved. She is basically shy, afraid, and sensitive. Allow her to feel these emotions without gruffness or reprisal on your part. She will require time alone or only with you and may feel uncomfortable with public attention or general recognition. Some Capricorn children are particularly slow and cautious as they move through life and they should not be forced to rush themselves or face the limelight if they are not ready.

Capricorn children certainly want your approval and, because of this need, will try to follow your rules and the rules of society without much resistance. Your role is not to abuse this facet of their nature. It is very easy to give additional responsibility to the child who seems best able to cope with it and makes no opposition to the rules. If you are the parent of a Capricorn, it is important that you read all of this chapter because so much of your Capricorn child's future depends upon the influence of her parents, as discussed earlier.

The father or primary disciplinarian will lay the foundation for the Capricorn child's interrelationships with all future people of authority; spouses, teachers, police officers, bosses, etc. She needs structure and order more than any other sign of the zodiac yet, as a parent, you walk a fine line in determining any abuse of her structure or discipline. You have a child who works comfortably within the rules but an excess of structure will hamper her self-image. She has an enormous need for love yet may experience a stinginess of affection or compliments in her early life. Her parents must keep a watchful eye on the balance of these energies in her early life.

Keep in mind, that she may easily become disoriented and frightened if there is a lack of order or system around her. Therefore, it is important that you do not swing to the extreme of unmeasured freedom. Discipline is her friend. It is because of this need for structure that the Capricorn child is usually ready at an early age to enter into the school, music lessons, and work. They also need a structured environment to help them excel in their studies. It would be a good idea to give them their own space, desk area or room for them to keep organized with their pursuits. They usually fare well with parochial or traditional systems of education and religious training.

It would not be unusual for the Capricorn child to have serious issues with her father. It is because of this quality, that the father must pay special attention to his interactions with this child. He needs to give his child structure and security without being overbearing or breaking her spirit. Both parents need to display warm affection toward her and encourage her to verbalize her own emotions. If your Capricorn child has difficulty with any of the "systems" such as the school, police, or work, it is important for you to help her look back to her childhood and examine her most influential relationships. This does not mean looking for blame! It indicates a time to look for clues in understanding her emotional makeup.

She needs responsibility early on because she is destined to assume positions of power and authority in her life and needs this training in her youth. The greatest gift you can give her is the acknowledgment of her sensitive nature and the tools needed to express herself emotionally.

In most of our lives, we watch the transfer of caretaker from parent to child turn to child to parent, but usually this is considerably late in our life. With the Capricorn child, she has the tendency to take care of her parents and other family members at a relatively early age. While this can be comforting and helpful during our own times of stress, you must be cautious not to exploit this aspect of her nature. She will look toward you to set her limits. Since identifying her responsibilities versus the responsibilities heaped upon her by others is one of her major karmic lessons, your example in this area can be invaluable to her.

Yours is a sensitive, wise child, sometimes mature and serious beyond her years. It is important for you to provide your Capricorn child with carefree elements in her childhood. Since she races toward adulthood before her time, it is your duty to reintroduce her to her own childhood periodically. She is certainly a child you can count on. If there is trouble in growing up, you can help her to correct it by offering careful observation of her relationships with the influential people of authority in her early life.

Give your Capricorn child an abundance of love, structure, and tradition, and she will have all the tools she needs to face the challenges of her sign. Not only will the world benefit from her strengths as an adult, you will also find comfort in her love and protection through your advancing years. She has the makings of a great leader whether it be on a small scale or large. Where would this world be without the Capricorns to hold us together?

AQUARIUS

January 20 - February 18

Male Energy

KARMIC LESSONS

♦ To dare to be different

♦ To bring change to our world

♦ To be nonjudgmental and unbiased

♦ To learn to work in groups without leadership

There are unique qualities to the Aquarian's karmic challenges which distinguish them from other signs. Therefore this foreword must be included in this chapter.

THE AGE OF AQUARIUS

We have entered into the Age of Aquarius which will influence the karmic growth of all of humanity over the following two millennia. The people who are born under the sign of Aquarius are experiencing karmic lessons which are similar to those encountered by all mankind. I see the Aquarians of today as the leaders of our world, not by the positions of power which they may or may not assume, but by the examples they represent through the way they live their lives. The lessons of the individual Aquarian are the same as those we must all learn as an indivisible mankind.

Our world is in dire need of change. Countries and political parties are reforming and disintegrating, age-old institutions of medicine, religion, and education are reshifting their basic structures and none of this is happening without the outside pressure of Aquarianism. We see that none of these changes are coming about with ease. Our world, at this writing, is wrought with anger, dissension, panic, and prejudice, overflowing with the desperate clamoring of people fighting the inevitability of change, for change is frightening to many who are unable to see the purging need to examine the old in order to eliminate the unnecessary and open their thoughts to the new. Change is unpleasant to many people. They would rather remain comfortably committed to the old simply because it is known rather than openly evaluate its usefulness. Tradition, as we saw in the Capricorn chapter, has its place in our world. It brings us continuity and comfort. The Aquarian energy helps to show us when change is needed, as frightening as that may be for many people.

Since our world now needs to experience change with the debut of the Age of Aquarius, we will be looking toward the Aquarians in our society to show us the way. Some Aquarians will assume positions of authority and lead us, as we experienced in our American politics with some of our most famous Aquarian presidents and leaders. Others will initiate change on a smaller level through their everyday lives which will serve as equally strong if not celebrated examples to us all. Great karmic responsibility, therefore, lies upon the souls of all Aquarians at this juncture of mankind's evolution. We look upon them as our signalmen and beacons through the sometimes dark chaos that inevitably travels with change. If the Aquarian is able to initiate, enjoy, and benefit from breaking away from the "system" in his everyday life, then, perhaps, we too, as a collective mass, can dare to change some of the greater establishments we created long ago. If an Aquarian can find improved health in non-traditional modes of healing then, perhaps, we can dare to question the authority of traditional medicine and demand change. If an Aquarian can grow intellectually through nonconventional forms of education, perhaps we can dare to topple the ivy walls of our traditional education system in order to try something new. The Aquarian example is forever around us. We, as a people, need our strong Aquarian individuals to show us the way.

This responsibility can sound intimidating to some people, but not Aquarians. They love to create change and disruption. To them, diversity is what makes the world go 'round, transition is their byword.

PRIMARY AQUARIUS

As much as the Aquarian energy revolves around change, this change is capable of taking many forms. You are vibrating on your primary level when you confuse change with rebelliousness. A perfect example of Aquarian rebellion is the typical teenager. The first people of authority in a child's life are his parents. In order to grow toward independence and maturity, the child must assert himself against the doctrines of the establishment, namely his parents. Here begins adolescent rebellion. This kind of antiestablishment may be quite crude and show a gross immaturity, yet it appears to be essential to that breaking away segue from childhood to adulthood.

An Aquarian is vibrating on his primary level when he resorts to shocking and rebellious behavior simply to gain attention or defy authority.

This need to electrify the world is a basic characteristic of all Aquarians but it is the motivation behind the actions that determines the maturity level. Granted, sometimes this world needs a little shocking to bring us back to basics, other times, jarring change can bring discomfort to people rather than awaken their sense of awareness. The teenager does not care whether he is awakening his parents consciousness, he only wants to create disruption and discomfort in their world. He is rebelling against the restrictions, as comforting as they may be, that his parents are imposing upon him.

Change is important to growth, and the teenager is aware that he must create change in order to establish his own individuality within his family unit. This is the premise of all dissenters or radicals who wish to put change into our world. Since this is the Aquarians' job, he must always remain aware of the motivations behind, and consequences of, his actions in order to determine the karmic level on which he is vibrating.

All change and protestations must be fulfilled with maturity, seriousness of purpose and with the soul's intention of bettering the system through change rather than simply rebelling against the establishment. When the daughter brings home her new boyfriend who has not shaved or showered in three weeks to meet her conservative, bank president father, she is rebelling rather than showing her independence. The protester who throws a Molotov cocktail through an abortion clinic window during office hours, is acting out against authority, most probably rooted in his childhood, rather than taking an affirmative stand behind his principles. These are examples of people who are fixed in their primary stages of Aquarius. They may appear to never grow up, they are now the graying flower children of the sixties.

These Aquarians enjoy being different from the rest of society and will change their causes as society changes. You will find these folks who once protested the Vietnam war now advocating different causes but still caught in the procedure of protesting and picketing. Their causes have lost their fervor; it is the protestation which has become their addiction. The Aquarian who vibrates on his primary level is one who will always remain outside the system in dissension rather than working within the system to effect change.

The primary Aquarian enjoys being different, looking and sounding different, standing on the outside on the rim of society. He basks in the attention of noncomformity. Every community has their Aquarian spirit who seems to be just a touch off the mainstream. He seems to walk a little bit to the right or left of the rest of society but not far enough off to be considered daft, just a little off-center. These people are interesting, although a bit frightful. We envy their ability to stand apart yet we do not want to get too close to them, nor do we want our children to emulate them. They are the interesting characters in our society who bring it color and usually do no harm.

Other Aquarians will be disruptive in their nonconformity and they can be frightening to us. These are primary Aquarian souls who have become slaves to their need to be different simply for the sake of attention, no longer aware of the distinction between positive and negative consideration. They become powerless to aid humanity's growth through change because they have been fixated in the monotony of their own nonconformity. They have now conformed to their own rebellion.

EVOLVED AQUARIUS

The evolved Aquarian will still be unconventional or antiestablishment on some level, but will go about the business of changing the structures of society by working within the system. Rather than being the one who is outside picketing or protesting, the evolved Aquarian is inside the organization creating opportunities for change from within. They often obtain all the credentials expected by the establishment to enhance their reputations and credibility which further aids their ability to promote modification. They are still seen as somewhat out-of-step with the rest of us, but this is now considered individualism and creative uniqueness. These traits become attached to labels of genius and innovator rather than dissenter or troublemaker. Once the evolved Aquarian has gained the respect of his target, he is able to move in with his formidable power to change and transform.

The evolved Aquarian will also be working in groups rather than alone. He will seek out other people who have similar interests and who agree with his methods of approach and will distance himself from the people or groups he sees as radicals or crackpots. This does not mean that he wears a cloak of deception, for he aims to deceive neither himself or those around him. He has learned, through experience, that it is more effective to join the cause you wish to convert and implement your changes from within. He knows that there is power and credibility in numbers and that the groups he chooses to join will become extensions of his own image, and in turn, affect his reputation. Do not confuse this evolved Aquarian with the image of a closeted liberal afraid of showing his true motives. He may be quite outspoken and dramatic in his pursuit of change. He simply goes about his work with the help of groups of like-minded people, working within the system looking to implement change.

The evolved Aquarian will also become actively involved in humanitarian causes. He is the true shepherd of all people regardless of religious, ethnic, racial or sexual considerations. He understands that we are all here on earth together with the common goal of soul evolution rather than the complexity of an earthly henpecking order. The evolved Aquarian will try to show the world, through his example, that we are all equals. He will show no prejudice or bias in his actions, deeds or words nor will he tolerate these negative behaviors in anyone around him. This can be accomplished through fighting for causes or by the quiet example of his daily living. His karmic obligation may not be to touch the masses but rather to influence a select few in his immediate environment. Most importantly, he will not need to prove his point through the techniques of shock or scandal but through the example of his own life.

The evolved Aquarian is like the ninth card of the major arcanum of the ancient Tarot, *The Seeker*. He is educated by the streets of life and acts as the bearer of the beacon for us as he guides us, through the wisdom of his example, into this wonderful Age of Aquarius. An age where we will all, eventually, realize the commonality of our diversity and the recognition of the treasure of our many uniquenesses; where we will learn to work in groups without dissecting ourselves into neat little cliques or ostracizing our neighbor; where we appreciate each other as equals each with unique gifts to share. This "utopia" is within our reach during this Age of Aquarius. If it seems a formidable goal for our diverse world, imagine the challenge it brings to the individual soul of the Aquarian. Small steps will bring us within leaping distance of this universal ambition and the evolved Aquarians will be leading our way.

REMEMBER, NO ONE IS TOTALLY PRIMARY OR EVOLVED. OUR KARMIC LESSONS ARE BEST LEARNED WHEN WE ARE DEALING WITH BOTH OF THESE ENERGIES.

WORKING IN GROUPS

When you dare to be different, you isolate yourself or set yourself apart from the rest of the group. When a teenager wants to show his parents that he is his own person and not simply a clone of their image, he dresses differently, wears outlandish hair styles, and refuses to conform to his parents codes of ethics or style. I remember when my son was a teenager, he had to have special, name brand, expensive sneakers. He could not be caught dead in those regular, no name, black ones he had worn before.

So, we started a sneaker fund, I put a little away each week, and he started mowing lawns and raking leaves. In no time the necessary money, which could have served as the mortgage payment, was put together and he bought his sneakers. He came home proudly sporting his new investment, which made him look like he was all feet, with the shoe laces untied. He looked like he would walk right out of them. Running for the school bus would have been totally out of the question. But would he tie the laces? Oh, no! That's not the way it was done. Boy, didn't I know anything? The next time I walked through town, I noticed that all the teens were wearing the same sneakers and none of them had their laces tied. Ah, I thought, this is an Aquarian thing. As much as the teens had to dress differently from the rest of conventional society, it was mandatory that they all fit uniformly into their own group. People who dare to be different will ultimately seek out other people who are exactly like themselves.

The flower-children of the sixties are another example of this Aquarian kind of grouping. The hippies of this generation all protested the establishment. They scorned the morals, ethics, and values of their parents and dared to look and act differently from everyone else. Yet, no matter where you were, whether it be New York, California, Canada or England, all the flower-children dressed, talked, and acted alike. They had established their own group and were totally uniform, conforming to their new association. This is an Aquarian need.

As an Aquarian, you will try to reform the establishment by, at times, rebelling against it. It is your karmic responsibility to the rest of us to help lead us from our own complacency through the direction of your rebellion. Yet, it is important for you to band together with groups of others like yourself in order to give yourself the support system and energy that you will need. It will help you to be aware of the need for sameness which you will crave when you dare to leave the comfort of society's traditions. You are a person who needs to be involved in groups and the company of kindred souls.

Many of the New Age groups being established are indicative of the intense Aquarian energy on our earth right now. The sign of Aquarius is compatible with the New Age philosophy along with the science of astrology and the concepts of metaphysics. These are society's ways of seeking a change from the more traditional spiritual beliefs which have become entrenched in our culture. Interestingly, these may be presented as new concepts and called New Age, but they are beliefs which have been around longer than our more established and socially accepted religious orders. Many people are therefore changing back to a belief or philosophical system which their souls embraced centuries ago.

It is only natural that people would attempt to organize these systems by forming groups, such as New Age centers or organizations. Traditionally, all groups are developed through constitutions and bylaws, leaders are elected and divided into categories of president, vice-president, and secretary. Individuals seek power through their positions and put their names upon the seals of their organization. This is not the *Aquarian* way although it is the *established* way of running a group. We know the pitfalls of this method, it can create cliques, attract power-seekers and eventually lead to acceptance of some people versus the alienation of others. But how else does one form a group? Doesn't every organization need someone to lead it? Who will be responsible for the decision making policies?

This is where the Aquarian comes in to work out his karmic lessons. Your job, as an Aquarian, is to enter into groups and help guide its members toward a nonpartisan, equal opportunity arrangement which affords no greater fame or power to one member over another. In theory, there would be no one leader, no battle of egos, no powerful cliques. The founders of democracy in our country were attempting this Aquarian format as they put together our country's constitution. What inevitably occurs is the intrusion of a powerful ego force, which has come to us through many of our leaders, and which must be fought against on a constant basis. This concept is not a simple one nor is it an especially easy one, yet it is necessary for you to touch upon in some capacity in order for you to comprehend this karmic lesson. You may experience your Aquarian role as the organizer of a group, as an anonymous member or as one who is oppressed by another group. Your karmic testing will come to you through your adherence to the Aquarian rule of equality within groups.

Some people feel that this cannot be obtained without chaos. How can a group be successful without strong leadership and exclusive rules, they ask. A group will lose its identity if it is open to all kinds of people. Here is an example of this exercise in Aquarianism.

THE AJNA METAPHYSICAL EDUCATION CENTER

In the 1980s two women and I organized an Aquarian, New Age center which brought together many different teachers in the Long Island area to bring their expertise to others without competition of egos. Many teachers shared their knowledge in astrology, tarot, meditation, philosophy, yoga and various health fields. The concept was designed so that the community members could learn from many different teachers; thereby, having the opportunity to learn more than they could from one teacher and having the influence of more than one instructor in their learning journey. The center was not named after any one person, it had no titles of president or director and was run by a board which was open to all members. Anyone could become a member which meant that they were willing to help support the Center through contributions of time and/or money. All mechanisms of running the organization functioned on a volunteer basis.

One of these members said that she would volunteer to make us thank you notes to send to all those who gave their help along the way. She designed some lovely cards but insisted that her initials be on the back of them because she would never do anything creative without her initials being a part of it. Here was a challenge to our Aquarian efforts. Up to this point no one had challenged the organization's purpose of equality of recognition through the process of nonrecognition. People had given much more of their time, talents, money, and expertise to the Center and had never asked for recognition. The proposal was put before the board, not because it was a monumental request but because it challenged the basic concepts of AJNA. It was determined that her initials would not be used which meant that her thank you notes could not be accepted. This was an uncomfortable challenge to all of us since we felt we were bordering on the concept of exclusion by our decision, yet it was a principle for which we felt an unquestionable allegiance. This was the basic concept of the Aquarian center. Those on that board who were born under the sign of Aquarius, of whom there were many, were experiencing a particular karmic lesson. The decision was important to all of us but especially so for the Aquarians.

It may be more difficult to implement these theories within already established organizations, such as Kiwanis, Girl Scouts of America, PTA's, Masons, sororities, and so on. Yet it is important that all groups eventually become sensitive to the Aquarian need for change. Your responsibility as an Aquarian is to remain attuned to your own ego's needs concerning your group or club affiliations. You must control yourself from any ambition to dominate others within the group or seek status which is detrimental to anyone else in or out of the group. You will find tests in these areas throughout your life until you make a commitment to equality and the greater purpose of serving humanity through your choice of memberships. The perfect groups for you are those which deal with humanitarian causes, world improvement, and environmental issues. You need not be the leader within your group, for it is through your actions that you advance your karmic growth, not the prestige of your position. If you achieve a position of power, your challenges will be even greater. It is here that you will confront your ego's needs versus the good for all. Most importantly, you need to involve yourself in group activity regardless of the conflicts or discomfort they may bring you. You are here to lead us in this area and many will be looking toward you for your example.

DEALING WITH PREJUDICE AND JUDGMENT

Your karmic responsibility, as an Aquarian, is to recognize your own prejudices, along with the prejudices of those around you, then go about the task of casting out these negative judgments through the example of your nonconforming behavior. You must first acknowledge the fears which your prejudices represent, for all bias is based on fear. Most people who need to hate have a fear of being trod upon or hated by someone else. It seems to be safer to keep one group of people in a lesser position in society in order to keep themselves in a higher position. As an Aquarian, you are instinctively able to recognize prejudice as one individual's fear of being abused by someone else. Power comes to the group who is on the top of this henpecking order. And the power diminishes as one is positioned further and further down. This type of classing has been apparent in all societies of mankind throughout the ages. It is not Aquarian in spirit and will take many years of Aquarian effort to eliminate.

What can you do as one Aquarian? You are able to show the world, through your example, that our society is able to function in harmony without abusing each other. You must first, and foremost, identify your own fears and prejudices. You must acknowledge them to yourself for you are a natural member of this world and have been tarnished as effectively as the rest of us by your upbringing, social standing, and the collective unconscious as taught by Carl Jung. We are products, not only of our experiences in this lifetime, but also by those of all mankind, present and past. You are a person of change. You have the ability to transform aspects of yourself and to influence many people around you by your actions. You can choose to put yourself in a position of power where you can affect masses of people or you can concentrate on your personal environment, the effect will be equally important.

HOW SOME FAMOUS MODERN AQUARIANS HAVE INFLUENCED US

➤ GERTRUDE STEIN - Writer and patron of modern art, Gertrude Stein encouraged the modern artists of her time, Jacques Lipchitz, Pablo Picasso, Henry Matisse and others to defy the tradition of artistic styles by daring to Aquarianize the world of art. She was a modernist author who dared to put her unconventional lifestyle into print by writing about homosexuality and interracial lovers. In her personal life she communed with the brilliant writers and artists of her time, dressed like a man and lived in an openly lesbian relationship with her lifelong lover whom she immortalized in *The Autobiography of Alice B. Toklas.*

➤ BETTY FRIEDAN - A highly intelligent woman who played an outstanding role in the women's liberation movement in the United States during the 1960s and 1970s. Her Aquarian energy sensed the injustice to women throughout time. She went about actively implementing changes into the traditional areas of employment, education, and medicine within our society. Her goal was to aid a repressed group of our society - women - and raise them to a position of equality and recognition in the male-oriented world. She sought to put an end to prejudice.

➤ TOMMY SMOTHERS - A comedic entertainer who, with his brother Dick, set upon shocking the nation with their rebellious weekly television hour called *The Smothers Brothers.* All America waited to hear what the television station VPs would censure on their show that week. Tommy Smothers loved to poke fun at the establishment, make fun of their mistakes and criticize their injustices. They had fun heralding in the Age of Aquarius by using their gift of humor, showing their vast audience where and how the system was not working, especially our political system. They defied that system and used it as the basis for their material. Still, the underlying message was always there. Change the old, get on with the new.

➤ OPRAH WINFREY - A talk-show hostess who uses her time and power to point out the samenesses in our differences as a people. She chooses material which shows us the universal similarities and challenges to all people regardless of race, religion, social standing, origin of birth, or sexuality. She has used her Aquarian energy to bring previously unspoken abuses out into the open. She has not used her forum to exploit those who have been wounded but has brought them the healing agent of sympathy and compassion. Women who were sexually abused and have lived alone with their confusion and shame are now made strong by Oprah Winfrey's willingness to share her own pains and to openly fight for their cause.

➤ **GARTH BROOKS** - A country and western singer who has made it to the top in his profession and has decided to use his position to speak out for the oppressed. He has dared to defy the, up until now, extremely conservative and traditional world of Country and Western music. Garth Brook's Aquarian energy is directed toward changing the style of his music along with some of his subject matters. Because he sympathetically addressed homosexuality in one of his songs, he was thrashed by many of his contemporaries and fans. His reaction was, *"too bad"*. One thing about being an Aquarian fighter for the oppressed, they do not get easily intimidated by the establishment. They are usually very good at saying *"too bad!"*

Perhaps the examples of these Aquarians will serve to strengthen you in the direction you wish to take in your Aquarian drive to end oppression and prejudice around you. Most of you are not in the positions of these celebrities. You must recognize that you are able to be equally beneficial exactly where you are. If you show the people around you that you have many different friends and acquaintances of varied backgrounds and lifestyles, if you show people that you refuse to combat or challenge the rights of others who are not as fortunate as you, if you give your example to others by stopping to help someone who others fear or hate, then you are living you karmic example of Aquarian equality. You must learn to believe in your own heart that all of us truly are created equal, no one is better than the other, as well as to recognize that we are not all equal in our opportunities due to positions of birth, parentage or karmic challenges.

Everyone is where they are for a purpose or many purposes which may never be known to us, nor do they need to be understood in order to be appreciated. The fact that your desk at work happens to be next to a fellow employee who is being persecuted by the rest of the staff may simply be your opportunity to test your karmic lessons in prejudice and bias. These kinds of tests will be all around you throughout your life and will always extend themselves as opportunities for your soul's growth.

Remember, Oprah Winfrey, Tommy Smothers and Garth Brooks could have taken their positions, their money and trotted off toward the easy middle road like many of their contemporaries. Betty Friedan could have chosen to fight her own battles for herself without sustaining the scars of abuse she must have suffered while serving other women of her generation. Gertrude Stein could have closeted herself, as many other lesbians had during her time and saved herself from the ridicule she must have experienced because of her daring. They were tested, each in their own way, and each chose their individual path.

Sometimes ego will give you that extra push that you might need. Aquarians enjoy being noticed. They revel in the confusion and turmoil created by their own part in turning the system inside out.

DARING TO BE DIFFERENT

Your gift to the rest of society is your ability to sense where change needs to be initiated within our traditional bases. We need your insight and stimulation to keep our world fluid and refreshing through the purging process of change. Part of your charisma is your daring nature, daring to challenge the musty structures of tradition and your fearless ambition to topple customs, replacing them with something new. The motivations behind your actions and the methods you employ to go about your modifications are of the utmost importance to your soul's evolution.

There is a child-like shock factor within all healthy Aquarians which must be kept under check or it will undermine your effectiveness in promoting change. If you appear too much as the radical who simply revels in the disruption of convention, you will quickly lose your credibility and potency. While it is important for you to dare to be an individual and nonconformist, you must also learn to work within the guidelines of the "rules", whether they be man-made law, nature's law, or law of ethics.

REBEL WITHOUT A CAUSE

There was a young man from a small southwestern town whose father wanted him to be a lawyer or doctor. The family had plenty of money and had always held a position of prestige within the community. But this young Aquarian, Johnny, had different plans for his life. He wanted to break free from what he felt were the confining limitations of traditions and expectations of this small-town community. He was more certain of what he did not want and not quite as sure of what it was he did want, yet he knew he had to defy the wishes of his father and go his own way. Being young and immature, he began his rebellion in a juvenile fashion. He wore outlandish clothing, shaved his head, leaving two braids, one behind each ear, dated all the "wrong" girls who he insisted on bringing to his parent's social affairs, and changed his college major from political science to English literature without informing his family. He then proceeded to fail enough courses that the dean of his college was forced to place him on probation during his sophomore year.

Johnny was enjoying the jolt his transgressions were giving his parents. He was fighting with all his might not to be a carbon copy of his father. All he knew was that he wanted to be his own person. He needed desperately to uncover his own identity and make that new image known to both his family and himself. All he knew at this point was that he needed to be different from the way he was raised. He needed to assert his individuality. Being young, he was rebelling exclusively against the establishment rather than riding on the crest of his own uniqueness. Johnny was searching for himself.

Opportunity was brought to him through a rather unlikely source. He was dating a girl who was a photographer for the college newspaper. Through this romance he began to spend more of his time at the paper's office and became involved in the daily issues on campus. The opening into his own identity and future came to him on an ordinary winter afternoon. A nuclear energy plant was being built only five miles from the school and Johnny went out with his girlfriend and another student reporter to cover a local demonstration against opening this plant. They expected a group of hippie radicals to be chanting and chaining themselves to link fences, ready sacrifices to the local paddy wagon which would be waiting to transport them to jail. What they found was a totally different atmosphere. Thousands of people were there in disciplined but vocal protest, determined to protect their community from what they felt was an unnecessary and potentially dangerous power source. The protesters were made up of average, middle class folks, senior citizens, public school children, and college students. They were all uniting with a common goal of combating a system that defied their ability to even scratch its armor. This power plant had already consumed millions of taxpayer's dollars. It was strongly backed by the federal and state governments. Who would listen to these few citizens? Johnny watched this crusade from that first afternoon's demonstration and followed it through the fights in the courts.

The growing strength of the lobbying done by the community was impressive. Against all odds, the power plant was forced to be closed and dismantled three years later. Through this entire process, Johnny learned the lesson of changing the system by using its own rules. He was greatly affected by the normalcy and average lifestyles of all those original protesters. Their example showed him that he did not have to make himself stand out in order to protest. He did not have to strike out at others in order to establish his own individuality.

Johnny went on to the world of journalism after graduation and became a respected writer known for championing causes which, while not always pro-establishment, were always humanitarian and ecological in nature. We would find him now wearing a conservative haircut and conventional suit. Yet we would also see the glint in his eye and feel the power of his pen as he follows the crusades which have become the illustrations of his own individuality.

As an Aquarian, you must always be attuned to the results and repercussion of your rebellious actions. Many times, the person you will hurt the most will be yourself. By fighting against a parent, community or tradition in severe rebellion you may undermine your own potential. Yours is an exciting sign with karmic lessons which will potentially add not only to your growth but also the evolution of our society. We need you to dare to be different. Creating change by working with groups of people with similar interests and by using your intellect you will discover that these are ideal keys to your successful rebellion.

AQUARIAN MALE

Several of the karmic issues of this sign are significantly important to the Aquarian male, one of which is the strong need for male bonding and friendships. Even as a young boy, he needs to involve himself with many friends and group activities in order to experience different kinds of personalities and comprehensions. In order for him to discover his own uniqueness, he needs to expose himself to the individualities of many people. Since all Aquarians need to work in groups, the Aquarian male will use the traditional group experiences of clubs and sports as his initial entry into group dynamics. It would be beneficial for him to join organizations like Boy Scouts, 4H Club, Little League and other such sports or social groups. As an adult, he may follow this direction by joining groups such as the Kiwaniis Club, Rotary Club, Masons, New Age organizations and any other type of organization that suits his personality. They may not be as traditional as these, which would also be typical of the Aquarian energy.

Since he has karmic lessons to learn through working in groups, he must expose himself to many different kinds of organizations during his life. He will also open himself to many different kinds of people through these groups. And it is here that he will find the opportunity to test his karmic goals of objectivity, humanitarianism, and eradicating prejudice. The ideal organizations for him would be those which are concerned with changing the system, helping others in need and fighting causes. Other groups may have less serious purposes behind them such as sports teams, fraternities and intellectual clubs. But let the Aquarian male not be fooled. He must always be mindful of lessons and tests which may come his way through any and all types of contact with his fellow human beings.

Our society does not always encourage male friendships. Girls are "allowed" to become closely involved in intimate relationships, telling each other everything, doing everything together. Our culture is not one that nurtures these kinds of important friendships in the lives of boys and men. Yet, they are especially important to the Aquarian male. He needs to have many friends, male and female, and some special, close friendships which he may carry with him throughout his life. Aquarian men today have a unique ability to guide their fellow men toward achieving and respecting the value of male/male friendships while acknowledging their emotional need for this bonding. This pleasure in relationships can cross lines of prejudice associated with race, sexuality, nationality, and religions. A wonderful example is the theory and principle behind our World Olympics, a particularly strong Aquarian male type of activity.

The Aquarian energy in the male form may sometimes bring with it some problems of fidelity. Aquarian energy, in nature, requires great freedom and latitude. Couple this with society's sometimes acceptance of male philandering, the Aquarian male can feel justified in experiencing sexual relationships apart from the person to whom he has committed himself. If he finds himself in a social setting that condones or even encourages extramarital relations, this may become a problem to him. Astrology, as a philosophy, does not involve any judgment of right and wrong in these kinds of issues. These rules are established solely by the society and culture of your time and place. Therefore, this need for freedom and ability to disassociate a sexual affair with his loyalties to his mate, may or may not be a conflict for the Aquarian male. His karmic lesson is not one of faithfulness but it may become a lesson in terms of playing within the man-made rules of his culture. To compound this issue, the Aquarian male is fully capable of maintaining friendships with women and even ex-lovers or spouses long after the sexual aspect of the relationship has ended. His mate will have to understand this facet of his nature and learn to differentiate between friendship and infidelity. This can be quite a challenge with honesty and trust being crucial to the success of their relationship.

Many Aquarian men enter into fields or careers which allow them to assert their uniqueness and individuality. They use their careers as their vehicle of bringing about change. The job itself can be devoted to nontraditional activities, New Age challenges or humanitarian issues. They may seek to change the world through science, technology, teaching or the fine arts. Aquarian men helped bring us the computer age, the space age, democracy and much of our unconventional artistic style. They often feel most comfortable using their Aquarian energy in their work rather than their lifestyle. They can also put changes into more traditional or conservative types of employment by working within the ranks. These are the Aquarian males who fought for fair wages, medical benefits, and decent hours within powerful businesses or governments unconcerned with the humanity of their workers. The Aquarian male need not be afraid of challenging the system. Karmically, that is his responsibility.

AQUARIAN FEMALE

Friendships and the groups an Aquarian female chooses to make a part of her life will have a strong influence on her values, character, and life direction. She must, therefore, choose her friends carefully. The people surrounding her will be indicative of her interests at that particular time in her life, and she will be able to mold herself into their physical and emotional sameness. This can sometimes be frightening to the parents of an Aquarian daughter, especially during her adolescence. The Aquarian female can lean toward either of two major directions as she is growing up: one is rebellious in spirit and the other in intellect. Sometimes she keeps a foot in both places. She needs to join intellectual groups such as those associated with computers, art, science or social causes. She is not afraid of rebelling against the establishment, so do not be surprised if she starts suggesting changes right away.

It is when the Aquarian female chooses the lure of free-wielding rebellion that she must be cautious of the causes she champions and the people with whom she associates. As a young woman she is learning to assert her independence, and in the process, discover her individuality.

She will naturally gravitate toward people who are declaring similar rebellions. An unhealthy deviance of law and order, for example, can place a trusting or immature Aquarian female in jeopardy. She must learn to choose her causes with care which will include discrimination on her part of the people with whom she chooses to affiliate.

Even though the Aquarian female, like her male counterpart, must choose her actions carefully, the basic make up of her sign can propel her toward radical causes and deviant behavior. She is a strong woman who is capable of placing great changes into her world through her work or family relationships. She is able to create great breakthroughs in some of the more traditional areas of society because she is easily admired and followed by others.

Women are the basis of most family units in our society. They are responsible for maintaining the structure of each family nucleus, the continuity and setting of the tone. The Aquarian female has the opportunity to teach her particular family members through her own example. If she is comfortable in her karmic role as the reformer and caretaker of humanitarian causes, then she, by her own example, will lead her family unit toward their obligations to question the unfairness and inequality of the system. She is skillful at displaying equitable and just action toward people who are oppressed by society. If she surrounds herself with many different kinds of people as her friends and if she displays her strength of championing the causes with her great passion, she is bestowing an invaluable gift of her example to all around her, especially her closest loved ones.

The Aquarian female is usually a particularly strong woman, and therefore, needs a mate who is equally strong without overruling her individualistic style. Her accomplishments may be grand, on the world level, or minute, on a personal level, but no one direction is less important than another. For example, she may influence a child's mind, if she is a teacher or a mother. That child may grow to achieve more celebrated attention through his lessons. Yet that child's accomplishments are as important to karmic fulfillment as those silent accomplishments of the Aquarian female who first influenced him. We must never underestimate the potential of the Aquarian female.

AQUARIAN CHILD

Your Aquarian child needs to be raised in an environment which encourages the fullest potential of his individuality and uniqueness. If one or both of his parents are severe traditionalists he will need to struggle and rebel in order to find himself. Your Aquarian child is different. You must accept that from the very beginning and then encourage that uniqueness rather than try to force him to conform. This does not mean that he will look different, or even appear different in personality right away. Sometimes it shows in infancy, other times it blossoms later in life. The ease by which your child is able to love and accept himself for his own differences is dependent on how much you, as his parents, have nurtured and accepted his individuality.

This is not to say that you must allow your Aquarian child to do whatever he wants without regard to rules and order. Quite the contrary. You will be assisting your child if you teach him the rules and the expectations of society and tradition so he will be able to live comfortably within them as he injects his changes. You must teach him respect of the rules and not fear of the system! To be totally rebellious will simply exhaust him. Complete freedom of self-expression will only create a spoiled child. Rules have their place. After all, he is here to change some of our rules. He needs to be comfortable with them so he will be able to choose where and how to assert himself.

The Aquarian child is creative and intelligent. It is through these two parts of his consciousness that he will discover himself. As he matures, these will become the tools he will use to assert himself. It is important to listen to the subtle messages he will give you to show you where his interests lie. Help him through lessons and activities which nurture his creativity and intelligence. Encourage his self-confidence by showing respect for his work and giving him your honest criticism. If you see him uncomfortable in a regimented program, then try to get him into a more liberal or progressive learning experience. Applaud his uniqueness and encourage him to assert his individuality.

If your Aquarian teenager comes home with green and orange hair and you have your boss coming over for dinner, do not put your child in the basement for the night. The greatest gift you can give him is to give your honest opinion of his hair and then sit him at the dinner table with pride. You will be teaching him that you encourage individuality and that you are not living in fear of traditional authority. You are also showing him that you accept him for who and what he is which is exactly the strong family base that a healthy Aquarian requires.

Sometimes, the Aquarian offspring can frighten you with the kinds of people he brings home or the unhealthy rebellious activities with which he may become involved. It is because of this ability to swing to great extremes that he will need the honesty of your opinions and the structure of the simple rules of society taught to him in his childhood. There will be times when you will have to place a firm hand on his activities and times when you will have to trust your judgment to let him play it out. The closer you are in understanding your Aquarian child, the easier this discrimination will be for you. Even with your greatest intentions, there will be times when you will simply have to hold your breath and wait it out. You must prepare yourself for the unexpected. Unusual friends, lovers and acquaintances will come through your front door on the arm of your Aquarian child. Friends of all backgrounds will be a part of his life. You will help your Aquarian child if you show that you are open to all kinds of people and that you are willing to give of your time and energy toward humanitarian causes and issues of equality. Any hint of bias or prejudice will be uncomfortable for him and it is especially difficult for the soul of an Aquarian to be raised to be a bigot or hatemonger. Since most of this kind of anger is initiated in early life, your beliefs will have a tremendous impact on your child's karmic growth in this area.

One final trait of the Aquarian child may be difficult on his parents, particularly if they are possessive in nature. He must have free reign to leave and go out on his own at an early age, if this is his desire. It is harmful to try to trap or control an Aquarian's demand for freedom. He needs to know that you are a constant and steady bond in his life and that he is free to come and go. If you have given him the background of encouraged free will, a healthy respect of authority along with the intelligence to question, a love and consideration of people, and a pride in his own uniqueness, then you have helped to nurture an Aquarian child and prepared him for his significant goals in life. Now you have to let him go and hope that society looks as favorably as you do on his karmic need to influence change in our world.

PISCES

February 19 - March 20

Female Energy

KARMIC LESSONS

- ◆ To give without being used

- ◆ To establish self-identity

- ◆ To learn to trust their intuitive natures

- ◆ To bring beauty and art to their world

- ◆ To deal with misunderstanding
  and abuse of their sensitive natures

- ◆ To be exposed to temptations of
  escape such as alcohol and drugs

THE NATURAL ORDER OF THINGS

Theory is that we all live lifetime after lifetime in each sun sign until we learn all the lessons that each sun sign has to offer. No one seems to agree on how many lives we must live in each sign or what order we go in as we travel from sign to sign. Some say we start at Aries, then go on to Taurus and so forth. Others believe that we complete all the fire signs first and then proceed to the earth signs until we are through. Philosophers and metaphysicians seem to thrill with this kind of debate. Yet most seem to agree that the last sign we will experience in our evolutionary journey on this earth plane is Pisces.

If you are a Pisces, you have already lived many lifetimes in each of the other eleven sun signs and are now facing your final challenges on this earth plane. This would account for the super sensitivity felt by those born under the sign of Pisces. There is a weariness that comes with the soul that has experienced so many encounters with life. The symbol of the fish most associated with Pisces is an excellent illustration of this exhaustion. One fish is swimming upward toward the spiritual realm and the other is swimming downward toward earth. There is a division within the Pisces soul based on reluctance. Reluctance to leave the comforts of its spiritual sanctuary where it exists between earth lives and its desire to return to earth in order to finally complete its education and tests on this level. A part of the Pisces consciousness knows that earth offers the experiences it needs and another part is weary, perhaps exhausted on an emotional and physical level and does not feel strong enough to cope with the difficult lessons which await. Often, Pisces children come into this life with weak physical stamina, strong desire to sleep, and a noticeable look of depth and wisdom in their eyes.

EVOLUTION VERSUS STRENGTH

There are some people who question this theory of evolution concerning Pisces because of their lack of strength. The question asked is, *"If a Pisces is the highest evolved of all the signs then why do they mess up so often? Why aren't they stronger by nature?"*

Let us look at those valid queries by using the analogy of school. We are all here on earth as students, each of us involved in our own personal program of study depending on the level of our soul's evolvement and the lessons we have chosen to experience this time around. When you were in kindergarten your lessons were simple and often fun. They were important because they were laying the foundations for all your future learning. Still, they were simple in nature and offered you little challenge. Your lessons became increasingly more difficult and complex as you went through elementary school, high school, and college.

A Pisces is similar to a Ph.D. candidate in that the lessons are most difficult and the expectations for success are particularly high. Like the student, the Pisces also experiences a weariness of school and alternating desires to quit or just get it over with. Obviously this analogy has nothing to do with intelligence. The Pisces is no more intelligent than any other sign. These are karmic lessons, not text book. Nor is the Pisces any better spiritually than other signs. No matter what our sign, we have a tendency to grade each others progress through the evolutionary process. In reality, we are qualified to evaluate only ourselves and therefore must control ourselves from judging the progress of the weary Pisces. As you will see from the remainder of this chapter, the Pisces' lessons are indicative of the vulnerability of the sign, and many Pisces choose to identify with that part of themselves that seeks to return to the higher ground by escaping their difficult challenges. Pisces are also vulnerable and often succumb to the abuses they experience in this life. When they are good they are very very good, and when they are bad they are horrid!

BAD PRESS

In astrology, Pisces is a sign which is associated with all the dark and gloom of life. It represents heartbreak, sorrow, disappointment, and general ill-fortune. It is certainly not the comedic sign of the zodiac. To add to this image, Pisces are often overwhelmed by their own karma and fall into the abyss of drugs, alcohol, and severe melancholia. Doesn't sound like much fun, does it? But there is a lighter side to this sign, which you will be learning about in this chapter. There is also that other fish which swims to the heights of spiritual bliss. This is the direction the Pisces soul is seeking in its journey toward karmic evolvement.

THE JESUS EXAMPLE

If you are one of those people who feel the hairs on the back of your neck rise in alarm when anything religious or biblical is mentioned, especially in regard to astrology, you can relax. The correlation between Jesus and Pisces is in reference to the teachings of a famous human being and how they can be used by the Pisces as a guide toward her karmic evolvement.

Many metaphysicians believe that Jesus was born under the sign of Pisces. His Capricorn birthday was given to Him by the early Christians. Some of His Piscean symbols point toward this argument. He chose His disciples from fishermen; the fish was the secret symbol of their order and many of His miracles and analogies revolved around fish and the sea. Jesus' birth also ushered in the astrological Age of Pisces. His messages were heralding the meaning of this New Age and are significant to all those born under the sign of Pisces. He was teaching the people of the world about their karmic evolutionary process and these words of guidance can still be directed effectively to the karmic challenges of the individual Pisces.

When I am giving a reading to Pisces I always counsel them to read all the words written in red in the New Testament, regardless of their religious beliefs. The words of this teacher are excellent guidance for the Pisces as she searches for her karmic growth in this lifetime. She needs to practice the wisdoms of turning the other cheek, caring for the meek and mild, standing tall for principles which herald human kindness, to remain strong in her convictions while honestly admitting her fears and weaknesses.

Some people may see Jesus as a weak man who wore clothing of low station, associated with troubled men, leaned heavily on women, and allowed himself to be killed rather than assert his powers. Others see him as a man who was not afraid to confront the most powerful authorities of his times, the Rabbis. A man who was comfortable in his passivism while strong enough in his beliefs to initiate changes in religions which are still followed today (although many argue that these original beliefs of Jesus are hardly recognizable in our modern churches). So we see Jesus as a positive example to Pisces of being able to use their sensitivities to their advantage while developing their strengths of character.

This is a difficult sign, like all the water people, and must be understood from both an intellectual and emotional perspective.

PRIMARY PISCES

The primary tendencies of Pisces are more often noticeable than your evolved traits. It is so easy to become that fish who does not want to participate in life's challenges. It is so easy to succumb to the fears which seem to thrive in your subconscious. Because of your weariness you must always be wary of your tendency to seek unhealthy escapes from the reality of misfortune or difficulty around you. Some of the typical self-defeating escapes used by a Pisces are addictions to drugs and alcohol, excessive sleeping patterns, and chronic depression. As one can see, these afflictions are also connected with illnesses to which the Pisces can be susceptible. In the primary stage, you can easily allow yourself to be swept up by these states of despair which then pull you out of the mainstream of life and away from the fullest extent of your potential. A segment of this chapter will be devoted to addictions.

The underlying emotion of all Pisces is insecurity. In the primary stage, you will have difficulty overcoming this self-defeating emotion and will react to most of life's challenges through the haze of your poor self-image. You will find it difficult to overcome this lack of confidence and may keep yourself in situations and relationships which perpetuate your self-doubts. You will then be easily used and abused by others who take advantage of your vulnerability in order to maintain their power. All Pisces have a basic desire to help others and care for the less fortunate. When you are vibrating on your primary level you misconstrue this desire to help with your feelings of poor self-worth which leave you as the caretaker for the abusers in your life rather than the angel of mercy you would prefer to be. You can become so consumed with your fears and neurosis, and so easily hurt on an emotional level, that you will become the slave of your own negativity. You will attract negative people, you will feel negative yourself, you may then absorb these nefarious energies into your persona and become the initiator of negative behavior rather than the recipient.

Here is where we see the Pisces disintegrate into the great abyss of darkness.

Other Pisces keep themselves protected from the weakness around them but they don a hairshirt as their defense. These are the Piscean martyrs. No one can beat their chest louder or more dramatically than a primary Pisces who is surrounding herself with weak people in order to feel stronger or better about herself. Most Pisces have a tendency to play the martyr now and then, but it becomes an integral part of your personality if you are caught in this primary level. Motivations behind your actions will always be of greater karmic significance than the actions themselves. Walking the little old lady across the street at midnight when no one sees you is far more favorable to your karmic growth than bringing all traffic to a standstill in the main street of town in the middle of the day to escort her grandly to the curb. You are really blowing it if you then go home and tell everyone how you put her safety first, even though it made you late for a very important appointment and probably cost you a much wanted promotion at work. Why we can hear the chest-pounding from here!

EVOLVED PISCES

Pisces are always sensitive to drugs, alcohol, and the poisons of our environment. If you are evolved in your sign you will probably have had some kind of contact with addictions either through your own experience or by living through or observing the addictions of other people around you. Armed now with the wisdom of experience, you are able to help others who are still caught in their struggles with these unhealthy types of escapes from the realities of life. If you combine your life experiences and your compassionate nature, you are able to help others through their difficult times. You would make a wonderful healer, medically, socially and psychologically.

Pisces, in its evolved stage, is the greatest of all healing energies. You have the ability to sense the pains and weaknesses of others and help lead them toward their own restoration. You are prepared to offer your love and compassion to all who need protection and guidance. Your special sensitive nature allows you to hone in on a person's particular difficulty and help show them the escape from their troubles. This will take the form of a healing on all levels, physical, spiritual, and emotional.

An evolved Pisces is capable of helping others without being pulled down or taking the role of the martyr. There is a power of helpfulness which also displays a strength of character, that sets limits, and refuses to be abused. You will teach those weaker than yourself to strengthen themselves and become self-sufficient rather than dependent on you for the long term. Your psychic energies allow you to sense the needs of others without needing to explain yourself to the technical world. This is the Pisces healer who sees a medical patient and "knows" that he is on the wrong medications without the aid of blood work or extensive testing. Hunches or instinct become your favorite allies. As an evolved Pisces, you are confident of your own strength and can no longer be misused by others. It is at this point that you are capable of truly serving others, as your sign is so perfectly equipped to do.

The evolved Pisces is true to both sides of its nature, of both fish, so to speak. You are in tune with your need to face life's challenges here on earth and your equally important need to maintain your spiritual balance. You realize that the full extent of your spirituality may not be totally appreciated or understood by others, that you live by the laws of nature rather than the laws of man. You vibrate to the spiritual meanings of life rather than the rules man has circled all around his understanding of spirituality. You will feel what is "right" for you even if you are unable to explain yourself or convince others. Because of this confusion, the evolved Pisces is not always seen as evolved. She may be persecuted by her society because she is different, because she seems to follow another voice rather than the shouts of man-made doctrines. If you find yourself at odds with the mores of society, you must follow your special instincts and feel confident that your spiritual guidance may be further evolved than even the most established traditions and ordinances. Remember, Jesus had to fight against the established, traditional faith of His time in order to teach His new philosophy of spirituality.

REMEMBER, NO ONE IS TOTALLY PRIMARY OR TOTALLY EVOLVED. OUR KARMIC LESSONS ARE BEST LEARNED WHEN WE ARE DEALING WITH BOTH OF THESE ENERGIES.

GIVING WITHOUT BEING USED OR ABUSED

A Pisces' basic nature is to be of service to others. As a Pisces, you care about the well-being of others around you. Since you were a child, this sensitivity to the needs of others has been an integral part of your temperament. The messages you receive from your family in your early life help to strengthen or weaken your effectiveness in this service. People around you will sense your need to please and serve, and therefore, may take advantage of this apparent "weakness." If your family lives by the doctrine of might makes right, or only the strong survive, they may see you as the weak link and take advantage of your giving, easy-going nature. They may attempt to keep you in a controlled position by exacerbating your insecurities and undermining your self-confidence. You are a delicate soul who is in tune with the feelings and moods of your environment and, because of this part of your nature, you can be easily intimidated and put aside by stronger willed or abrasive personalities. It would be easy for you to pick up the message of power-makes-right and be subdued by aggressiveness. This Pisces is taught to feel that they are here to serve those who are mightier than they, which, in turn, creates an attraction to those who may abuse and misuse their serving nature.

WENDY HAD TO LOVE HERSELF FIRST

Wendy's older brother, Jeff, was a terror in the family. He was strong-willed, spoiled and quick to anger. Wendy, being a typical Piscean child, learned to withdraw from his outbursts by keeping to herself. She found pleasure and companionship in the recesses of her own imagination and the company of animals. She was always finding birds with broken wings and motherless kittens to take care of and nurture. Wendy's sensitivity made her especially vulnerable to Jeff's constant belittling. She grew up hearing she was stupid and homely, that no one really wanted her in this family. Her father felt his son could do no wrong, *"boys will be boys"* and her mother seemed to prove powerless against the emotional abuses she and Wendy endured. These messages were particularly harmful to Wendy since her basic nature was one of insecurity and poor self-image.

When Wendy began dating she found herself seeking the broken and unloved souls she had always found comforting in her youth. She easily transferred her love for injured and motherless animals into her choice of men. To her disappointment, these men did not greet her kindness with the gratitude and love she expected. They, like her brother, took advantage of her soft nature and continued to exploit and abuse her. Wendy's closest friends told her to look for a better quality of men, the achievers, the movers and shakers. But Wendy did not feel that she would be attractive to these men. It was far safer for her to set her goals on the weaker men who she felt would be easier to obtain. Her lack of self- confidence, garnered through the many years of her belittling childhood, left her feeling that she deserved no better. Her emotional abuses had all the potential of escalating into physical abuses if she did not take control of her life. By the time she had graduated college, she found herself at a crossroads. She was intelligent enough to see that her relationships, as she knew them now, were unhealthy and held little future for her, yet she did not know how to restructure her patterns toward improvement. Wendy stood at that crossroads and pictured her life with a series of weak relationships and unfulfilled needs. Her friends told her she deserved more. They encouraged her to love herself as much as they loved her. If she believed that she deserved better then she would attract better. Wendy knew it had to begin within herself. Her Piscean insecurities had bought into the verbal abuses she endured in her childhood. She had allowed herself to believe she was not worthy of a strong, healthy relationship. So, Wendy set out to strengthen her own self-image. She learned to like herself until, eventually, she was strong enough to rebuke her brother's negativity and forgive her mother's weakness. She took responsibility for herself and discovered her own strengths which were inherent in her Pisces energy. Wendy chose her path on those crossroads which was very different from the path she had known. It took courage, strong desire, and help from good friends but she did it. Her future relationships held a greater potential for her now.

As a Pisces, you will need to overcome those nagging voices of insecurity from within and stand up to the bullies in your life who try to take advantage of your fears in order to gain power and control over you. You are kind and gentle by nature, looking for the road of pleasure and ease rather than easily accepting a course of conflict; coupled with reluctance to do battle and your underlying nature of insecurity and self-doubt. This leaves you vulnerable to the abuses and misuses of other people's power. Karmically, you are here to learn to love yourself, to develop your own strengths and feel that you are capable and deserving of the best. You have so much to give to the rest of this world but you are only capable of bringing your healing energies to us if you are first able to heal yourself. It is important for you to be helping and serving mankind without becoming a symbolic doormat upon which to be walked by others.

Yours is a karmic lesson which deals with powerful emotions. You need to be loved but must first feel that you deserve the best in your love relationships. Some Pisces try to buy love by always taking care of others, therefore making themselves indispensable. This can also lead to abuse.

MOTIVATIONS BEHIND LOVING KINDNESSES

Jerry seemed always to be attracted to the same kind of woman. All his relationships seemed to end the same way. He had experienced several love affairs in a row which indicated his pattern of being abused, or so it appeared to the outside world. With each of these women, Jerry had found people who were down and out on their luck and needed someone to help them get on their feet. He helped Joy earn her high school equivalency diploma and encouraged her to go on for her college degree in elementary education. He protected Martha as she went through a turbulent divorce, paying her mortgage and electric bills when she was unable, and helping her to deal with her three children's seemingly endless problems. His last relationship was with Alice who seemed different from the others in that she was educated, independent, and successful in her career. But it was less than six months into their courtship that Jerry began to notice a strange twist in Alice's behavior. Within two months, Jerry found himself in the midst of Alice's manic cycle of her manic/depressive illness. He stayed with her during her wild sprees of spending and paranoia only to find that she wanted no more of their relationship once she had achieved balance through the proper medication. In fact, each of these women had eventually ended their relationships with Jerry after they had achieved their strengths and no longer needed him. It seemed to be such a sad pattern to all Jerry's friends. Why did he choose such needy women who took him for all he was worth and then left him?

Jerry's self-image was so poor that he felt he was only worthy of relationships with women who were weak or destitute. He feared that self-reliant, strong women would not be interested in him. He also allowed his Piscean sensitivity to rule his heart by seeking out those who needed his nourishing personality while they were at a weakened state. Once these women, with Jerry's help, achieved their strengths, his continued presence in their lives became a constant reminder to them of their vulnerability. They wanted to move on with their lives. Jerry was a Pisces who was allowing himself to be abused by choosing just the right women to bring him this karmic experience.

THE HAIR SHIRT SYNDROME

You must always stay attuned to your motivations and behavior while in the process of helping others. You may look like a demigod to the outside world but may be hell to live with within your relationships. You are meant to be caring and nurturing of others but you must watch out for your tendency to play the martyr. If you were to outline fact-for-fact all that you have done for someone, you would come out looking like a saint. But, if you are pounding your chest and wearing the hairshirt of the martyr, you are succeeding in filling your loved one with guilt which will karmically tarnish the goodness of your actions while also creating the demise of your relationship. People might think you got a raw deal, there your love walks out on you after all you have done. They may never be aware of the heavy price of guilt your lover had to endure due to your Piscean manipulation. It is important that you remain aware of this tendency within your personality. Remember, the karmic reward of an action comes from the intent, not the overt image.

LEARN TO TRUST YOUR INTUITIVE NATURE

Yours in one of the most intuitive and psychically sensitive of all the signs. From infancy, you will feel the moods and personalities of others long before you can express yourself in words. This ability comes to you because you are an old soul and have already experienced many lives in each of the other signs. When someone comes to you with a problem, and they will, you will psychically recall your experiences with the same situation many lifetimes ago, and will naturally sympathize and relate to him. This psychic sensitivity is the basis of your loving compassion and kindness to others. Karmically, you are here to bring loving and healing energy to our planet. You must be cautious not to allow yourself to be overcome or consumed by the dark moods of others because people who are troubled will seek you out.

If you are in a terrific mood as you walk into a room of people, you can be brought down easily by the negativity of just one person who is also in that room. You can psychically zoom into that one person who seems kind of sad, mad or withdrawn. You start to wonder what is wrong with him, why is he so sad? Soon, you see nothing else in the room except that one tortured soul. In short time, your terrific mood will ebb away and be replaced with a sad and pensive energy much like that which you feel from this melancholy stranger.

Karmically, you must learn to develop your psychic sensitivity to a point that you can trust the messages it brings you without allowing yourself to become consumed by any negative factors around you. This is indeed a challenge to your Piscean nature, but well within your capabilities. The stronger you are, the more you can help others. Allowing yourself to be brought down to the negative depths of the people you are trying to help will only defeat your purpose.

When you receive a signal that brings you warning through a dream or simply a "feeling", learn to trust that intuition. You have many guides or guardian angels around you who are constantly sending you messages of help and direction. Be sure to thank your spiritual support system either through prayer, thought or deed. Yours is a spiritual sign which needs reinforcement from time to time.

LEARNING TO DEAL WITH MISUNDERSTANDING AND ABUSE

So far we have looked at your need to give to others without being abused and to be aware of your own motivations behind your actions which may lay you open to hurt. The fact is that you do wear a vulnerable aura due to your psychic sensitivity. Now we must look at the times in your life when you may need to bear the misunderstanding and abuse of others regardless of your actions and motivations to the contrary. Many Pisces have chosen to reincarnate in order to serve others and sometimes to bring them some rather difficult but important experiences. Pisces are answering to nature's laws not the laws of man. They may bring different, unusual circumstances into their realm which may have them looking bad or wrong, but they are really sacrificing their ease on earth in order to bring lessons and experiences to those around them. This is truly the Jesus-Christ syndrome.

➤ Helen and Ralph had waited many years for the birth of a child. Doctors had told them that pregnancy was most probably out of the question for them for medical reasons. So they were thrilled when Joey was born on a wintry night in March. He became their whole world; their marriage was now complete. No one knew why Joey just died in his crib when he was 18 months old. They just found him there, dead, for no apparent reason. Why was he born to live for such a short time?

➤ Sabrina was underweight and listless when she was born. The doctors assumed it was because her mother was poor, uneducated and had received no prenatal care. Sabrina's health continued to decline requiring further testing which revealed that her mother was a heroin addict and they both were suffering from AIDS. Sabrina died a painful death two years later in a foster home away from her mother who had already succumbed to death the year before her.

➤ Mike was a Pisces who was always in trouble. He was truant from school and lost in drinking binges by the time he was 14 years old. On his nineteenth birthday he was sentenced to prison for killing an innocent bystander during a gang shooting. No one could understand why Mike's mother was so unfortunate to have a no-good son like Mike when she was such a sweet gentle woman.

➤ Mary, a Pisces, married, had two children, and lived the typical life of a suburban American until she finally decided her true life calling was to the church. She tearfully left her family and moved to France where she entered a convent and took the strict vows of poverty and silence. Her family never saw her again. Why were her children punished by this unexplainable loss of their mother?

We often see Pisces choosing unhealthy, illegal, seemingly selfish directions in their lives. Or we see them being dealt an unfair hand in this game of life. They may succumb to addictions, poor health, crime or a multitude of physical or emotional malfunctions. Or their lives may lead them in an unconventional, socially unacceptable direction. We are at a loss to explain the reasons behind the fates of these Pisces. So many times, other innocent people are affected by their turn of events. This is where the mystery of karma enters and the rigidity of social law exits. We may never understand why things happen to us and other people. First, we must acknowledge the simple yet hard to comprehend fact that we do not need to know the explanation behind these karmic lessons. This is hard for us because we are a society who wants to know everything.

Secondly, we must try to dissuade ourselves from taking the role of judge as we watch the Pisces go through her learning experiences. The one whom we may choose to blame may be the soul who has entered into this lifetime to sacrifice her happiness for the sake of others. In each of the cases previously discussed, a Pisces soul came to earth in order to bring lessons and karmic experiences to those around him or her. Helen and Ralph's Pisces child lived a short time on our planet. Perhaps his purpose was to bring the experience of loss and death to his parents in order to encourage their evolution. He, like the AIDS baby, Sabrina, touched many people's lives, family, doctors, nurses, foster parents, and others we may never realize. Mike's family may have needed the frustrating experience of losing a child to the harsh world of the city streets just as Mary's family may have found karmic opportunity for evolution through the rejection of their mother as she devoted her life to the church. Yet, we tend to judge people, particularly Pisces, rather harshly. We expect them to be close to perfection because we acknowledge them as evolved souls. How can they fall from the graces of society, how can they stray from our laws? The Pisces soul is governed by a law and order far beyond our understanding. We must be careful not to judge them or any other sign, for that matter. We do not always comprehend the purpose behind karmic events.

TEMPTATIONS OF ESCAPE THROUGH ADDICTIONS

Pisces is the most addictive of all the sun signs. Of course you will always find a Pisces who has had no problem with addictions in her life, but this is rare and we can assume that her soul has already experienced this challenge in a previous lifetime.

Most Pisces will touch upon addiction in some form during their lifetime. Keep in mind that this is a sensitive sign which carries difficult karmic lessons. Add to this the Pisces' natural reluctance to become earthbound and the weariness due to the soul's number of previous incarnations, and you will find a Pisces who is often looking for avenues of escape and modes of relaxation which are associated with drugs, alcohol, nicotine and caffeine.

As a Pisces, you may find your life touching upon addictive behaviors through several means. You may be born into a family where one or more person may be addicted to drugs or alcohol, and/or you may be attracted through your love relationships to a person who is struggling with an addiction. You yourself may need to face this challenge through your own addictive personality. Your karmic lessons lie in what you learn from these experiences rather than how they come to you.

THE SECRET LIFE OF ALCOHOLISM

Ned was used to coming home from school alone. He knew he could never bring his friends back to his house after basketball practice so he always went to one of their houses until dinner time. Only then would he reluctantly drag himself home knowing he would find both of his parents either passed out or in the midst of a violent argument. He would eat the dinner his older sister had prepared and then they would both retreat to their rooms where he would study and read. Ned's goal was to be as good as he could be. Maybe if he excelled in his studies and sports, his parents could finally be happy and stop drinking and fighting.

Throughout this complex family psychology, Ned did learn one thing, how to keep a secret. He never let anyone know about his problems at home and he was an expert in making up reasons why his friends could not visit his house or why his parents never came to watch his games. He became skilled at covering up, lying, and making up tales.

His industriousness as a student paid off when he won a scholarship to a prestigious New England college. After graduation, he was sought after by some of the most powerful brokerage houses on the New York Stock Exchange. Ned married his high school sweetheart, who hated the taste of alcohol, and together they proceeded to raise a family while he quietly climbed the corporate ladder of success. He continued to play his usual role of the good boy by portraying the perfect husband and father image in his community. His old study habits also found their place in his world of work as he became the youngest vice-president in his company's history.

Ned never faced the issues surrounding his parents alcoholism and the prominent role it played in his early life. He was trained effectively in his childhood to maintain the family secret and he continued along his quiet, lonely road as he journeyed into his adulthood. Ned made many excuses to himself as he started his own drinking patterns. He felt that beer he enjoyed in the bar car of the local train that brought him home was simply a way of taking the edge off the pressures he felt from work. After all, it did make him a better father and husband when he walked in the door of his suburban house. Those martinis he savored at lunch were simply a necessary part of those power business lunches everyone shared in his line of work. Even as his drinking increased throughout the years, he never associated his drinking with the alcoholism of his mother and father. He was used to lying, even to himself.

Years passed with his drinking bouts increasing and his work performance slipping. Within ten years, this wonderboy of Wall Street had lost his job and the respect of his wife and children. He noticed, during his lucid moments, that they sometimes looked at him the same way he used to look at his parents. His body became bloated with alcohol and his mind became soft, sometimes failing him altogether.

It was during Ned's hospitalization in a rehab clinic that he finally faced the place alcohol had taken in his life from his early childhood to now. In being forced to face his addiction, he was also finally coming to terms with his Piscean karmic issues. In reality, Ned had the opportunity to explore the part addictions played in his life by taking a good, hard look at his childhood, the breakdown of his family, his desire to please through excellence and his conditioning to keep his feelings secret. Instead, Ned continued his experiences with alcoholism into his adulthood. It was certainly a sign of his desire for healthfulness when he choose a wife who would have no part of drinking. Her intolerance for this destruction of her family was the strength that put Ned into a rehab clinic and provided a clear environment for him to develop a new life clean of alcohol.

Ned may have looked like a Pisces who had succumbed to his addictions rather than an evolved soul of strength that we would expect from this "old soul" sign. And this story may not have turned out with a happy ending. Ned could have lost everything and wound up on the streets somewhere, alone, dying young. We cannot determine the extent a Pisces has to go in order to face his experiences with addictions. But we do feel joy when we see a Pisces overcome the power of alcohol, nicotine, drugs or any mood-altering substance. These seem to be the Pisces who are capable of bringing a special wisdom and guidance to others through their own personal battles and experiences. Although they may appear to be the weakest sign at times, they are also the strongest when they face their challenges and overcome their own temptations.

Life can be hard for the Pisces. Their sensitive natures have them *feel* and *sense* more than others and sometimes this extreme sensitivity has them seek unhealthy escapes. Your karmic testing, as a Pisces, is to face your difficulties with addictions and to seek healthy escapes from the harshness of life. You may feel that you are not responsible for a childhood involvement with alcoholic parents, it was simply bad luck. Karmically, you chose those parents because you needed to experience this environment in order to aid your soul's growth. Your parents were confronting their own karmic battles which brought to you the necessary circumstances to encourage your karmic growth. Some of your greatest challenges will come to you through your struggles to stop drinking, taking drugs, smoking, working so hard, or drinking so much coffee. These are all escapes which prohibit you from facing important issues in your life.

At the same time, you must acknowledge your sensitive nature and realize that there are times when you must escape from some of the harsher realities of life. It is how you go about this escape that creates your karmic testing. Some positive avenues for you to explore would be daydreaming, reading, creative expression, the fine arts, music and, if not in excess, peaceful sleeping. Your dreams will bring you bountiful guidance and meaningful messages to help you in your travels. You need to keep your mind free of harmful substances which may limit your psychic potentials.

BRINGING BEAUTY AND ART TO OUR WORLD

Here is a karmic responsibility that can be fun and bring much pleasure to you and others. Ours is a world which requires work, seriousness of purpose and continual maintenance by all twelve signs of the zodiac. But we must remember that we also require nourishment of our souls through the dimensions of art and spirituality. When local schools reduce the budgets of their art and music departments because of budgetary deficits, they are overlooking their students needs for these important subjects. We human beings are not satisfied solely by the mathematics, sciences, and geographies in life. We desperately need the soothing comfort brought to us by the fine arts.

Your job as a Pisces is to struggle against this prejudice by pursuing your instinctive drive to create beauty for beauty's sake. Others may call you lazy or unproductive unless you make a lot of money at what you do, but your success in the area of arts cannot be determined by your financial reward nor should you be judged by others in this manner. We need the output of your creativity as much as your soul needs to be a part of the creative process. This may be another area where you obtain nothing but scorn, yet you must be strong in your mission. No one knows better than you of the healing powers of a melody, a gentle poem or brushed oils. Your karmic challenge may be to confront those who are governed by the power of materialism by showing them the potent beauty of art and music and the benefits they can bring to all of our souls.

Special talents often accompany your sign. Some of you may have skilled hands to create objects of beauty with clay, wood, flowers, precious metals or anything else that catches your eye. Others of you may possess the wondrous talent of expressing feelings through the medias of painting, sculpting, writing. photography or music. Whether these special talents are used as your source of income or your hobby is totally your choice. The results of your energies will be gifts to mankind regardless of your motivating needs. These talents will enrich your own soul as well as inspire a potential for spiritual growth for all who experience them.

TO ESTABLISH YOUR SELF-IDENTITY

As you can see from the karmic challenges already discussed in this chapter, your identity may appear to be weak in the eyes of others, and to some extent, also to you. You can be easygoing, lay-back, and carelessly led by others which will make it easy for anyone, including yourself, to doubt your strength of character and individual identity. You may have a tendency to follow the easiest path, or succumb to the dictates of your passions without proper regard for your own growth or well-being. Since other people may try to take advantage of these aspects of your personality, your karmic responsibility is to determine your goals in this life and to develop your strengths in this direction. Let us look at an example.

A young teenage Pisces, who is easygoing, may go along with the crowd rather than assert herself because she does not have any strong goals of her own. She is always there for her friends, especially when they are sad or struggling with unhappiness in their lives. They see this as weakness because she never asserts herself within the group. As she grows up, she decides to direct her compassion toward a career in nursing which enables her to continue her need to help others while establishing a commendable position in the community. She is still there to help her friends, but now has learned to limit her availability and assert her authority. Her training within the nursing profession has taught her to strengthen her character and define her objectives.

As a Pisces, you must be proud enough to recognize that your compassionate and easygoing nature is an attribute as long as you channel it with disciplined direction and sure purpose. In order to establish your unique personality, you must set your goals for yourself and these goals must reflect the sensitivity of your nature, rather than try to cover it over with an image that is untrue to your inner core. Some Pisces feel that their sensitivity is a fault, a sign of weakness, and they try to compensate for this aspect of their nature by entering into goals which require ruthlessness and are based on cold materialism.

Karmically, you need to establish first a love and respect for yourself, then an understanding that what may be considered signs of weakness by others may truly be traits of your greatest strengths. Lastly, acknowledge that you are an old soul who may be here to lead some of us toward different, unexplored paths through your daring to defy some of the morals and ethics of our society. This takes strength of character which may never be acknowledged or applauded by your peers. This takes courage. Only the evolved Pisces can do this for us. Sometimes, where you think you are weakest in your personality is more accurately the source of your greatest strength. Do not allow yourself to be judged by others when your inner self tells you that you are right!

PISCES MALE

When people ask me what is the most difficult sign of the zodiac to live, I answer, the Pisces male. This is an exceptionally feminine, passive energy put into a male's body. Our society is not especially tolerant of boys and men who vibrate on their feminine side. We teach them from early age to be strong, do not cry, do not be a wimp, boys do not play with girls' toys, boys play baseball, they do not take ballet. Consequently, the Pisces male, from the beginning, is taught to deny, and even to be ashamed of, a large part of himself.

As a Pisces male, you need to be able to incorporate both the masculine and feminine or the yin and yang of your identity. You must know that it is alright for you to cry during emotional scenes in movies, to find joy in the beauty of nature and art, to express your fears and insecurities, and most importantly, to trust your intuitive sense. There may be times in your life when you will be scorned or ridiculed because of your sensitive nature, and consequently, labeled queer or girlish by less sensitive people. In fact, many Pisces men talk about questioning their sexuality during their developing years of adolescence. Your feminine nature has nothing to do with heterosexuality versus homosexuality. Statistically there are no more gay Pisces than of any other sign of the zodiac. You are simply more sensitive than society usually allows you to be, and this may be an uphill battle for you throughout your life. The Pisces male who is secure in his masculinity will be able to show his feminine side without fear of retaliation. He will enjoy the insight provided to him by his intuition, the inspiration given him by his creativity. He will comfortably nurture his loved ones, especially children without fear of displaying his compassion and devotion. The insecure Pisces male will become what many call a *manly-man*. He will enter life with great competitiveness whether it be with his friends, sports, work, or hobbies. He will need to assert his strength and masculinity by overpowering those who are weaker than himself. Many of these Pisces become homophobic or abusers of anyone weaker than themselves, including women and children. As a Pisces male you must remember that Jesus, the greatest of all Pisces, was never ashamed of His compassionate nature and always placed the weaker of His world in the highest positions.

In terms of relationships, women are usually drawn to evolved Pisces men because they innately understand the way a woman thinks and feels. They are known for being passionate lovers who seem to know how to love a woman. They are not afraid of caring for and nourishing their children through the depth of their own emotions and also show great compassion for the sickly or elderly in their family. Sometimes, as a Pisces, you can feel overwhelmed by the emotional needs and demands of your loved ones simply because you are so attuned to their pain. When this happens, you need to allow yourself to escape through healthy means. You may want to take off to a hunting cabin or isolated fishing spot, or retreat to a spiritual refuge. Your artistic talents can also take you away from the harshness of your reality by allowing yourself to get lost in your work. You must be cautious not to escape through drugs or alcohol which is so readily acceptable for men by our society. A man is encouraged to have a drink after a hard day of work, but this can be dangerous to you as a Pisces male. As you can see from this chapter, there are many healthy ways for your escape which will bring you much happiness. Addictions are your downfall.

You will need to be aggressive enough to succeed in this male dominated world of business and career. Do not ever let your feminine side fool you. You are still strong enough in your masculinity to compete and sensitive enough in your feminine to trust your hunches which will help you evaluate the characters of others. Some typical careers for Pisces men are those of healers, caretakers, artists, musicians, writers and anything which combines the creative with the compassionate. As the insecure Pisces male grows up, he realizes the strength of his character and moves quickly up the ladder of success. Only self-hatred, insecurity or addictions will hold you back.

PISCES FEMALE

Certainly women are more comfortable in the sign of Pisces than men. This is a feminine sign of great sensitivity and compassion which is socially identified in a female's character. As a Pisces female, you need to surround yourself with people who are soft, caring, and thoughtful or you may find yourself abused or misused by others. In our society, women are the caretakers, and many times, the enablers within problematic relationships. As a Pisces, your natural temperament is to help the weak, side with the oppressed, and nurse the sick. Because of these traits, people who are weak in character or especially needy may be drawn to you. This can create lopsided relationships for you which have you caring for people who are unable or unwilling to give you back the love and support that you deserve. These relationship patterns can begin in early life with you protecting a parent who is an alcoholic, or ailing physically or mentally, or weakened through circumstances of life. You may find yourself attracted to men who are also destitute, weakened by illness or addictions, or considered outcasts by society. Your obligation to take in the weak, injured or oppressed, along with your own feelings of inadequacy, may propel you into relationships which take much from you and offer little toward your growth. Be cautious of this tendency to save the world. It can lead to a feeling of martyrdom and deep unhappiness.

You must devote time to yourself and the development of your greatest potentials. The first step is to set your boundaries with everyone, family, and friends. Since it is your nature to be giving and loving, you must place these traits in high priority within your relationships without losing your self-respect and identity. Determine your goals, and insist that the people who love you play a part in helping you to achieve those objectives. If you devote yourself totally to the success of someone else what will you have left if this relationship should fail? If you have also channeled your energy into yourself, you will always have the results of your labors with you. You must first love yourself. You must develop self-respect and a feeling of worthiness while knowing that this is not always easy for a Pisces female.

You are a creative, spiritual being who has magnificent abilities to heal the human body, mind, and soul. The greatest healers of the ancients have been women. It has traditionally been the women who carried the secrets of wisdom through the ages. The energies of these spiritual healers have been stored in the psyche of the Piscean female. If you choose to enter into a field of healing or caretaking, you will be bringing with you endless generations of stored energy. You must always guard yourself against being drained or exploited by others but must never underestimate the power of your healing energy and the sixth sense of knowledge which reinforces your capabilities. Your Pisces energy qualifies you for jobs in medicine, psychotherapy, social work, and all areas of the arts.

You, like all Pisces, must be cautious of your addictive nature. You may find yourself, due to your enabling tendencies, attracted to relationships with mates or lovers who are alcohol or drug abusers. You may tend to withdraw from the tensions of life through these unhealthy escapes including the addiction of cigarettes. The Twelve Step program is ideal for you, in its basic concepts, to help to strengthen your self-esteem, and bring you to a higher spiritual awareness of yourself. It is my belief that the Twelve Step program was the final gift of the Age of Pisces before it was replaced by the Age of Aquarius. Through your experiences with addictions or addictive people in your life, you will be able to feel your own power and add great benefits to our society. Yours is a sensitive sign that can be easily abused, yet has the strength to rise above all obstacles because of the evolved power within your soul. Many will look toward you for their guidance and power.

PISCES CHILDREN

Most parents think of their children as new souls who need the wisdom of their teachings and experience which, to a certain extent, is true. But when you are parenting a Pisces child you must remain cognizant of the fact that your child's body houses an old soul which may be here to teach you a thing or two. This antiquity may not be easy to notice especially since the underlying personality characteristic may be insecurity. Still, never underestimate your child's potential or try to second guess why she is here in your life.

Let us begin with her shy nature. Other aspects of her astrology may show her as outgoing and social, but all Pisces have a corner of their personalities reserved for the quiet demons of insecurity, fear, phobias, and inadequacies. Your job as a parent is to help build her confidence and self-reliance. Try to stay away from negative expressions such as, *"you're a bad child"* or *"don't even try that, you'll never be able to do it."* Negativity seems to attract itself to her already floundering self-image. It is important for you to praise her and encourage her to pursue her greatest potential even if the direction she seems to be taking is not to your liking or of your choosing. Your Pisces child is here for very special reasons which may not ever be fully understood by you. She must be encouraged to follow her path regardless of your expectations or societies' demands. The greatest gift you can give her, as her parent, is your unconditional love and support throughout her life but particularly during her formative years.

Yours is a gifted child who needs to follow her own direction. Her love of the arts is important to her emotional balance. Therefore, it is important for you to encourage any interest she may show in art, music, or writing. Help her to develop these talents by bringing her to theaters, movies, museums, and art galleries. If you are financially able, take her to classes or teachers who can aid her development in these areas.

If you are raising a Pisces male it is important to encourage him to be comfortable with the feminine, passive, intuitive side of his nature. Many times, Pisces males are raised with fathers who are nervous about their son's passivity and try to beat or intimidate their "sissy" natures out of their personalities. This kind of action is particularly destructive to the child's nature and will teach him to dislike himself. This may later cause him to turn on himself through the destruction of alcohol, drugs or other abusive actions.

Give your Pisces child, male or female, the encouragement she needs to express her emotions without the restriction of bias or guilt. It is important to keep the lines of communication open concerning feelings and fears. Give her the benefit of your praise and physical comfort. Keep in mind that yours is a sensitive child who needs an abundance of love and support and has the potential of becoming an adult who is sensitive to the wants and needs of her fellow man.

Pay attention to the dreams and made-up stories of your Pisces child during her early years. She may be relating her remembrances of past lives feeling as though they are merely dreams. Many messages can be brought to us through the seemly trivial conversations of a Pisces child which can help us to understand better the workings of the universe, and certainly, the comprehension of universal law. She has come to this world with a powerful psychic sensitivity. Teach her to trust her instincts by paying attention to them yourself. You may hear your Pisces child come out with advice for you that seems to show a wisdom far beyond her age. This is typical for the Pisces youngster. They are able to *feel* their way through problematic situations which cut through the emotional complexities of adulthood.

It is important for you to provide a place of quiet and isolation for your Pisces child. This can be the privacy of her own room, or a work area or a quiet room. She needs to socialize as much as any other child, but she also has a great need to be able to retreat into a place where no one else will intrude. This is because she is so psychically attuned to others that being in groups, even family groups, can be overwhelmingly draining at times, and she will need to retreat to a place where no one will intrude on her as she recharges her energies. Many Pisces children also retreat through their imagination, daydreams, and the world of sleep. Many a Pisces teenager seems to go into their dark bedrooms when they are thirteen and come out again when they are twenty. Since they are prone to depression and drugs, you, as a parent, may become quite concerned. You have a responsibility to investigate the extent of her isolation while keeping in mind that because she is a Pisces, this self-imposed confinement may be necessary for her well-being.

As mentioned, her predisposition for alcohol and drugs along with her easily led nature, can become a worry for the parents of teenage Pisces. You must pay special attention to the kind of friends with whom she associates and act on any clues you may turn up which indicate a possible problem with substance abuses. You must also be heedful of extreme mood swings, since she tends toward the painful escapism of depression. Remember that this is a difficult sign due to its extreme sensitivity. The more you are able to encourage her to be comfortable with herself and the more you show her your love, the better equipped she will be to adjust to her karmic challenges. Sometimes music and art play an important role in the Pisces life by providing a healthful escape which also soothes her soul. The tone of her art and music will be an indication to you of her state of mind without her having to say anything to you.

Your child is a spiritual soul. She needs to be in contact with her spiritual self. A possible suggestion is to introduce her to a religious background in her early years. She may not be comfortable with a dogmatic, intimidating belief system, which her soul knows is filled with man's ego. She will be better served with a spiritual foundation based on humanity and symbolism. She will find great pleasure sitting quietly in a church listening to the choir sing and feeling the warmth of the sun as it shines through the colorful stained glass windows. This setting will uplift her soul.

Do not expect your Pisces child to follow your direction in life by growing up to be what you want her to be. She is here to lead a special life and follow her own path. If you expect her to be a clone of your expectations she will disappoint you. Be proud of her differences and uniqueness and always remember that she is the teacher whether her life takes a direction of social approval or social condemnation. She has many pitfalls to beware of in her journey and may trip several times along her arduous path. Always have faith in her that she has the strength to pick herself up and keep going. The greatest gift you can give her is your love and support and fullest acceptance of her life's direction.

You have been chosen to parent a special sign of the zodiac and will receive great reward from the universe for the role that you play in her life. Many positive karmic consequences will come to you, especially the joy of being loved by the most powerful of loving signs, a Pisces child.